2

PSYCHOTHERAPY 2.0

The Library
Aneurin Bevan Health Board
St Cadoc's Hospital
CAERLEON
NP18 3XQ

GIG CYMRU
NHS

Bwrdd Iechyd
Aneurin Bevan
Health Board

Tel 01633 436758/60

United Kingdom Council for Psychotherapy Series

Recent titles in the UKCP Series
(for a full listing, please visit www.karnacbooks.com)

PSYCHOTHERAPY 2.0
Where Psychotherapy and Technology Meet

Volume One

Edited by
Philippa Weitz

Series Consultants

Aaron Balick
Alexandra Chalfont
Steve Johnson
Martin Pollecoff
Heward Wilkinson

KARNAC

First published in 2014 by
Karnac Books Ltd
118 Finchley Road
London NW3 5HT

British Library Cataloguing in Publication Data

A C.I.P. for this book is available from the British Library

ISBN-13: 978-1-78220-048-2

Typeset by V Publishing Solutions Pvt Ltd., Chennai, India

Printed in Great Britain

www.karnacbooks.com

CONTENTS

ACKNOWLEDGEMENTS

Thank you!

This book is a team effort. First of all I must thank UKCP for allowing me to lead on this book and having faith in me.

Second, the series consultants, Aaron Balick, Alexandra Chalfont, Steve Johnson, Martin Pollecoff, and Heward Wilkinson, have worked tirelessly with me, as well as my co-authors, and this book is all the stronger for their involvement. In particular, Aaron Balick and John Knott have spent many hours digging out bad English, grammatical errors, and repetitions, to ensure the book is easy to read and fits well together and I thank them for this. Alexandra Chalfont has been available at all times for support and has been an inspiration and shrewd in her analysis of the knotty problems I have presented.

I'd like to thank all those people over the years who have helped me to get to where I am today professionally—my partner Elizabeth, colleagues, family, and friends.

Finally, a thank you to our digitally native grandchildren, Jessica, Danielle, Adam, and Zoe, who are highly amused that I should be editing a book about the digital age and who usually patiently explain the obvious when I haven't quite "got it"!

ABOUT THE EDITOR AND CONTRIBUTORS

Chapter authors

Kate Anthony is the leading UK expert on the use of technology in mental health services. She is a fellow of the British Association for Counselling and Psychotherapy (BACP) and co-CEO of the Online Therapy Institute, a think-tank and training organisation for mental health/coaching professionals using technology to deliver services. She is co-editor and co-author of four textbooks on the topic and holds the first doctorate based on developing counselling and psychotherapy in the age of technology and the Internet. She is co-founder and co-managing editor of *Therapeutic Innovations in Light of Technology* (*TILT*), a quarterly publication for professionals with an interest in innovative thinking in providing life-changing interventions. She is also on the UK's Responsible Gambling Strategy Board (RGSB) studying the impact of online gaming on gambling behaviour.

Email: info@onlinetherapyinstitute.com

Website: onlinetherapyinstitute.com

Aaron Balick is a UKCP registered psychotherapist, supervisor, and a media and social networking consultant working in London. Aaron is also an honorary lecturer at the Centre for Psychoanalytic Studies at the University of Essex where he participates in the postgraduate MA and PhD programmes in psychoanalytic studies; he also lectures and runs workshops in a variety of psychotherapy trainings in the UK. As a founding and executive member of The Relational School UK, he works to develop and promote relational thinking in the UK and abroad. Dr Balick writes for both academic and lay audiences, having published several academic articles and book chapters while at the same time contributing a psychological angle on national press and radio, particularly the BBC. Aaron is the author of *The Psychodynamics of Social Networking: connected-up instantanteous culture and the self* (Karnac, 2014) and a self help book for children, *Keep Your Cool: how to deal with life's worries and stress* (Hachette, 2013).

Email: aaron@mindswork.co.uk

Website: www.mindswork.co.uk

Twitter: @DrAaronB

LinkedIn: uk.linkedin.com/in/draaronb

Chris Blackmore is a researcher in mental health at the School of Health and Related Research, University of Sheffield. He is lead for innovation in teaching in ScHARR, and course director of the MSc in Psychotherapy Studies, an e-learning programme. He has a special interest in the role of emotions in e-learning, and offers educational consultancy in this area. Recently published research has included a systematic review of group analysis and analytic/dynamic group psychotherapy for IGA/GAS and a scoping review of psychological treatments for long-term conditions/medically unexplained symptoms for IAPT.

Email: c.m.blackmore@sheffield.ac.uk

Website: http://www.sheffield.ac.uk/scharr/sections/list/mh/
sectionstaff/cb

Twitter: @chrisblackmore

Alexandra Chalfont is a UKCP registered psychotherapist, a trainer, supervisor, and executive coach. She works integrally relationally in private practice with individuals and couples in West London. Recent specialisms have been mixed-culture relationships and intergenerational trauma. She is an associate editor of *Self & Society* and serves as co-chair of The Association of Humanistic Psychology and chair of the book editorial board of the UKCP.

Email: chalfont7@icloud.com

Website: www.alexandrachalfont.com

Divine Charura is a senior lecturer at Leeds Metropolitan University in counselling and psychotherapy. He has years of various work experience in diverse psychiatric/clinical and therapeutic settings. He works as a UKCP registered adult psychotherapist within the NHS, the voluntary sector, and as a consultant in private practice. Divine is also a supervisor who offers supervision to trainees and experienced psychotherapists. As an independent trainer Divine has facilitated many workshops and presented keynote lectures at conferences and training events nationally. He has contributed chapters to various published books and is currently editing two books within the counselling and psychotherapy profession. Divine is a keen saxophone player and a lover of food, art, music, and photography.

Email: psychotherapyinleeds@gmail.com

LinkedIn: uk.linkedin.com/pub/divine-charura/87/8a7/a28

Kate Dunn is a senior counsellor with the Counselling and Well-being Services at the University of Portsmouth, where she has worked since 2005. She initially qualified as a primary school teacher in the 1970s, working in an innovative and progressive open-plan, child-centred educational setting in West Sussex. She went on to study psychology with the Open University and to work in health and social services settings before studying psychotherapeutic counselling at the Universities of Sussex and Brighton. In 2007 she developed and established an online counselling provision within the services at the University of Portsmouth. This has subsequently provided an alternative psychotherapeutic approach to more traditional face-to-face counselling for significant numbers of students. Kate has carried out research into the nature of the online counselling relationship which has been published in *Counselling and Psychotherapy Research* and she is a frequent speaker at events where this topic is of interest.

Email: kate.dunn@port.ac.uk

Stephen Goss, PhD, has over twenty-five years' experience in the helping professions. He is principal lecturer in the postqualification doctorates department at the Metanoia Institute (Middlesex University) and an independent consultant in counselling and support service development and research. He provides clinical and research supervision worldwide. His specialist interests include pluralism, online service provision, suicide prevention, and the development needs of counselling and psychotherapy practitioners and services. Previously chair of the BACP research committee and BACP's first research development officer, among his 100 publications are *Evidence-Based Counselling and Psychological Therapies: Research and Applications* (Routledge, 2000), *Technology in Counselling and Psychotherapy: A Practitioner's Guide* (Palgrave, 2003) and *The Use of Technology in Mental Health* (CC Thomas, 2010). He is also associate editor for research for the quarterly journal *Therapeutic Innovations in Light of Technology* and is co-editor of the *British Journal of Guidance and Counselling*.

Email: stephenpgoss@googlemail.com

DeeAnna Merz Nagel is a psychotherapist, consultant, and international expert regarding online counselling and the impact of technology on mental health. She is co-founder of the Online Therapy Institute and managing co-editor of *TILT* (*Therapeutic Innovations in Light of Technology*). She specialises in text-based counselling and supervision via chat and email. DeeAnna's expertise extends to assisting individuals and families in understanding the impact of technology in their lives from normalising the use of technology and social media to overcoming Internet and cybersex addictions. She has co-authored/edited two textbooks and written several book chapters and articles on topics related to technology and mental health. DeeAnna graduated from the University of Georgia with an M.Ed. in rehabilitation counselling and is licenced to practice in New Jersey, New York, and Georgia. She is also a certified rehabilitation counsellor and a distance credentialed counsellor and a board certified coach. In addition to creating curricula for the Online Coach Institute she serves as faculty at the Institute for Life Coach Training.

Email. info@onlinetherapyinstitute.com

Aqualma Murray has international experience in social work spanning twenty-five years. Her career started in residential care with young people with challenging behaviour, and she has worked with a wide range of client groups of varied ethnicity, abilities/disabilities, and ages, including young offenders. Her work with these client groups has centred on addressing issues of sexual abuse and child protection. Aqualma has held the roles of social worker, probation officer, independent reviewing officer, and child protection conference chair. She has also worked as a local authority designated officer (LADO), where she worked alongside police officers, teachers, and other professionals, investigating issues of allegations against professionals, including issues of online abuse. Aqualma is also a trainer and consultant addressing issues of abuse, challenging behaviour, children's mental health, children's rights, anti-discriminatory, diversity issues, and attachment theory as well as implementing policies and procedures for young people with disabilities. She is also an ordained interfaith minister. Aqualma believes that professional participants and service users, including children and young people, know what they want and with appropriate guidance and support are able to realise this and gain achievements.

Email: mannaaqualma@hotmail.co.uk

Websites: www.aes-inc.co.uk www.aesinc.co.uk

Martin Pollecoff describes himself as a "jobbing" psychotherapist and supervisor, one who has served in the trenches of Exegesis, several mental health charities, the NHS (the Soho Centre), and private practice in London W2 and Empshott in Hampshire. He founded www.thelongboathome.co.uk, the National Psychotherapy and Counselling Service for Veterans and their families and is currently an elected board member of the UKCP.

Martin welcomes comments, queries, brickbats, and praise.

Email: martin@psychotherapyW2.co.uk

Anne Stokes is a senior BACP accredited counsellor, a supervisor, and a trainer, and throughout her career has integrated her interests in both education and management. As well as maintaining an independent practice, she taught on diploma and masters programmes at the University of Bristol for fifteen years. In the last decade, Anne has been at the forefront of developing online counselling and training in the UK. She is a director of Online Training for Counsellors Ltd, and also the supervision editor for the online journal *TILT* (*Therapeutic Innovations in Light of Technology*). As well as publishing a number of articles and contributing chapters to several books, she has co-authored: *Online Counselling: A Handbook for Practitioners* (Palgrave, 2009), *Setting up in Independent Practice* (Palgrave, 2011), *Therapy for Beginners—How to Get the Best Out of Counselling* (Sheldon Press, 2011). She has an MSc degree (counselling supervision and training) from Bristol University and an MBA from the International Management Centre, Buckingham.

Email: anne.stokes4@btinternet.com

Digby Tantam is an emeritus professor at the University of Sheffield, and an honorary visitor senior research fellow at the University of Cambridge. He and Emmy van Deurzen own the Septimus group of companies, one of which (the New School of Psychotherapy and Counselling) provides higher education in psychotherapy, counselling, and coaching leading to doctoral and masters level degrees. Another Septimus company, Dilemma Consultancy, provides psychotherapy and psychiatric services in Sheffield and London. Digby is currently chair of the Society of Psychotherapy and is on the executive of the Society for Existential Analysis. He has been founding chair of the Universities Psychotherapy and Counselling Association, chair of UKCP, and registrar of the European Association of Psychotherapy. He is a fellow of the Royal College of Psychiatrists, the British Association for Counselling and Psychotherapy, the British Psychological Society, the Higher Education Academy, and UKCP. He has worked in the NHS for over forty years, and has been a member of the Institute of Group Analysis in London for thirty, and of the British Association of Cognitive Psychotherapy for twenty. Digby is the author or co-author of 170 scientific articles, and the author or editor of twelve books, including *Psychotherapy and Counselling in Practice: A Narrative Framework* (Cambridge University Press, 2002).

Email: digby.tantam@googlemail.com
Website: www. nspc.org.uk
Twitter: @therapytraining
LinkedIn: uk.linkedin.com/pub/digby-tantam/9/34b/679/

Janet Weisz is chair of the United Kingdom Council for Psychotherapy (UKCP). Janet has worked in both the public sector and private practice for the past twenty years. As well as maintaining a private practice, she works in the NHS as part of multi-disciplinary teams and has experienced first-hand the demanding pressures for change and evolution in the provision of psychological services. More of her time is now spent focusing on management and funding strategies, and on fighting to retain the service.

Philippa Weitz is a qualified teacher and psychological counsellor with twenty-five years of private practice and primary care experience, and training and mentoring within mental health. She is currently commissioning editor for the UKCP book series, managing director of Philippa Weitz Training Ltd., and co-founder of the London Online Therapy Centre. She was executive director and co-founder of the Counselling and Psychotherapy Forum for Primary Care. She was head of The Conference Unit (Mental Health Sciences) at St George's Hospital Medical from 1990–1997 and subsequently director of Mole Conferences.

She has written and trained widely around bereavement counselling, general practice, and primary care counselling, and more recently has been working online as a practitioner. She has an MSc in psychological counselling from the University of Surrey (Roehampton). She has published a number of articles and books including *Setting Training Standards for Primary Care Counsellors* (Douglas Hooper & Philippa Weitz (eds.), Karnac, 2006) and, more pertinently for this publication, *Setting Up and Maintaining an Effective Private Practice: A Practical Workbook for Mental Health Practitioners* (Karnac, 2006).

Email: pweitz@pwtraining.com

Website: www.pwtraining.com

Twitter: @PhilippaWeitz

LinkedIn: uk.linkedin.com/pub/philippa-weitz/19/b98/698

Commentators

Tamara Alferoff is a facilitator, psychotherapist, and supervisor of over thirty years' wide study and experience in the integrative and transpersonal fields. She bought her first computer the day after her mother's funeral in 1999. In 2001–2003 she completed both the basic and advanced certificates in online counselling with OLT, and together with fellow students, established online both a therapeutic group practice (www.cocooncounselling.com) and her own practice (www.tamara.alferoff.com), which now specialises in a form of transformative inquiry. She works much more with live one-to-one than email these days, using Skype or Google video calls for individual, couple, and groups, as well as teleclasses on various topics such as symptoms, illness, body issues and death, fear and anxiety, creativity, relationships, and transformative inquiry.

Website: www.tamara-alferoff.com

Facebook: https://www.facebook.com/TheWorkwithTamara

LinkedIn: http://www.linkedin.com/in/tamaraalferoff

Michèle Bartlett, MA Dip ICP, is a UKCP registered integrative arts psychotherapist and child psychotherapist. She is chair of the Faculty for the Psychological Health of Children. Michèle works with both adults and children using creative arts, storytelling, and imagery. She has extensive experience of working with young people in educational settings. Having recently undertaken training in outdoor therapy, Michèle is developing her practice to include the metaphors extant in the natural world, with a view to extending the therapeutic space into the wild outdoors. She also runs workshops—"Transformational Spaces in Nature".

Websites: www.creativetherapy.org.uk www.wildoutthere.org.uk
Twitter: @wildoutthere

Tim Bond is a counsellor, educator, and practitioner, specialising in teaching research methodology and professional ethics (education, counselling, and research). He continues to offer a small counselling and supervisory practice. He is internationally renowned for his contributions to counselling and research ethics and particularly his interest in dialogue between different cultural and moral positions. He has extensive experience of leadership, management, and policy-making in higher education and professional associations.

Ian Gilmore has worked for nearly forty years in therapeutics in one capacity or another: as practitioner, as trainer, and as supervisor. He has also travelled widely pressing those principles developed by the psychotherapeutic community to use in various less traditionally or less obviously psychotherapeutic circumstances, such as from the immediate aftermath of terrorist attacks to the terrorism inherent in industrial relations. In addition to critical incident response work, he has undertaking international and forensic assignments, and has also worked in private practice and in medico-legal contexts.

Email: Ian@IanGilmore.com

Jen Hyatt has worked as a consultant and social entrepreneur in over twenty countries, and helped establish or founded more than thirty social purpose organisations internationally. She founded Big White Wall in 2007 and now functions as its chief executive. Big White Wall is transforming mental health services through technology, delivering safe, online self-care, with 24/7 access to professional staff on demand.

Jen is amongst those spearheading the development of a national digital mental health system.

Email: jen.hyatt@bigwhitewall.com
Website: www.bigwhitewall.com
Twitter: @bigwhitewall1
LinkedIn: www.linkedin.com/in/jennyhyattbigwhitewall

Susan Iacovou is an existential therapist and counselling psychologist with a private practice in Cheshire. She has published widely and most recently co-edited a book on existential relationship therapy with Emmy van Deurzen. Susan teaches on a range of psychotherapy masters courses, and was a research associate on the European-funded Continuing Education in Psychotherapy project, which was designed to improve access to quality psychotherapy training across Europe. Susan received an MA in psychology from Edinburgh University and will shortly complete her doctorate in existential counselling and psychology with the New School of Psychotherapy and Counselling.

Email: therapy@susaniacovou.com
Website: www.susaniacovou.com

Steve Johnson heads up Oxygen Professional Risks and has been an insurance broker for the last forty years. Since 1988 he has specialised in providing professional liability insurance to psychological professionals including, psychotherapists and counsellors. For much of the last twenty-five years, Steve has been in the front line, helping and supporting practitioners when things have gone wrong and they find themselves faced with a complaint or a claim for compensation. Steve has presented workshops and given talks at conferences and on training courses. In the late 1990s he was a founder member of a forum group looking at standards in primary care counselling and psychotherapy and, for a time, sat on the professional standards committee of BACP.

Email: steve.johnson@oxygeninsurance.com
Website: www.oxygeninsurance.com
Twitter: @Oxy4Therapists
Linked in: http://uk.linkedin.com/in/stevejohnsonpsychology
          insurer/

Gordon Law is a teaching and supervising transactional analyst, and a UKCP registered psychotherapist. He has maintained a small training, supervision, and psychotherapy practice since 1972 and has an interest in integrating TA, gestalt, Ericksonian hypnotherapy, and meditation. He is currently acting chair of the UKCP Ethics Committee and co-chair of the ethics committee of the International Transactional Analysis Association.

Email: gordon.law1@btopenworld.com

Eduardo Pitchon, initially from Argentina, trained as a child and adolescent psychotherapist at the Tavistock Clinic, is a member of the ACP, and has worked in special schools and CAMHS clinics. He is currently a child, adolescent, and adult psychotherapist in private practice, having worked for many in the public and private sector. He set up and chaired Link Psychotherapy Centre which specialised in work with the Jewish community. He has written many articles on different topics and has lectured extensively at home and abroad.

Email: Eduardopitchon@ yahoo. co.uk

Kate Thompson trained in London and at The Center for Journal Therapy, Denver, Colorado after a first degree in English Literature at the University of Cambridge. She is a registered psychotherapist in the state of Colorado, a journal therapist and writer, faculty member at The Boulder Psychotherapy Institute, The Therapeutic Writing Institute, and The New School of Psychotherapy and Counselling.

Email: kate@KateThompsonTherapy.com

Website: http://katethompsontherapy.com/

Biljana van Rijn is a head of clinical and research services at Metanoia Institute in London. She is a transactional analysis and integrative psychotherapist, supervisor, and tutor who combines her academic and research work at Metanoia Institute with a private practice in West Sussex.

Email: Biljana.Vanrijn@metanoia.ac.uk

Diane Waller is emeritus professor of art psychotherapy at Goldsmiths, University of London, visiting professor in the Centre for Mental Health at Imperial College, and a UKCP registered group psychotherapist. Her background is in art and art history, psychoanalytic psychotherapy, and ethnography. Her recent research has explored the potential value of art psychotherapy groups for people with dementia, addictions, schizophrenia, and stroke, with other main interests being in the history and sociology of psychological therapies and the ethnography of the Balkans. In 2007 she was awarded an OBE for services to health.

Email: diane.waller@virgin.net

Tom Warnecke (ECP) trained in gestalt therapy and subsequently with David Boadella in somatic and psychodynamic-oriented psychotherapy. He is a tutor and lecturer in various psychotherapy education settings, facilitates small and large group events, and developed a relational-somatic approach to BPD. His publications include several journal papers and book chapters. He was a vice-chair for UKCP from 2008 to 2013 and he is a board member of the European Association for Psychotherapy (EAP).

Heward Wilkinson is a UKCP honorary fellow, chair of the UKCP Humanistic and Integrative Psychotherapy College, based in London. Author of *The Muse as Therapist: A New Poetic Paradigm for Psychotherapy* (Karnac, 2009). He focussed on the interface between religion, philosophy, the arts, and psychotherapy. He edited the *International Journal of Psychotherapy*, the journal of the European Association for Psychotherapy, from 1994–2004. Heward loves people, also the natural world, butterflies, the sea, moors, and mountains, as well as music, soccer, and cricket.

Email: hewardwilkinson@gmail.com
Website: http://hewardwilkinson.co.uk

UKCP BOOK EDITORIAL BOARD PREFACE

Alexandra Chalfont
Chair, UKCP Book Editorial Board

Philippa Weitz
Commissioning Editor, UKCP

The UK Council for Psychotherapy (UKCP) holds the national register of psychotherapists, psychotherapists qualified to work with children and young people, and psychotherapeutic counsellors; listing those practitioner members who meet exacting standards and training requirements.

As part of its commitment to the protection of the public, UKCP works to improve access to psychological therapies, to support and disseminate research, and to improve standards, and also deals with complaints against organisational as well as individual members.

Founded in the 1980s, UKCP produces publications and runs meetings and conferences to inform and consult on issues of concern to practitioners and to support continuing professional development.

Within this context, the UKCP book series was conceived to provide a resource for practitioners, with research, theory, and practice issues of the psychotherapy profession at the heart of its aims. As we develop the series, we aim to publish more books addressing issues of interest to allied professionals and the public, alongside more specialist themes.

We are both extremely proud to be associated with this series, working with the UKCP Book Editorial Board to provide publications that reflect the aims of UKCP and the interests of its members.

PREFACE

Janet Weisz

This book on psychotherapy in the digital age is most timely. Despite some of us being luddites with the digital age, the Internet, Skype, etc., most of us have some form of online presence, some professionally, some for personal use only. What is certain is that many of our patients live elements of their lives online. For those for whom "Psychotherapy 2.0" is a new term, Web 2.0 refers to relatively recent developments online, shifting from the Internet as a source of information to a nexus involving a two-way means of relating.

This book, *Psychotherapy 2.0*, will mean a great deal to some UKCP members, as well as to psychotherapists and psychotherapeutic counsellors from other professional organisations. Some will view the arrival of this book as timely; others will view it as a source of puzzlement and, maybe, will even initially dismiss it as irrelevant. But I urge those of you whose instinct is to dismiss it to pause and think again, as, whether we are fully equipped, or planning, to work online as practitioners or not, our clients and patients are possibly fully integrated with the online world, some in ways—both positive and negative—we may never have thought about.

I therefore ask you to read this book with an open mind. The impact of the nternet on all aspects of our lives is irreversible. We can't go back.

We can't "unknow" what we know. We cannot put toothpaste back in the tube!

The Internet can never replace the physical presence of social interactions, including face-to-face encounters in the consulting room, but it can lead us in new directions, for example through social media; within the world of psychotherapy it opens up the possibilities of working online, and existing research has already proved this very successful. Whilst many will never wish to practise psychotherapy online, hold in mind when reading this book, that Web 2.0 can give many a lifeline back to life, a chance to develop a new online social network where geography, illness, stigma, disability, and isolation are no longer an issue. Psychotherapy 2.0 can play an important role by providing new opportunities for formerly excluded groups to receive the psychological help they need.

At UKCP we have already run a number of days around how psychotherapy and the Internet integrate, and now have our own special interest group which is proving very popular. We know this is a fast moving field of clinical practice and research and we are committed to providing our members with the resources necessary to keep them up to date, for example through training, so that psychotherapy in the twenty-first century can make use of the new tools available and we can continue to provide support, help, and understanding to those in need of psychotherapeutic help.

FOREWORD

Philippa Weitz

The human being is an evolutionary creature … and change is a necessary part of evolution: the challenge of change is an eternal crisis of the human condition. The arrival of the digital age is merely another step along the road of evolution, albeit a huge step in a short number of years, evolution in fast-forward mode.

Psychotherapy is an intensely private activity as well as being a microcosm of the society we live in. Our responses need to reflect both.

I have called this book *Psychotherapy 2.0* because, for the first time in over 100 years, technology is really changing the way in which psychotherapy is delivered and experienced. The subtitle—*Where Psychotherapy and Technology Meet*—alludes to the nexus of the two, and just as when you put two chemical elements together (e.g., H_2O makes water), so the combination of psychotherapy and information technology leads us to a new field of knowledge and clinical practice, which must be embedded and confirmed by research.

The digital age is far from new; it's just that psychotherapy has been late coming to the digital discussion. It is refreshing to note the recent growth in references to the digital age in the professional journals and to observe how the profession is now engaging in the conversation about the way forward.

Some view the relationship between psychotherapy and all things digital as a marriage of convenience, whilst for others it was "love at first sight", the land of food and plenty for those minded to go in that direction. What is certain is that, for better or for worse, there is no going back. The toothpaste is out of the tube!

Is therapy online a pleonasm? With therapy involving many different methods, formats, and situations, online may just be seen as an extension of these, and some may say "What is all the fuss about?" Others will call for specific training, regulation, ethic guidelines, and more. Who is right? Time will tell. What is sure is that your clients are most likely to interact online via the Internet and social media as a matter of course, using a mobile, the Internet, gaming, or other devices.

This book is therefore written for all practitioners and allied professionals working in mental health. How far we have come in such a short time! I was in my late twenties when affordable computers first appeared on the high street. And I'm not that old either! There are some distinct groupings in our society and, of course, amongst practitioners as a sub-section of society: those that were born in the digital age and have never known anything else "digital natives" (Buckingham, 2013); those, like me, who were young enough to take it on board though there are always gaps in our knowledge; and skill "digital immigrants" (Buckingham, 2013), as it were. There's another group who cannot, or refuse on principle, to engage with the digital age. This book aims to address all practitioners: Web 2.0 is having a major impact on society and on the individuals living within our society, for better or for worse.

Why "Psychotherapy 2.0"? The Internet initially was viewed as a passive resource that you consulted like an encyclopaedia. More recently, with the advances in speed, technology, and the broadening of how, when, where, and why we use the Internet, and now that so many people own hand-held devices such as ipods, smart phones, laptops, "Web 2.0", the interactive web in which the reader also becomes broadcaster and shaper of ideas, has become a hub for communication, a vehicle for two-way exchanges, living in a new and virtual world (for example, through online gaming, or second-life, virtual, reality) and social media. The Internet has become an important form of social communication involving relationship—a two-way process. It's full of bloggers, citizen journalists, and global groupings, and it is changing the nature of psychotherapy and mental health. You only have to turn to sites such as www.madnessradio.net, theicarusproject.net, or www.hearing-voices. org to see how "patients" are shunning the mental health system, and instead forming global self-groups which have agency, pride, and power. In Chapter One you will see how Big White Wall is transforming the way in which individuals can access help. Chapter Seven will show how people use virtual reality facilities such as Second Life to build new confidence. It's a whole brave new world!

It is not the advent of the Internet itself that provides the challenge for psychotherapy—it's a great tool and resource—it's the move to Web 2.0 that provides both the challenges and the potential for psychotherapy. Some are already using Web 2.0 to create very successful tools and resources for providing new methods of, and routes to, working online in Psychotherapy 2.0.

This book aims to present the background to the current situation and some of the current strands of thinking going on—it is never going to be a polished masterpiece, since to achieve that would take years and everything in the book would be out of date! It's very much "work in progress" in this fast-moving virtual climate and will be followed by further volumes with more emphasis on the application of therapy online.

The definition of society is continuously evolving. With the advent of the digital age the world has become a village, the walls of our world have elasticated to become worldwide, and it is affordable to all. Families living on the other side of the world are now joined up via the various social media and forms of communication available online. It's great news for families and friends! We'll come to the negatives in later chapters.

This book is a compendium with a number of different chapter authors, all with different styles and traditions. You will, naturally, engage more easily with one style than another, depending on your own tradition and experience. Some are more practical, some are more academic. What I have done is to ask, more or less, for a standard format to each chapter: a case study, the chapter content, and finishing, in most cases, with short comments from two different psychotherapeutic traditions, to help weave the different psychotherapeutic traditions together.

You do not need to read this book in a linear way—dip in to the parts that most interest you to start with, get engaged with the material—it will make it easier to look at the other chapters afterwards.

I will always be a digital immigrant and face the same challenges as so many of my colleagues. I hope this book will help deepen your understanding and provide some insight on directions to take. Above all, I hope you will enjoy it!

Finally, a request: as this book is always only going to be "work in progress" in such a quickly changing world, if you would like to contribute to our future volumes or online forum, please contact me at philippa. weitz@ukcp.org.uk. Together we will build the future volumes.

A note about all case studies and scenarios throughout the book

The case studies and scenarios may be drawn from clinical work but all chapter authors have been asked to present these in ways to disguise any identities, and have confirmed that they have done so.

Reference

Buckingham, D. (2013). Making sense of the "digital generation": Growing up with digital media. *Self & Society*, 40: 7–15.

PART I

PSYCHOTHERAPY EVOLUTION
IN CONTEXT

CHAPTER ONE

Psychotherapy 2.0: for better or for worse?

Philippa Weitz

Psychotherapy 2.0 reflects and parallels Web 2.0 as an active participation in the digital world, providing us with new forms of social communication. Through Psychotherapy 2.0 comes the opportunity to work therapeutically in the digital world: a multi-faceted virtual world, almost a parallel universe, where we communicate and are in human relationship. It is the space where psychotherapy and technology meet: technology is merely the conduit in this new world. These relationships may be rooted in the real world, or only in the online world—such as through Second Life—or may cross the borders of both. As a society, our active participation is what makes the Web 2.0 world revolve.

This book aims to engage with this rapidly changing interface to ensure that we make the most of the opportunities as practitioners, and at the same time, protect ourselves as necessary from the inevitable negative elements that go along with this new world. We must ensure, as in other parts of our practice, that we lead the way in the development of online practice through mentoring, training and research.

We are all aware of the "evils" of the digital world. Whilst this book will be focusing heavily on developing a robust online practice as well as exploring the development of the online therapeutic relationship, it will not ignore the negative elements currently at play, for example, of cyber-bullying, trolling, sexting, misuse of Facebook, abusing confidentiality, these are particularly addressed in Aqualma Murray's chapter on protecting children and young people from online abuse. It will draw our attention to all that can go wrong, and at the same time embrace the potential for positive progress. All these "suspects" are currently making waves internationally and there is some pressure for Internet Service Providers (ISPs) and software developers to take responsibility for the "evils" that exist online. As practitioners we are likely to be confronted by these issues on a regular basis amongst our clients, whether or not we work online. We need in our practice to address issues of cybersafety as well as promoting it throughout practice and with our clients.

Given that we are where we are, in a technologically based world, it is imperative that we study in detail how we can make this work well for us and how we can overcome the limitations of this new world. These are the underlying themes of the book.

The arrival of the digital era is hugely exciting for psychotherapy, but not without its threats and challenges. This book explores our interactions, as humans, with our complex emotions; Web 2.0 and how we, as a society and as individuals, interact with this; and how Psychotherapy 2.0 can emerge successfully, vibrantly, and professionally as a new pathway in psychotherapy in the twenty-first century.

Web 2.0 is perhaps the greatest opportunity, challenge, and threat to psychotherapy since its foundation: until now psychotherapy has flourished very successfully, within western society, with the traditional tools of the "couch" and the consulting room. Many will be resistant to this challenge, citing the evidence that if it isn't broke why fix it. This is the tension that now exists within our profession, but this tension can provide a rich opportunity for developing new ways and deep discussion about what works best and for whom.

And now to begin with some clarifications and definitions

The language we use: as *English Vinglish* (Gauri & Nalki, 2012), the Bollywood comedy-drama, so hilariously demonstrates, language is a fickle creature, dependent on context, culture, and a variety of verbal, non-verbal and visual cues. The English that we will be using and discussing will be standard British English (whatever that is) but those of us who read English language textbooks produced in the USA or Australia already know to be wary of the use of language ... put very simply, we *die* in the UK, we *expire* in India. Even regionally in the UK the nuances of English vary ... further on in this book we'll have a wider discussion about the use of language. The digital age has changed language, and as we work across borders we will need to think about the context of, and geographical variation in, language.

What are psychotherapy, psychotherapeutic counselling, and counselling? Here's another hornet's nest that fills academic libraries, which we'll need to sidestep by deferring to the professional associations' definitions. Traditionally, both the UKCP and BACP definitions of psychotherapy have included the phrase "talking therapies", but the digital era is resulting in its own "definition transformation" to include therapy by text, email, messaging, and other written formats, apps such as moodmeter, and CHT automated program, as well as the virtual uses of VSee, Skype, and others. It is, therefore, time to check that our way of working fits with the code of ethics and the ethical guidelines that we adhere to, and that is fit for purpose. I intend to use the word "the practitioner" in order to sidestep the nuances of differences between the different roles, styles of therapy and traditions.

The term *"Information Technology"* summarises the multitude of *hardware*, including gismos, gadgets, and telecommunications systems, computers, hand-held devices, and *software* including Apple and Android apps, programs and packages such as the Microsoft suite, and websites to include social media to "store, retrieve, transmit and manipulate data" (Daintish, 2009). Software and hardware need to live together as companion plants rather than one as a parasite plant feeding off the other. Just as companion planting provides a fertile environment for good growing potential, so digital companion planting can provide the same: the result is what we can produce, the relationships that develop, how "companion planting" helps us engage in our lives, and, in the context of this book, in our professional work.

The *digital age* describes the era in which we currently live, starting seriously in around 1985, although history shows us much earlier antecedents.

What's in a word?—e-therapy, psychotechnologies, Psychotherapy 2.0, teletherapy, mediated technology, i-therapy, online therapy, the digital age, iDisorder ... and many more expressions ... I am reluctant to come down and choose any one of these expressions over another as they all have their place. Let's see what evolves.

In other words, I am not cornering definitions per se. The world of the digital age is too fluid to be captured: it would be like trying to catch bubbles. Even "new media" is now not new!

The emergence of the digital world and its impact on society

Society has been undergoing a major revolution in its relationship to the digital world, where globalisation is just one major theme. There is a plethora of research, books, and articles on the subject of society and the Internet. As just one example, in 1978, Nora and Minc's report— "*L'Informatisation de la société*" (Nora & Minc, 1978)—prepared for the French president, Valéry Giscard d'Estaing, described how computerisation was going to change and upset our lives irreversibly, leading to a new society, where maintaining national independence would be critical, so much so that France would need to alter its strategy towards telecommunications and satellites! It was their view that the future of French democracy depended on successfully adapting. We now recognise and take for granted the strands of thinking highlighted in this report: how far we have come, whatever our nationality, tradition, and viewpoint.

To illustrate this point we are in crisis if the email server is down for more than ten minutes, the hole-in-the-wall doesn't deliver our cash, the very simple transaction of buying some fruit in a shop fails because a till machine isn't working, or the announcement boards at the railway station lose electricity: everyday situations which can lead to chaos and meltdown for thousands, and sometimes millions. Big Brother is alive and well!

Today we never leave home without our mobile phone and credit/debit cards. Whilst the advent of the mobile phone has changed our connectivity, the Internet too has transformed every aspect of our society. In 1980 virtually no one except a large business owned a computer. In the early eighties Alan Sinclair launched one of the first computers, the ZX Spectrum. Lord Alan Sugar is responsible in the UK for the first fully functioning computer available to the mass market at the right price: in 1985 he launched the Amstrad PCW 8256 which retailed at over £300, a fortune at the time.

I was the first woman in Kingston-upon-Thames to buy an Amstrad! The man in the shop looked astounded when I asked for one. I had to ask a nuclear physicist friend of mine to help me set it up ... but I was on my way and I never looked back. This personal testimony describes the IT journey of most of us in our fifties and older. It is poignant to remind ourselves about just how far we have come in a relatively short time, and, often, without any formal training. Younger generations have never known anything different and are not afraid, in the way that I was never afraid of the telephone. We must, however, be careful not to pigeon-hole. Not all young people are adept at all things digital, and to lump them all together as digital natives can be presumptuous.

Most of us have grown up reading, watching TV, going to the cinema, playing CDs, records, writing a diary, or poetry, chatting on the phone, writing letters, sending postcards. Many of these activities already involved digital aspects and even the now-defunct telegram was a digital activity.

Nothing much has changed in *what we* do, but it is *how* we do things that has changed dramatically. We can now do all these things online, assembled within our mobile or computer. There's nothing more exhilarating than getting good quality BBC radio programmes directly from TuneIn Radio, or *The Archers* podcast downloaded, whilst driving along a French motorway—an Apple app on my iphone, working via Bluetooth using my car radio as a speaker. Instead of feeling very much in foreign lands I feel connected to my home. It's merely the medium that has changed.

The digital age has brought changes to family dynamics, some welcome and some unwelcome. Whilst we may be able to communicate freely with our loved ones in Australia on a daily basis at no cost, Buckingham (2013) points out that technology may change the family dynamics and alter the balance of power between parents and children: as an example, where there was once only one TV in the house and an evening in front of the TV would be a family activity, we all now look at what we want on our individual screens, with its subsequent impact on family dynamics. On the other hand it probably stops the "marital" about who manages the remote control! Dunn (2013) pointed out in a lecture on the therapeutic relationship that a photo of students sitting on a lawn all peering at handheld devices could be perceived as a breakdown of communication, but in fact it was precisely the opposite—they were communicating via social media. This same point is well illustrated by Chalfont in the case of Tommy (Chapter Five), whose father cannot understand how Tommy's social community was online, leading to a serious confrontation.

Society only really works if we abide by the rules. Social networking sites themselves create their own micro-society with both implicit and explicit rules. But who creates the rules? And who abides by them? We are dependent on a convergent agreement by the majority, otherwise we have anarchy. But these rules, as in society at large, are continuously being negotiated and changed, as is the netiquette that we should contribute to and follow if we wish to fit into the online world of acceptable online behaviour. As I write, we are currently seeing the power of society and governments putting pressure on the major ISPs and search engines to manage and control pornography.

The cynic will tell us the power of the Internet and cyberspace is all about consumerism and profit. And I am sure it is certainly true in some respects. I will not be the first, or the last, to download a free app for train times only to discover that the full version is £6.99! We do need to wise up and be alert to how we are being commercially exploited and find a balance about what we can accept and also what we cannot afford both financially and emotionally. Not everyone is aware of the Big Brother aspect to this brave new world. Balick (2014) alludes to "data mining"—the exploitation of the data gathered through tracking people's social networking habits—and the fact that most research regarding social networking is focused on "how to utilize social networking data for commercial advantage" (p. xxvii), rather than using these resources to increase our understanding of people better.

I mentioned above that I find the Internet and all my gadgets very important as a means of communication and connectivity when I am out of my comfort zone. My office and world travel with me in the smallest of bags, wherever I am in the world. Naydler (2013) sees this differently: "the virtual world may be best understood as being due to its offering an alluring counterfeit to real human relatedness and authentic spiritual experience that can long satisfy this hunger". Counterfeit or complement ... I raise this merely to show that there is not a one-size-fits-all answer. Human nature is very varied and whilst some will thrive in the online world, others will not.

In terms of the time scale of the digital age, few of these gadgets, gizmos, software, and apps are new. So why has psychotherapy been so slow to embrace the available technology? I wonder if we can see a parallel in the French attitude to the Internet. I have already mentioned Valéry Giscard d'Estaing's vision in the late 1970s to develop the Minitel (Schofield, 2012), which was launched nationally in 1982—you could book your train, consult your bank account, register your milk results (farmers), apply to university.

The Minitel was an ugly beige machine attached to the phone. The French were the envy of the world and were proud. I remember looking at one of these machines with awe and amazement in the mid-eighties. They were supplied free by France Telecom, ensuring even the poorest households had access to information in very remote areas. Minitel closed in June 2012, but its very success made the French come late to the Internet.

Teletext in the UK was comparable to Minitel and we have recently seen its demise. The parallels with psychotherapy, where we are wedded to our successful way of working in the consulting room and see no reason to change, are evident.

It's for your security! Really?

Everything we do online has an impact on our digital security, with emails, texts, etc. all stored electronically deep in cyberspace. We're now being told that there will be micro-chips in "smart" appliances such as fridges and ovens under the European Network of Transmission System Operators for Electricity's (ENTSO-E) report as some way of controlling use of electricity (others are more cynical). If you choose to step outside the "digital identity" (i.e., no credit card, no phone, probably no car, etc.) you are considered at best deluded, at worst a weirdo. It's a real Big Brother situation and actually if we wish to continue to situate ourselves within society we have little choice but to comply.

CCTV, biometrics in our passports, and tracking devices are now everyday items. Some love them, some hate them. I'm sure none of us would wish to criticise Sussex police for investing in tracking devices for those with Alzheimer's ... making it easy for them to find those who go missing and saving thousands of pounds. Whilst this may appear a reasonable use of technology, how far do we take this? The digital industry is now involved in developing the "Central Nervous System for the Earth", leading to a linking-up, on a cosmic scale, of technology and human activity and thought.

What has this to do with Psychotherapy 2.0?

Rather a lot, as all that develops in the digital world impacts on our society, and we as practitioners operate within our society, and develop our own "mini-society" within which we operate. The digital world therefore can at no point be ignored as an irrelevance to our consulting rooms. To illustrate this point, Kate Anthony and DeeAnna Nagel, in their chapter on "Avatars", use a case study in which Lucy, the practitioner, is initially out of her depth when Alice is talking about Second Life, with the resulting negative impact on the client who felt unheard and exposed. It is how we rise to these challenges that so often determines the outcome, as we shall see further on in Lucy and Alice's story.

One central theme in this chapter is to demonstrate that, as practitioners, our relationship to the digital world will result in either a happy or an unhappy marriage: we're in it for better or for worse. It is early days to make any hard and fast statements about what will work for whom and how, and this is a prime area for future researchers to work on. Like all marriages, certain ingredients are required for lasting success. What will these ingredients be for the practitioner? Will they be related to your chosen modality, or your personality, or the personality type of the client? Or something else?

At an organisational level, psychotherapy in the UK has been slow to engage with the digital age and needs to move quickly or it will be left behind. To misquote Nora and Minc (1978) concerning the Minitel, we need to alter our strategy towards all things digital. UKCP is now leading the way with its "digital first" policy, its special interest group for new media in psychotherapy, and its support of this book. Curiously, what I view as being "better", may make some clinicians shudder and of course the opposite is true—what I view as "worse", others may view as important or better. So we are at a complex moment in the profession, with tensions pulling in different directions, a time of transition.

The potential of Psychotherapy 2.0

Psychotherapy 2.0 provides an open market for those with a commercial eye to develop new ways of working online for our clients, with the potential to reach many new clients who have not previously engaged with counselling and psychotherapy, both within the charitable and the commercial sectors. It can help address some of the issues of availability and cost and provide an invaluable resource within the mental health sector. Big White Wall (www.bigwhitewall.com) is but one example where digital routes have successfully facilitated access to new client groups. It is a one-stop shop for online help, offering input from "Wall Guides" (24/7 trained counsellors who moderate and facilitate all conversations and work for BWW) right through to therapists, depending on what you need. What's great about this is that it gives the power back to clients to choose how they work, where they work, when they work. This may be very challenging for certain group of practitioners.

Needless to say Big White Wall has received a number of prestigious national awards and is clearly a service that is going places. This provides the evidence that there is a demand out there. Psychotherapists and counsellors often find the idea of thinking commercially distasteful, or as a conflict of interest, as it is a caring profession. I am a firm believer that just because we think commercially does not mean that we are any less caring. Big White Wall is but one example, and they are here to stay. The challenge for you, the practitioner, will be to decide *what* can work for you and *how* this might work. The opportunities are out there, and our potential clients use them. Jenny Hyatt, Big White Wall Chief Executive comments:

> "Big White Wall (BWW) offers a multitude of safe, therapeutic services, all of which place the person seeking help at the centre of their own care. As an online service BWW can offer the client access to safe, anonymous support in the moment that they experience the need, via tablet, smartphone or computer …. It's a commercial service, but one which puts the patient, and their path to recovery foremost, by creating an environment that allows them to be active and supported in their health journey by their peers—rather than seeking help alone, whilst potentially stuck on a long waiting list for treatment."

Currently seventy-five per cent of people with a mental health problem receive no treatment (The Centre for Economic Performance's Mental Health Policy Group, 2012).

MindFull[1] is another example of the broadening of help available through online support. In this environment of increasing demand and unmet psychological need, this but one example of a growing number of organisations answering the call for therapeutic support in a way that reflects our ever-increasing use of technology, demonstrating that the Internet has the power to transform the way that healthcare is delivered. This provides safe access, anonymous support 24/7, combined with quality therapeutic interventions, all from the comfort of the client's own home. Kooth.com is an example of an integrated online and face-to-face service for young people.

The Internet is here to stay, and we need to change and adapt, developing resilience as practitioners in our relationship with the digital world. There is plenty of research and literature on the subject of resilience and the psychology of change: some blossom with change, others really struggle. There is nothing new about this. Resilience and change are themes that resonate for us as practitioners and recur for our clients. "The concept of resilience has as its starting point the recognition that there is huge heterogeneity in people's responses to all manner of environmental adversities" (Rutter, 2012). This is good news for us as a human race, and for us as therapists in this process of change.

In addition to the new pathways to help online, there are new horizons and ways of working that are emerging for teaching and training online. Consider the exploration of identity through the use of an avatar in online role-playing, the impact the digital world is already having for those in the autistic spectrum or with schizophrenia, or the use of computerised self-help, just to name a few. It's a really exciting moment for those practitioners and clients who want to go in those directions. But that does not mean we are all forced to work in these new ways. Becoming aware they exist may be all that you wish to do as a practitioner so that you do not land up feeling inadequate as a practitioner or out of your depth, as Lucy did in Chapter Seven.

The digital era and psychotherapy as "modern" inventions

Whilst the digital revolution has taken place over only thirty to forty years, psychotherapy is also a new activity within the scale of our human evolution. How far we have come in less than 140 years! When Freud was starting out in the 1880s, communication was largely through meeting together, or by writing letters. The telephone was just a new gadget feared by many, though it is documented that Freud was fascinated by the telephone, and used the telephone as a metaphor (Freud, 1912; Rickels, 1989). My great-grandmother, one of the first people in the UK with a phone, was terrified by it and when one day there were cows on the lawn she only just managed to use the phone to call my great-grandfather and shout "Arthur, cows!" ... an expression that endures in our family to this day to let someone know there's a crisis afoot. People talked about the dangers to human health through travelling on a train, declaring that such speeds would kill us. These are just two examples of the effects of major technological transformational moments on our society. Trains and phones are now at the heart of our society, and there is a crisis when one or the other doesn't work, showing how an initially marginalised invention can later become central to the effective running of our society. Fear is a funny thing, and fear of the unknown, and fear of being shown up, provides the backcloth for conflicting feelings about new and existing social media and gadgets. Nothing new here, then.

Perhaps some of the discussion may connect to the never-ending debate about whether psychotherapy is an art or science. It is curious on re-reading Storr's (1980) excellent book *The Art of Psychotherapy* to see that in only his second paragraph of the preface to the second edition he says, "Psychoanalysis bade goodbye to science in 1896 ... However the gulf between science and psychotherapy is gradually being bridged." At the end of this same preface he foretells that "New techniques and new approaches to psychotherapy" are on their way. How right he was!

Although the digital age impacts on every moment of our waking day in some way (TV, texts, telephones, social media, online gaming, chat rooms, use of apps, right down to the train timetable and Weight Watchers), it is evident when trawling through currently advertised psychotherapy conferences and trainings, or recently marketed Apple and Android apps, that its impact on our industry is token. Fortunately this is starting to change, though there are still very few specialists to lead us, with notable exceptions such as Kate Anthony and Stephen Goss who have been publishing and training in this field for at least ten years.

Regional differences in acceptance of new media for psychotherapy provision

Elsewhere in the world, and in other allied professions in the UK such as psychology and medicine, IT has been an integrated tool of the trade for a much longer time.

For example, in the USA the situation is very different and the psychotechnologies—the term used by Maheu (Maheu, Pulier, Wilhelm, McMenamin, & Brown-Connolly, 2005) to define online clinical practice to deliver therapeutic dialogue at a distance—have played a central part in mental health care provision for forty years. This is possible because their mental health care system is more integrated than our own, with physicians working collaboratively together.

Maheu (Maheu, Pulier, Wilhelm, McMenamin, & Brown-Connolly, 2005) opens the book with a case study of Alice G, showing how her care is managed through the shared use of IT between all the professionals involved in her care. Whilst it is impressive, this would be unlikely in the UK. On the other hand, we are almost unique internationally, and extremely fortunate, to have an independent psychotherapy profession that does not automatically derive from the medical profession or psychology and is a healthy vibrant profession in its own right, with clinicians coming from all walks of life and cultures.

The challenge to trainers

In the realm of training, both pre- and post-qualification training should be seen as essential to practice online in this fast-changing online world. It's very interesting to note that Professor Digby Tantam, Professor Emmy van Deuzen, and Chris Blackmore have, in fact, been providing quality training since 2003. Interestingly, there are only limited numbers of pre-qualification courses available and, surely, modules on the digital age and online working need to be integrated into all pre-qualification courses, though the general view of those already training and practicing is that training to work online is a post qualification specialism that in no way can replace initial pre-qualification training.

Good quality post-qualification courses have been developed over recent years, but more are needed. These courses should be essential for anyone setting up an online practice. These will include consideration of ethical frameworks, contracting, choosing which technology to use, the development of the therapeutic relationship, thinking about the issues of transference online, issues of dissociation, security, how to present your identity, software you may use to drive your business/online practice, and many other vital pieces of information.

Let's take Skype or VSee to explore this idea further: many of us use Skype in our personal communications, but do we use it well? It may be a very small point but twice this week I have had to ask people to move themselves so that I could see their whole face—in both instances I could only see part of their face as they had no awareness of the need to check that they were looking at their camera. Such a small point. Such a big impact. But it is so important that we use the technology well if we intend to practice this way and charge for it, as part of our professional business strategy. Specialist training in online practice will help develop the practitioner's confidence, overcome the technophobe moment, develop policies (such as what happens when the technology goes wrong), and provide training and feedback about our online presence that will help us develop a flourishing professional practice.

Engagement with the online world requires us to think about the distortions and challenges that confront us whilst also realising that this is a gateway to many riches.

The riches that the digital age has brought us

We may not have been looking but the digital age has been, and is, engaging effectively in many ways with mental health needs within the UK. Just a few random examples:

- John Mellor-Clark and his team in the 1990s developed the CORE System (CORE IMS Ltd) as the first UK standardised quality evaluation system for psychological therapies. This tool is being widely used, particularly in primary care settings and has helped create one of the single largest databases of practice-based evidence in the field.
- In the 1990s Samaritans (www.samaritans.org) discovered that the Internet was an ideal way of engaging with suicidal young men, who were able to avoid perceived stigma whilst accessing the help they needed. Levels of suicide in this client group were reduced.
- There are countless websites offering self-help that date back as far as 2000, and indeed the more recent IAPT (Improving Access to Psychological Therapies, Department of Health [www.iapt.nhs.uk]) programme uses online support as part of its stepped care programme.
- Telephone counselling has been available professionally for a very long time in the voluntary and commercial sectors, being used by organisations such as Employeee Assistance Programmes.

- Distance learning programmes in psychotherapy (2003) through the University of Sheffield with European Union grants (www.septimus. info).
- Professor Isaac Marks ran a computer-aided self-help clinic at Imperial College (2000–2003) and was instrumental in the foundation of Triumph Over Phobia (TOP UK, www.topuk.org).

The challenge to researchers

Research on working online has already been taking place and is referred to within this publication. This book deliberately does not include a detailed research section, as this merits its own volume, which will follow. Whilst good research already exists there are a rich number of strands to explore and research into further, including: the wide varieties of support available online; the development of the therapeutic relationship; the role the digital world can play within the psychotherapy profession; the catastrophic consequences of the misuse of available social media; how the dynamic changes; how the law impinges or what we can and can't do; cross-borders issues of jurisdiction; contracting; how we can train online; how we can support each other as professionals online and take part in supervision; how we are online; the use of avatars; how our personalities fit in with this new world; how we do our research online; how we confront the issues raised by differences in culture and language.

A multi-dimension bricolage

The world of psychotherapy and counselling is challenged in this online multi-dimensional bricolage (Lévi-Strauss, 1966) where the rules of engagement are continually developing in new ways. Anthropologist Claude Lévi-Strauss (1966) defined the bricoleur (from the French word for a DIY worker, usually with a slight suggestion of questionable quality!) as someone who uses convenient implements and ad hoc strategies to achieve his ends, pulling together systems from what is available. Is this our current position in respect of working online in psychotherapy? I'd like to think we are a bit more systematic, but in reality many of us are using, ad hoc, what works for us and our clients, but let's use this opportunity to research in this field and provide resources for practitioners and clients.

A door opens onto new vistas of psychotherapeutic help

The advent of Web 2.0, Psychotherapy 2.0, and the massive changes in the NHS for the provision of services, may mean that the days of purist psychotherapy are threatened but, as Jenny Hyatt has pointed out earlier on in this chapter, current developments in IT and in the online world offer new potentials and will open counselling and psychotherapy and other forms of online support to those who could not previously access it because of constraints of geography, finance, stigma, psychological block (for example, agoraphobia), or if you are a carer limited in the time available to leave your home. It may simply be that in this new era you can access the service and help fulfil your need from the privacy of your computer, when you want and how you want. Some practitioners may hold the view that actually this immediacy is not therapeutically constructive and that it is the challenge of the getting to the meeting, the pain of the time between sessions, and the boundaries that all combine as grist to the mill for the therapeutic process and that somehow the immediate availability panders to a "have it all now" trend.

Not everyone needs the support of a practitioner, and indeed many people worldwide already consult the Internet to understand physical and psychological symptoms better, and to look for answers, and, where appropriate, assistance and treatment. Self-help has always been a strong market in the UK, as a trip to the appropriate book-shelf of any major book-shop will show. The digital world offers an unlimited opportunity to extend the options and resources available to those who either cannot afford or do not wish to engage traditional services.

New business opportunities

For those practitioners wanting to develop new directions and gain different groups of clients, Psychotherapy 2.0 offers new platforms for working and new markets to tap. The Internet and social media have led to a more collaborative way of being online, both in general and in the ways we seek help.

The challenge for psychotherapy in the twenty-first century, with particular reference to the digital world, is to ensure that it is fit for purpose, robust, and feasible and that the profession and its professional bodies have regularly amended and updated codes of practice and ethical guidelines to ensure best practice.

This book does not aim to be the ultimate scientific tome on the subject: it would be out of date before it was printed. It is "work in progress", with further volumes planned to ensure that we continue to engage with the rapidly evolving world of IT.

The aim of this book is to raise some good questions and provide some substantial leads which the profession can continue to ponder upon and work through; questions that will continue to be advanced and worked through in future volumes.

I was recently asked what would be my dream list in order to make online therapy work, within the UK context, more robust. There were four key items on my shopping list:

1. Professional membership associations' guidelines and codes of ethics fully integrated for working within the digital age, and specifically online.
2. Professional associations' templates for contracting that are fit-for-purpose within the digital age.
3. A UK-based Internet platform, a one-stop-shop for practitioners, what Chris Blackmore and Digby Tantam in Chapter Three call the virtual therapy office—the online consulting room, a website and office, that can be purchased, bought into on a monthly fee, that provides you, the practitioner, with all you need to work safely and professionally. This would include a diary, secure storage of notes, the means of communication via email, text and web-conferencing, a resources library, and a business section to include accounting, invoicing, and receipts, and a credit card/PayPal facility for receiving payments. Organisations will need to develop their own in-house systems fit for purpose.
4. Training courses and CPD fit for purpose to take UKCP members and other practitioners forward and provide them with the necessary knowledge, skills, and tools to work effectively online *and* to be knowledgeable about the online world that our clients inhabit.

Some of these are in development, none are complete. There are many opportunities available here to take the profession further into the twenty-first century. That is why this book will ever only be "work in progress".

Commentator one: Jenny Hyatt

The future of online healthcare lies in finding new ways of providing support that suit people's lives, needs, and expectations. My organisation, Big White Wall (BWW), is a thriving service used by thousands weekly, whilst constantly innovating in response to the needs of its community and the professionals who support them. These are points that Weitz makes in this chapter. In response BWW has developed personalised support and recovery pathways. Apart from self-management and peer support, there are guided therapy groups and traditional face-to-face therapy online through BWW's LiveSupport platform. This is a secure digital platform where therapy can be delivered through any combination of webcam, audio, text, and whiteboard, and where outcomes can be reported directly to the client's GP. This new way of working has benefitted the expertise of BWW's staff and approved counsellors and therapists who are highly experienced in working online as well as training from the Tavistock and Portman NHS Foundation Trust. BWW has opened up this online therapy space to other NHS practitioners, allowing them to truly embrace the digital-first strategy, reduce the burden on primary care, and save the NHS money. Indeed, a conservative estimate suggests Big White Wall provides cost savings of £370 per member to the NHS, due to reduced demand on other services as clients actively self-manage their conditions. The need for safe and easily accessible digital services in an age of squeezed budgets and increasing demand has never been more obvious.

In a few years, it will seem strange to imagine that once our only option to get therapeutic support was to travel to a set location, finding time and transport, and making arrangements at home to ensure we could attend. Rather, this model will be one option amongst many, and people will also have access to a range of support online, with many options for therapy available.

Commentator two: Diane Waller

When Pippa invited me to make a response to this chapter, I was both delighted and a bit scared! I still place myself in the category of "technologically challenged", as anyone who has observed me struggling to set up PowerPoint would attest. However, like Pippa, I am convinced it is vital to embrace all the potential for communication we are lucky enough to possess. It's a long time since I attempted to give away an electric typewriter in the former Yugoslav Republic of Macedonia—in the 1970s nobody wanted it due to the constant power cuts! In Bulgaria, making a phone call to another city was expensive and difficult and making an overseas call required a visit to the central post office. Now, most people have access to laptops and can email and Skype at any time, although there are still power cuts.

In reminiscence mode I smiled at Pippa's comment that she was the first in her town to buy an Amstrad. I remember being "strongly encouraged" to get an Amstrad whilst doing my PhD and declaring that I couldn't cope with that on top of the research … but now working with an elderly author, in her mid-eighties, who can master the electric typewriter but not a computer, I am so glad I was "persuaded" to get that Amstrad and to have had the help of my brother, an IT whiz, who taught me the language of computers, emphasising that once the basics had been mastered, it was a "question of practice". For my friend, not being able to send files electronically has meant trips to local IT stores for expensive scanning, trusting disks to the post, and a great deal of forbearance on behalf of her publisher.

I realise how much I take for granted the ability to send things back and forth, all over the world, but that this still can remain too much of a leap into a different world for an older generation. Yet, initiatives such as the Social Exclusion Unit have promoted easily accessible computer training, so that everyone can benefit from the amazing online services that now exist.

So, what about psychotherapy and counselling online? I first heard about this from a presentation by Irish colleagues who had designed a CDT package. They had put it on trial, finding it highly successful in reaching people in rural areas, people who worked shifts, and especially men. Not having to visit a place with a stigma attached, such as a clinic, was both convenient and safe. The majority of people who used the package were, of course, IT literate and found the almost "impersonal" relationship very beneficial. Several of us present were very sceptical, as this seemed to go against the proven importance of "the relation-ship" in therapy. However, as time goes on, we are increasingly using social networks, communicating through Skype and email, using ever more sophisticated mobile phones, and in spite of the well-publicised dangers of the Internet, forming and maintaining strong relationships with others.

I've concluded that increasing access to psychotherapy and counselling, which was a major aim of the IAPT project, can definitely be achieved through becoming familiar with IT. This doesn't mean that face-to-face individual and group meeting and "traditional" psychotherapy is no longer valid. It can be helpful to have such a meeting to begin with and afterwards other media can be used if all parties are agreed. This applies to training as well, as one Northern Irish institute demonstrated through having weekly video-link presentations by some of the world's most distinguished therapists, followed by an interactive session and by staff conducting therapy by phone and Skype to remoter parts of the region. It will be good to see these issues brought into training and for psychotherapy professional bodies to provide training, as this is a new approach and needs to be well supported.

Note

1. http://www.mindfull.org/more-about-mindfull/

References

Balick, A. (2014). *The Psychodynamics of Social Networking*. London: Karnac.

Buckingham, D. (2013). Making sense of the "Digital Generation": Growing up with digital media. *Self & Society, 40*: 7–15.

Daintish, J. (Ed.) (2009). *"IT", A Dictionary of Physics*. Oxford: Oxford University Press.

Dunn, K. (2013). The therapeutic alliance. A paper given at the symposium "Psychotherapy 2.0: Meeting the Challenges and Potential of the Digital Age", London, 12 October 2013.

Freud, S. (1912). Recommendations to physicians practicing psychoanalysis. *S. E., 12*: 111–120. London: Hogarth.

Gauri, S. (director), & Nalki, R. (producer). (2012). *English Vinglish*. India.

Lévi-Strauss, C. (1966). *The Savage Mind*. London: Weidenfeld & Nicolson.

Maheu, M., Pulier, M. L., Wilhelm, F., McMenamin, J. P., & Brown-Connolly, N. E. (2005). *The Mental Health Professional and the New Technologies: A Handbook for Practice Today*. New Jersey: Lawrence Erbsum Associates.

Naydler, J. (2013). The advent of the wearable computer. *Self & Society, 40*: 17–24.

Nora, S., & Minc, A. (1978). *L'informatisation de la société: rapport à M. le Président de la République*. Paris: Seuil.

Rickels, L. A. (1989). Kafka and Freud on the telephone. *Modern Austrian Literature, 22.3/4*: 211–225.

Rutter, M. (2012). Resilience as a dynamic concept. *Development and Psychopathology, 24*: 335–344.

Schofield, H. (2012). "Minitel: The rise and fall of the France-wide web". BBC News, Paris, 27 June 2012; http://www.bbc.co.uk/news/magazine-18610692. Retrieved 12 May 2013.

Storr, A. (1980). *The Art of Psychotherapy*. London: Taylor & Francis.

The Centre for Economic Performance's Mental Health Policy Group (2012). A report: *How Mental Illness Loses Out in the NHS*.

http://www.who.int/mental_health/advocacy/en/Call_for_Action_MoH_Intro.pdf

CHAPTER TWO

How to think about psychotherapy in a digital context

Aaron Balick

A funny thing happens when psychotherapy and technology meet: all too often, thinking stops as a result. This is a curious situation to find in a field where thinking occupies such an important position. For many psychotherapists, technology is an anathema. After all, though psychotherapy was invented at the tail end of the nineteenth century in the intense coal fire-heat of a burgeoning mechanical age, it ultimately relied on devices no more complex than a couch, a chair, and a door that closed. Even today, the *optimal* condition for a traditional psychotherapeutic space is that it lacks modern technology completely, and it is all the better for it. The consultation room is meant to be a "safe place" where impingement is minimised so the client can simply *be* with his/her therapist. Shielded from the intrusions of pinging phones, email alerts, and Facebook event notifications, the client can come into himself/herself, and thereby come into relationship with another for the psychotherapeutic work.

Psychotherapists know from experience that a large proportion of the psychotherapeutic work comes by way of the multi-natured layers of the psychotherapeutic relationship (Clarkson, 2003), and there is much research, some of which is described by Cooper (2008), that bears this out too; a space free of technological infringement is ideal in order for the therapeutic relationship to grow. However, while traditional psychotherapy remains blissfully unplugged, its therapists and clients generally are not; outside the therapy room they are always "on", plugged in and connected. Whether or not the ubiquity of connected-up culture features as an explicit theme in therapy, it is no doubt an intrinsic part of the field in which psychotherapy occurs. More and more, as I have pointed out previously (Balick, 2012), world is one in which one has the capacity to pierce the off-line clinical encounter in the form of virtual impingements. I have defined "virtual impingement" in the broadest sense as "any event that happens to a person by way of the virtual world, which is experienced as an intrusion on the self" (p. 125); this can include anything as benign as an unwanted photograph posted on Facebook by another, to the more pernicious activity of cyber-bullying.

Such impingements are part of everyday life outside the therapy room, and I have argued (ibid.) that the therapeutic environment enables a possibility for a deeper discovery of this process, not only in the clinical sense with our clients, but also as a way into understanding broader social and cultural issues in relation to the digital world; this is a way of developing therapeutic thinking as applied to the digital world, for which I will be advocating in this chapter. Whether this application is with regard to traditional individual psychotherapy in the context of our own rapidly developing technological world, or psychotherapy within and mediated by it, that is, online psychotherapy (Anthony & Nagel, 2010), we need to know how to think about it critically, with psychotherapeutic acumen and precision.

For many psychotherapists and other mental health professionals, technology, when considered at all, can feel threatening. Not only is it perceived to interfere with psychotherapeutic boundaries (texting or emailing between sessions; mobiles ringing in purses or pockets; projected fears of social networking being destructive to relationships; etc.), but it also changes the rules of engagement, provoking traditional psychotherapists to ask questions they may prefer not to have to ask themselves. These questions can be assembled by theme.

Direct questions that come up as problems arise

- Do I have to have a website? If so, how do I wish to present myself, and how might I be perceived by potential clients?

- How can I be sure I remain within my registering body's ethical framework?
- How do I deal with therapeutic material sent via email or text message?
- What do I do with a text message that has come out of hours?
- I have found that my client is a friend of a friend on Facebook, what do I do?

Questions that we should be asking but may not know to ask

- What information might potential clients get about me from Google and how might this affect our therapy? Is it ethical to Google my clients?
- What kind of decisions am I making about my private online life that may affect my professional one? How aware am I of my "digital dossier"[1] and how might this passive online identity (Balick, 2014), as it appears in a Google search, affect the way my clients see me?[2]
- Can I use social media in ways that do not interfere with my clinical work or should I abstain from it all together?
- Do I use the same mobile phone for private and professional reasons? Are there consequences for this choice? What do I need to consider if I'm doing Skype sessions?
- Are emails to my clients encrypted? Do they have to be? What about the notes I keep on my computer?

Questions we may be asking on our clients' behalf

- How do I better understand a client who is involved in technologies in ways I don't comprehend?
- Am I fully accounting for generational differences in the clinical judgements I am making about my clients' Internet use?
- How much do I understand the online worlds in which my clients are engaging?
- How much knowledge do my clients expect me to have with regard to the world of technology?
- What is my own psychological response to technology and how might this response affect my relationship to my client?

*Fundamental questions about the meaning that
technology and the digital world hold for individuals
and society as a whole*

- What are the unconscious meanings that we give to online experience and what are the consequences of this "new age" of ubiquitous connectivity?
- How does our modern technological world influence and mediate our own relational connectivity both within ourselves and with others?
- Is our technological world a real paradigm shift in human interrelating, or are we just getting caught up in the hype?
- How do we, as a society, make meaning of new media and new technology?

These questions, though numerous and begging varied and complex answers, merely scratch the surface of that confusing nexus where psychotherapy and technology meet. The profusion of such questions is often the cause for our thinking to shut down. The onslaught of potential consequences, combined with the gaps in our knowledge, have the capacity to induce an inundation of anxiety in which therapists either defend themselves by not properly thinking things through or by avoiding the situation completely by burying their heads in the sand. However vast the notion of modern technology, it is, nonetheless, an object (like any other) that takes our projections, phantasies, and transferences. In relation to such an object, Seligman (2011) calls upon the "analytic postulate" in which "most anything can stand for anything", maintaining that

> particular objects, forms, and media will lend themselves to certain particular uses, and it seems more likely that the social situations that such objects embody will be imported into the analyses along with them: The Internet and its media carry the contemporary crises of privacy, overstimulation, and the broad questions of where and by whom reality is adjudicated. There is a kind of groping for the core that seeps into each of the cases, a search for intimacy amidst tension and alienation, that gets organized around the social media, even as those new forms are amplifying these problems in the culture and the analytic dyads that it sustains. (p. 502)

This text was created to acknowledge what online life provokes in us while attempting to undo the resultant assault on thinking invited by the complexities of modern technological life in their relation to psychotherapy. All the while we might remind ourselves that we will have developed skills to think things through in a different way while at the same time being able to hold the unknowable in a way that is relatively contained. To put it simply, all that we need to do is apply our usual way of psychotherapeutic thinking (though, admittedly, with somewhat less abstraction) and apply it to the material at hand, the online world in all of its manifestations and complexities.

Online life is not singular

One of the biggest mistakes that anyone encounters when confronted with thinking about "the Internet", "the digital world", or "technology," is imprecision. From psychological theorists to cultural commentators, we hear an awful lot about why we should be worried about the "virtual world" or "the Internet" without being told precisely what we should be worried about. This lack of precision encourages sloppy thinking because it disables us from being precise about the *particular* operations that we should be thoughtful about, and *how* we should be thoughtful about them. As I have said elsewhere:

> While we should acknowledge that in some ways the virtual world offers a different category of experience than the public domain, we also need to bear in mind that *different actions* across the online world also offer fundamentally different expressions of identity and self within that context (e.g., taking on the identity of another in a networked fantasy game or interacting with known others on an SNS [social networking site]); simply because one is doing the interacting through the interface of a computer terminal or smartphone does not make these interactions homogeneous. (Balick, 2014)

Morozov (2013) similarly argues that utopian (or dystopian) thinking about "the Internet" is essentially misguided because "the Internet" is not a singular knowable thing that can be theorised. For example, though more and more we find our lives occurring *online*, we must think about this *being online* as a sort of quasi-public environment—in some situations it is more public than others.

The way one may express oneself in a variety of online environments will differ depending on that online environment. For example, self-expression on a social networking site such as Facebook, amongst online friends, is different from actions one may take on a professional social networking site such as LinkedIn. While self-expression on social networking sites such as Facebook tends to correlate pretty closely to offline self-image (Back et al., 2011), the way in which an individual may choose to play with an identity in a virtual environment such as Second Life or a massive multiplayer online role-playing game such as World of Warcraft will be very different. Furthermore, the way in which one presents oneself on an online dating site will be different from how one represents oneself in a professional discussion forum.

The presentation of self in everyday life (Goffman, 1959) is as varied online as it is offline. To consider "online interaction" as a singular register of experience is the first problem that we must immediately sweep out of the way. From this perspective, the first rule of psychotherapeutic thinking in relation to the online world is to be precise. Are we talking emails or social networks; actively created online identities (e.g., Facebook profiles) or passive online identities (such as those created on our behalf by way of a Google search, for example); a public tweet that may lack context, or a private text message that may be lacking nuance? While all of these *events* are particular manifestations of modern technologies (in which I include the whole of the Internet in conjunction with mobile technologies such as smartphones, tablets, and laptops), they are not the same as each other. In many important ways, a status update on Facebook is no more the same as a private text message than a response to "How are you?" in mixed company is the same as a different answer given to a close friend in private. While many cultural commentators complain that Facebook, for example, represents a false and rosy picture of any given individual, they do not at the same time consider that most actions across Facebook are essentially interpersonal interactions within a *public context*. While these cultural commentators may not take issue with an individual "putting their best face on" for a dinner party or other public social event, many of them do project their rancour about Facebook narcissism where, equally, individuals are "out in public" engaging with their public-facing personas. In order to think about this psychotherapeutically, it is crucial not to respond with a knee-jerk fear-induced response to a narrative of perpetual relational shallowing; rather, we can think in terms of public-facing aspects of the psyche as exemplified by Jung's (1966) conception of the persona or Winnicott's (1960) notion of the false self. It is important, however, to hold in mind that these concepts and terms need to be deployed with a depth and thoughtfulness that prevents them from being a kind of psychological jargon that is simply tacked onto various aspects of "online relating". For example, while it is crucial we understand many aspects of online relating as employing outward-facing aspects of the ego such as the false self, as I have summarised elsewhere:

> We all develop a false self in relation to our strengths and capacities, so it is not "false" at all, but as real as any other part of ourselves. It is however, deployed with the aim of social compliance and is therefore not a fully free expression of our authentic selves (which is itself a complex and problematic concept). When the ... functions of false/true self and the motivation for mutual recognition are combined with the ease, convenience and architecture of the online social network, you can see how the social network is replete with opportunities and challenges. In one sense, recognition is so easily acquired over the social network (Look! He "liked" my comment; Great, she followed me!) Many of these acquisitioned [sic] are gained by the persona or false self. Does the true or "real" self get neglected in this transaction? (Balick, 2014, p. 30)

By thoughtfully applying insights from the depth psychologies we add a profundity and complexity to our exploration of the *meaning* of our online lives rather than dumbing-down and responding in ways that are inadequate to the task of either psychotherapy or the application of psychotherapeutic concepts onto cultural artefacts.

While it is important to hold in mind that most online environments can be broadly compared to public environments, there are some important principles that do indeed differentiate *online* identities from their *offline* equivalents. These include:

1. The instantaneous nature of online engagements
2. The ease of replicability of information online (enhanced by point one)

3. The ease with which privacy can be compromised (enhanced by points one and two)
4. The way in which information logged online may never be erased and may be accessed at any time (synergises with points one, two, and three).[3]

These categories work synergistically, with each one creating an enhanced effect for the rest of them (Balick, 2014, Chapter Six, p. 137).

While these principles were developed with particular reference to online *identity* they are useful in thinking about any sort of online interaction because each of these principles, alongside their synergistic engagement with one another, are applicable across the board of online interactions. It is the nature of these principles and the consequences of them that, I believe, causes such consternation to psychotherapists when confronted with the issue of technology and the Internet. This consternation results from the feeling of overwhelm that assaults therapists when they think about technology and the Internet as a singular and incomprehensible behemoth rather than as simply an alternative environment through which relational events are occurring, albeit differently. By breaking down the thinking into these terms, psychotherapists and others in related fields can approach the material more thoughtfully. While there remain many unanswered questions (another state of affairs with which psychotherapists should be familiar), some of the questions are answerable, and those that are not can be engaged with in a more thoughtful and grounded way.

The psychodynamics of the extension of the self into virtual space

I have found it helpful to consider "virtual space" (meaning anything that is occurring online, from emails to avatars) as an extension of the self. The idea of extending ourselves through the various media is not new, as Marshall McLuhan noted as far back as 1964:

> Today ... we have extended our central nervous system itself in a global embrace, abolishing both space and time as far as our planet is concerned. Rapidly, we approach the final phase of the extensions of man—the technological simulation of consciousness, when the creative process of knowing will be collectively and

corporately extended to the whole of human society, much as we have already extended our senses and our nerves by the various media. (pp. 3–4)

The concept of the self and its extension outside the immediate physical body is one with which many psychotherapists should be familiar, because the very functioning of the therapeutic relationship relies upon how the therapist and the client, within the therapeutic dyad, extend, in one way or other, into the psychic world of the other. The therapeutic relationship is held in such high regard because it is recognised that object constancy, the therapeutic alliance, and attachment are all fundamental aspects of what make psychotherapy work. This is because the nature of empathy is embedded in the ability to *extend the self into the mind of the other*. Perhaps it is the tradition of object relations that theorises this notion the most cohesively. By looking at early relationships and the development of the self, the object relations tradition sees the very nature of the self as a product of external influences that are brought inside the self via the internalisation of external objects. This internalisation occurs in the context of what Winnicott (1953) refers to as the facilitating environment between the primary caretaker and the infant that offers a sort of intermediate space whereby the infant works out the nature of the world between internal experience and other people. In Winnicott's words, "The intermediate area to which I am referring is the area that is allowed to the infant between primary creativity and objective perception based on reality testing" (p. 266). In other words, this intermediate space is one that allows the infant to begin to distinguish the limits of her selfhood, from an initial experience of omnipotence to a later, more developed position of limit in relation to the external world. Central to this is the development of intersubjectivity in which the infant comes to realise not only the limits of the outside world but that those others in the external world have minds of their own. In Winnicott's admittedly confusing language there is a shift from "object relating", in which the other is viewed simply an aspect of the self, to "object usage", in which the other is viewed as a subject in her own right. Jessica Benjamin (1988) paraphrases Winnicott's view of this development succinctly:

At first, Winnicott says, an object is "related" to, it is part of the subject's mind and not necessarily experienced as real, external, or independent. But there comes a point in the subject's development where this kind of relatedness must give way to an appreciation of the object as an outside entity, not merely something in one's mind. This ability to enter into exchange with the outside object is what Winnicott calls "using" the object. (p. 37)

The online world also functions as a kind of facilitating environment in which the limits of self and other are tested; an environment that is vulnerable to objectification or "object relating" in Winnicott's words, or intersubjectivity, which is more akin to "object use". Lingiardi (2011) makes a lovely parallel between this transitional space and online relating:

> computer-mediated communication allows the user to play with realities and identities. It can thus contain transitional elements as defined by Winnicott; the transitional object, in fact, lies halfway between Me and not-Me, between reality and fantasy, between near and far, between what we create and what we discover. Serving as a potential space between subject and environment (a space for experimenting with the Self between me and myself, and between me and the other), the online experience—which in many cases facilitates and feeds dissociation—can also help us illuminate the difficult path between separation anxiety and being engulfed by the object. (p. 487)

While there is not enough room in this chapter to detail the myriad ways in which the online world functions as a transitional space or facilitating environment, suffice it to say that conceptualising it as such will allow the doors to be opened for a depth psychological approach to this important zone of interpersonal interaction. By applying a broad-based multi-modal conceptual psychological framework (akin to the frameworks developed by Dreher (2000), Hollway and Jefferson (2010), and Frosh (2010) for psychoanalytic applications to society and culture) psychotherapists can offer broad insight into the social media and technological complex that so engages our global attention. Individual applications to online phenomena may be as varied as the psychotherapy modalities; however, it will be the responsibility of psychotherapy researchers to dutifully deploy their theories upon this complex area with due diligence, grounding their research in data, and enabling its influence to reach beyond the narrow confines of fellow psychological thinkers.

Conclusion

The varieties of experiences that are open to us as therapists and citizens in this brave new world of ubiquitous connected-up technologies are immense. To paraphrase Huxley by way of Shakespeare, we may, upon entering this new environment exclaim, "Oh brave new world, with such *things* in it!" In this exclamation, we may forget that though they are indeed things, it is indeed people who have made these things, and though these things exude quite an influence upon us, we are part of the feedback system that enables these things to come into existence in the way they have. This notion of a relationship between technology and society is a function of what Baym (2010) refers to as the "social shaping hypothesis". Rather than seeing technology as something that happens *to* us, we may rather look at it as something that develops in tandem with our expectations and needs. However, there are consequences to this shaping of technology that, in many ways, has produced a system that favours weak tie communications over strong tie communications, as weak ties are more amenable to twenty-four hour a day "touch in/tough out" contact via the expansion of mobile smartphone technology. While many of us think we want this sort of contact, Turkle (2011) warns that "if we pay attention to the real consequences of what we think we want, we may discover what we really want, we may want some stillness and solitude" (p. 285). From this perspective, the Winnicottian (1958) notion of the "capacity to be alone" is also thrown into jeopardy.

While my aim in this chapter is not to raise unnecessary anxiety (in fact, in many ways I am positive and optimistic about technology), it is to throw light on the rather less conscious aspects of our brave new world, a light that a psychotherapeutic perspective can bring to bear on it. Sand (2007) notes that "We [psychoanalysts] need to expand our analytic boundaries to incorporate these new aspects of self [provoked by the online world], or risk becoming stagnant and outdated as we lose the interactive richness of what will soon be an integral part of all our patients' experience" (p. 87). On this point I heartily concur with Sand, but I would also choose to expand it. Applications of psychotherapeutic thinking in relation not only have the capacity to shed further light on technology and our culture (rather than just our patients' experiences), but by expanding our psychotherapeutic thinking into this area, we also stand to revitalise psychotherapy as a discipline itself.

Commentator one: Gordon Law

Behind the front end of the underlying logic and denouement of Balick's argument there lurks an operating system of fundamental ethical principles. In brief these are:

Autonomy: respecting the patient's right to make his or her own decisions emphasises the importance of the patient's commitment to participating voluntarily in the services offered by the practitioner.

Beneficence: a commitment to promoting the patient's well-being by acting in the best interests of the patient, based on professional assessment.

Non-maleficence: a commitment to avoiding harm to the patient by striving to mitigate any harm caused to a patient even when the harm is unavoidable or unintended.

Fidelity: honouring trust by judicious exploration of expectations; making explicit that which is implicit.

Justice: the fair and impartial treatment of all patients and the provision of adequate services—as well as considering conscientiously any legal requirements and obligations.

Self-interest: appropriately applying all the above principles as entitlements for self.

Foremost of these principles is the exponential explosion of *justice*. Clearly the digital age radically changes the extent to which psychotherapy services may be offered.

But which principles apply to Balick's themes? Project yourself into the virtual world and imagine little text boxes popping up. Here's a sample:

- Do I have to have a website? *Self-interest*
  If so, how do I wish to present myself? *Autonomy*
  And how might I be perceived by potential patients? *Fidelity*
  How can I be sure I remain within my registering body's ethical framework? *Fidelity, Justice*

- Are emails to my patients encrypted? Do they have to be? *Non-maleficence*
  What about the notes I keep on my computer? *Fidelity*
- How do I better understand a patient who is involved in technologies in ways I don't understand? *Justice, Fidelity.*

Tagging the text in this way identifies the ethical underpinnings of the themes chosen by Balick. He emphasises the need for precision. Technology is not to be regarded as a catch-all phenomena largely beyond one's control; it needs to be embraced yet not introjected without differentiation.

"… all that we need to do is apply our usual way of psychotherapeutic thinking …. *Autonomy* … and apply it to the material at hand … *Beneficience* … the online world in all of its manifestations and complexities."

In other words apply principles to contextual factors—the target:

	Target individual(s) and/or group(s) to be addressed					
Ethical Principles	Practitioner	Patient	Other professionals	Other statutory agencies	Other relevant parties	General public
Autonomy						
Beneficence						
Non-maleficence						
Fidelity						
Justice						
Self-interest						

All of this applies to a pre-digital era—so here's the "service pack one upgrade" for the digital age.

He adds a third dimension for new technology: land lines, smart phones, tablets, PCs and within the capability of each, a mode of delivery—phone calls, text messages, emails, and online audio-visual sessions.

Technologically speaking, Balick has created a relational database—a nexus of synergistic engagements. This is *a way of thinking*—not a tick box matrix. As Balick asserts, you can use everything you already know and simply deploy it via technology. "Moreover, because most online environments can be broadly compared to public environments, there are some important principles to hold in mind that do indeed differentiate online *identities* from their offline equivalents" and "computer-mediated communication allows the user to play with realities and identities". This expands the psychotherapist's *autonomy*.

Likewise, the "analytic postulate", in which "most anything can stand for anything", nuances all other principles. Obviously, one has to adapt to suit particular circumstances. For example, one may choose to be more explicit about a patient's expectations by specifying "no text messages". This addresses *fidelity* but constrains the patient's *autonomy* by invoking the *self-interest* of *autonomy*. As ever, one has to balance the relevance of one principle against one or more others.

I think Balick's notion of "virtual space" is a crucial contribution. In this domain and because "the nature of empathy is embedded in the ability to *extend the self into the mind of the other*" the psychotherapist (like Optimus Prime, the main character in the online *Transformers* game) now has an increased ability to morph into the virtual reality of another's psyche. And, as Balick concludes, the digital age encourages manifestations of virtual self in an asynchronous environment. By taking on both conscious and unconscious extensions of self (both real and virtual), we have the opportunity of exercising *self-interest* and thereby, authoring or, at least, influencing a revitalisation of psychotherapy.

Commentator two: Tom Warnecke

The digital world has crept up quietly onto the practice of psychotherapy. Information technology mushroomed from a convenient tool to facilitate communication and research into digital and virtual worlds. These may, in multiple ways, impinge on the therapeutic space or provide access to a therapist's personal information at the click of a mouse.

Balick rightly argues that we can—and should—use our well established psychotherapeutic tools to think about the great technological upheaval that is changing many aspects of the world we live in.

Applying depth psychology paradigms to the "confusing nexus where psychotherapy and technology meet" makes for thought-provoking read and left me wondering about perceptions I commonly hear of the digital world as the uninvited visitor knocking on the door of our treasured therapeutic space.

What drives such views? And why can we not dare, collectively, to welcome and embrace these modern variants of human endeavour? Did psychotherapy not learn to manage, make good use of, and find symbolism and meaning in an earlier invention that changed the ways people lived—namely the telephone?

It is a primary purpose of psychotherapy's formal frame to create a space where client and therapist can safely cross psychological boundaries. Should that not equally apply to any digital impingement? I expect I am not the only psychotherapist whose client has insisted on reading a text message that has arrived during a session. On the particular occasion I recall, the event facilitated a hitherto absent personality aspect to appear in our relationship. My intervention that challenged my client's action made for a difficult yet powerful session that became a turning point for this person's therapeutic process. At the other end of the spectrum, another client—too anxious to leave the house unaccompanied—created an ingenious, round the clock and spanning the globe, supportive environment with the aid of an array of digital communication, and social and virtual networking tools. This client's creative use of new technology achieved a resource that would have been unimaginable only a decade ago.

Considering Balick's thoughts about how the Internet and digital technology are not a single knowable thing, I am struck how this observation seems to parallel dynamics commonly observed with regard to minority concerns in psychotherapy: I am referring to common tendencies to either ignore the unfamiliar or to reduce some rich and pluralistic "many" into simplistic frames, or, worse still, to pathologise an unfamiliar "other".

Both digital and minority experience share an intrinsically pluralistic nature, and both appear to instigate the inundation of anxiety that shuts down thinking, as Balick describes.

Most of us will only ever become familiar with a number of digital or social media phenomena, just as we are unlikely to develop good working knowledge of all minority concerns. But should that really be an issue for good psychotherapy practice?

While it is probably recommendable that therapists only use digital technology they are comfortable with and knowledgeable about, there seems indeed little rationale for psychotherapy to approach digital impingement in any way differently from other aspects of human life and endeavour, namely with curiosity, openness, and thorough appreciation for the complexities and multi-layered-ness of individual experience.

Psychotherapy is the art and science of exploring the deeply personal, of weaving threads of meaning that may help a person to recover his or her vitality and autonomy. New media technology and its manifestations, are an ever-growing part of the diverse, multi-layered, and pluralistic world we live in and, as such, they have every "right" to be included in our thinking and welcomed into the therapeutic space.

Notes

1. Palfry and Gasser (2008) define a digital dossier as "all the personally identifiable information associated with … [a] name, whether that information is accessible or not …" (p. 40).
2. If you have not Googled yourself to find out what your passive online identity looks like, perhaps you should take the opportunity now.
3. Since the publication of these four principles in my book *The Psychodynamics of Social Networking: Connected—up Instantaneous Culture and the Self* I have added a further two. These are "scalability", that is, one's potential to exposure to vast audiences, and "the online disinhibition effect" (Suler, 2004), which reduces online inhibition either by way of anonymity, or the emotional distance that is enabled by online interfaces.

References

Anthony, K., & Nagel, D. M. (2010). *Therapy Online: A Practical Guide.* London: Sage.

Back, M., Stopfer, J., Vazire, S., Gaddis, S., Scmukle, S., Egloff, B., & Gosling, S. (2011). Facebook profiles reflect actual personality, not self-idealization. *Psychological Science, 21*: 372–374.

Balick, A. (2012). TMI in the transference, LOL: psychoanalytic reflections on Google, social networking, and "virtual impingement". *Psychoanalysis, Culture and Society, 17*: 120–136.

Balick, A. (2013). The real motivation behind social networking. *Therapeutic Innovations in Light of Technology, 3.*

Balick, A. (2014). *The Psychodynamics of Social Networking: Connected-up Instantaneous Culture and the Self.* London: Karnac.

Baym, K. (2010). *Personal Connections in the Digital Age*. Cambridge and Malden, MA: Polity.

Benjamin, J. (1988). *The Bonds of Love*. New York: Pantheon

Clarkson, P. (2003). *The Therapeutic Relationship* (2nd ed.). London: Whurr.

Cooper, M. (2008). *Essential Research Findings in Counselling and Psychotherapy: the Facts are Friendly*. London: Sage.

Dreher, U. (2000). *Foundations for Conceptual Research in Psychoanalysis* (Trans. E. Ristle). London: Karnac.

Frosh, S. (2010). *Psychoanalysis Outside the Clinic: Interventions in Psychosocial Studies*. London: Palgrave.

Goffman, E. (1959). *The Presentation of Self in Everyday Life*. New York and London: Penguin Books.

Hollway, W., & Jefferson, T. (2010). *Doing Qualitative Research Differently: Free Association, Narrative and the Interview Method*. London: Sage.

Jung, C. G. (1966). *Two Essays on Analytical Psychology* (Trans. R. F. C. Hull). Princeton, NJ: Princeton University Press.

Lingiardi, V. (2011). Realities in dialogue: commentary on paper by Stephen Hartman. *Psychoanalytic Dialogues, 21*: 483–495.

McLuhan, M. (1964). *Understanding Media*. London and New York: Routledge.

Morozov, E. (2013). *To Save Everything Click Here: Technology, Solutionism and the Urge to Fix Problems that Don't Exist*. London and New York: Allen Lane Books.

Palfrey, J., & Gasser, U. (2008). *Born Digital: Understanding the First Generation of Digital Natives*. New York: Basic Books.

Sand, S. (2007). Future considerations: interactive identities and the interactive self. *The Psychoanalytic Review, 94*: 83–97.

Seligman, S. (2011). Psychoanalytic ideals, new technologies, and the expropriations of the corporate self: commentary on paper by Stephen Hartman. *Psychoanalytic Dialogues, 21*: 496–507.

Suler, J. (2004). The online disinhibition effect. In: The psychology of cyberspace. Retrieved 1 November 2013 from http://users.rider.edu/~suler/psycyber/disinhibit/.

Turkle, S. (2011). *Alone Together: Why We Expect More from Technology and Less from Each Other*. New York: Basic Books.

Winnicott, D. W. (1953). Transitional objects and transitional phenomena: a study of the first not-me possession. In: P. Buckly (Ed.), *Essential Papers on Object Relations* (pp. 254–271). New York and London: New York University Press, 1986.

Winnicott, D. W. (1958). The capacity to be alone. In: J. Southerland (Ed.), *The Maturational Processes and the Facilitating Environment: Studies in the*

Theory of Emotional Development (pp. 140–152). London: The Hogarth Press, 1982.

Winnicott, D. W. (1960). Ego distortion in terms of true and false self. In: J. Southerland (Ed.), *The Maturational Processes and the Facilitating Environment: Studies in the Theory of Emotional Development* (pp. 140–152). London: The Hogarth Press, 1982.

CHAPTER THREE

Thinking about training fit for the digital era

Chris Blackmore, Digby Tantam, and Anne Stokes

Working with the next generation: training for online counselling

Anne Stokes

BACP's guidelines for online counselling and psychotherapy (Anthony, 2009) strongly recommend that if counsellors are going to work online, they should undertake further training. This makes sense to me as working online has differences from face-to-face (F2F) interactions. As is demonstrated in the case study in Chapter Eight, counsellors can find themselves in both therapeutic and ethical difficulties, not to mention legal ones, if they have not fully considered these differences. The areas training may cover are discussed in the second section below.

Because so many of us use the Internet regularly for administrative aspects of our work, it is easy to believe that it is simple to transfer to meeting clients online. It is quite scary to trawl the Internet for counsellors offering online counselling only to find that they do not mention any online training amongst their credentials.

Page (1999) considers how the "shadow" may affect interactions with clients and that, although when we start to experiment with a new part of ourselves we may feel tentative and uncertain, we may in fact appear very powerful to our clients. If we haven't understood this and worked with it, our clients may be left in a vulnerable place. Although it may not entirely eliminate this factor, online training will help to bring it in to the light and safeguard our future online clients.

Goss, Anthony, and Nagel (2012) posit that proper training is a prerequisite to ensuring client safety. This is to make certain that there is proper preparation and consideration of ethical issues before embarking on client work. I believe that clients should be encouraged to discover the qualifications of a counsellor when considering working online (Bor, Gill, & Stokes, 2011), and to use a directory of trained online practitioners such as the one that ACTO[1] offers.

While the International Society for Mental Health Online (ISMHO) does not endorse any specific training, it supports the importance of competence. Its website[2] lists some training organisations, though recommends that you also undertake an independent search. It is wise to also look at the background of those providing the training—are they themselves trained in this area? Do they also work online with clients and so really understand the issues?

The early training for online work, which began in the late nineties meant that providers inevitably had no training themselves—there was none! However, sound online organisations put their own tutors through their training to establish whether or not it covered what was needed, and then have refined and added to the curriculum over the years. Initially most training was concerned with using emails to counsel clients, with a very small amount of time being given to working synchronously. The balance in training has now shifted, so that both synchronous and asynchronous communication is routinely considered.

Another aspect to consider when selecting a training organisation is whether or not it is externally validated or endorsed. For some counsellors, that will be a very important consideration in terms of their CV. Certainly when an organisation is funding the training, this may be one of their criterion. For other people, the length of time the organisation has existed and has been offering online training, as well as its reputation in the field, will be the deciding factors. Blackmore and Tantam (below) raise the question of how the quality of training can be assured. While external validation cannot guarantee that a course will offer the experience that you find most stimulating, it does give some assurance as to its standard and quality.

Whether or not they are externally validated, courses should offer clarity about what is involved, access to previous students if asked for, a rigorous assessment process, and a complaints procedure, at the very least. This information is not necessarily to be found on websites, as it can make them too cumbersome, but be prepared to ask the admissions tutor for any reasonable information. If you cannot get a response, it may tell you something about the course!

Blackmore and Tantam also raise the question of the impact of e-learning on a trainee's mental health and well-being. This is a valid point, as I am well aware that both the de-skilling process of learning to work as counsellors in an online environment and the impact of group dynamics through the ether can be a deeply upsetting experience initially. This can happen equally easily in F2F training, though tutors appear to feel that they can monitor and support students more in F2F training. I might argue the opposite. F2F training happens on one day a week, so that is usually the only time that students and tutors have real contact. Online, we can easily meet students seven days a week (if we so choose!). I say to students, "If I am online with my 'available' sign showing, then please do feel free to contact me." Most do if there is an issue. Tutors can also contact participants in the same way. It's also possible to pick up and attend to trainees' wellbeing from journal entries and teaching and learning sessions. In the organisation I direct,[3] we have a campus counsellor and every student is entitled to a certain number of free sessions with her if they would like to use them.

How does training happen?

There is no one way in which training for online counselling is delivered, except that it will be online. The types of experience given below reflect a generality, and no single training course will necessarily offer all of these.

Choosing a training course

Some courses are delivered to groups, and some are for individual learning. Personally, I favour learning in groups, as the collaboration and the diversity of ideas, experiences, and issues raised seems to enrich the process and also, importantly, provides a network of colleagues also working online for postcourse support. However, not everyone enjoys working in a group. Another disadvantage of group learning is that it will only begin at specific times (e.g., January, April, and September). This can be frustrating if it doesn't fit your schedule. One-to-one online training can often be arranged to suit a period when you are less busy.

Some training organisations offer just an introduction to counselling online, while others offer initial training, a diploma, and short workshops on aspects of online work, as well as online supervision training. So if you think you might want to go further, this could be a consideration. Would you want to be able to stay with the same organisation, or if you decide to change, would the second training organisation be prepared to APEL or APL[4] your previous course?

The majority of current online training happens in courses that are not a part of a large commercial organisation but were started by online practitioners who wanted to ensure good practice and share their passion! (Jones & Stokes, 2009). As a result they are usually welcoming of enquiries about how courses happen, what is in them, what the prospects of working online afterwards are, and many other questions counsellors want to ask before signing up for a particular training. It is not uncommon for a large number of emails to be exchanged and/or a live discussion on Skype to take place before an application is actually made.

What is likely to be included in an online training—and why?

Most online training courses will include a mixture of synchronous and asynchronous methods, thus mimicking the ways in which counselling takes place. So there will be email exchanges, as well as live sessions using text, or voice or video.

There will almost certainly be teaching and learning sessions. These synchronous sessions may be held in whole cohort groups, smaller groups, or one-to-one. In group sessions, there will be usually be as much input from students as from tutors, as topics and issues are discussed. As well as learning about the focus of the session, participants experience how interpersonal dynamics play out online. While this does happen in one-to-one sessions, it is rather more apparent in a group. This enables people to experience disinhibition, transference, countertransference, projection—the whole gamut—in an online environment, and to reflect on how they will process this when working with a client.

It can make for tricky and discomforting times for students and tutors, but is immensely useful learning.

Often training groups, or their subgroups, continue to meet long after courses are over. They have worked through the difficulties and dynamics of forming online groups and can provide support for each other. Evans (2009) discusses the importance of case study groups and peer support forums, and, in my experience, these are frequent outcomes of online trainings.

There are a number of elements that parallel F2F counselling courses, but which may also include a different aspect. Tutorials focus on how the participant is experiencing and coping with the online environment including technology, as well as with the more typical reflections on learning, group processes, and assessment. As tutorials will take place live online, technological problems in particular can often be resolved in the moment. While this is one of the most frustrating and common difficulties in online work, and a cause of great exasperation, there is nothing like it for being prepared for the same happenings in the real work with clients. Contributions and ways of resolving problems are shared between group members, so that, by the end of the course, confidence in dealing with the whims of technology is based on reality rather than an untested hope. A sense of "it will happen at some point, and the important thing is to be prepared for it and have discussed back-up plans with the client" has been established through experience.

To ensure that the differences between F2F and online counselling are considered, there can also be a "practice lab". Here learners will respond to an ethical dilemma, a legal issue or a "client" email. A few of the typical areas would be:

- Empathic response to a client enquiry
- Replying to an email which requires boundaries to be kept in place
- Responding to a client presenting with mental health issues
- Replying to an email asking about your counselling model or approach
- Working with difference and diversity
- Beginnings, middles, and ends online—what is different from F2F?
- Who might I choose *not* to work with online?
- Working with suicidal online clients
- Online contracts
- Encryption

- Working across geographic regions and jurisdictions
- The security (or not) of online synchronous platforms
- Compiling a list of online websites, agencies, and resources that will be useful for online counsellors and their clients.

There may also be an area in an online campus where students sign in or register every week. There might be a "task" to respond to—something to do with the online training of a more personal nature. This helps the tutors know that everyone is still on board, and helps create group cohesion. I think it can help counsellors to understand and grapple with the fact that working online can be very isolating if there is not some contact with other practitioners.

A heartfelt cry of people on online training courses is that they feel as if they are drowning under a sea of course emails. The learning in this is to consider setting up a separate and securely encrypted email address for course, and then client, work. It eliminates the possibility of opening your inbox during leisure time and being overwhelmed by course/client emails. It also prevents work emails being apparent to others if your inbox is opened while in a non-work setting. Clearing the inbox regularly into folders representing different aspects of the course also helps. In my training organisation, we have moved to discussion threads, begun by tutors or students, located on our campus website, so that people can choose more easily when to read and add to these.

Weekly journals are a part of the majority of training courses whether F2F or online. A difference with online training is that there is often an expectation that course tutors will read these throughout the course, rather than just the overall summary presented in a course portfolio. There is debate around this practice, being fairly criticised as preventing students from writing openly. On the other hand, it can enable tutors to spot difficulties and offer support as they do not "see" students each week, or pick up nuances from physical presence and interactions. We expect clients to be able to write or speak online openly to us as counsellors, so maybe it is helpful to experience sending something off into the ether in this way.

Sending things off into the ether, not knowing how they will be received, brings me to the final part that most courses have in common, and that is role-play. This gives participants the chance to experience being an online counsellor in a safe environment, where their "client" will understand that this is a learning environment and all may not go according to plan. It can be rather daunting for experienced F2F counsellors to go back to that place of conscious incompetence, but it is much better than experimenting on a real client. It gives an opportunity to begin to develop an online counselling approach based on that used in the individual's F2F counselling practice. What needs to be added? What cannot be used? And what simply needs tweaking?

Hopefully, the course will also enable counsellors to be a client to another trainee. An important part of my development as an online counsellor has been based on the experience of being an online client. I have learned what works for me and what doesn't; what it is like not to hear back from my counsellor when I expected to do so; and what to do when technology fails. That is not to say that what I find useful as a client will always work for my own clients. However, it has sharpened my understanding of what it is like to be at the receiving end of online counselling.

I don't particularly like the concept of role-plays, and the nearest alternative I can get to is "real plays". If someone is role-playing a client, they are not being themselves and it can be difficult for the counsellor to know who they are working with. Without visual cues, it is hard enough for counsellors to adjust to online work, without the added complication of a fellow student "making it up as they go along".

Just before writing this part of the chapter, I was driving home listening to *The Life Scientific* on Radio Four. Elizabeth Stokoe was describing CARM (Conversation Analytic Role-play Method), an approach that she has developed for training police, mediators, and lawyers, amongst others. Towards the end of the interview she spoke about the unreality in working with role-plays, and suggested a way forward based on using real client material, in methodological terms sounding rather like a Gilmore Group (Inskipp, 1996). While I don't think that online training has quite got to the point of adopting that, it chimed with me in terms of the importance of encouraging the use of material that is as real as possible.

> How can you construct an entire hypothetical role play and make it look anything like the situation you're really going to deal with? Yet people are trained all over the public and private sector to interact amongst the public through role play. (Stokoe, 2012)

In most introductory courses, role or real-plays are the norm. At diploma level, online trainees usually work with real clients, though still closely monitored and supervised. For anyone who is going to set up their own independent online practice, I would contend that undertaking a longer course, such as a diploma, ensures that the counsellor is "'fit for practice". Participants are also encouraged, or in some case required, to undergo their own therapy with a trained online counsellor who is not attached to the training organisation. Once more, this adds to the understanding of working online as a practitioner.

Future developments in training counsellors to work online

Currently, training for online counselling is almost solely available for counsellors who have already qualified to diploma level and who have some experience in working in a F2F setting. There are a few initial training courses that include a session or a weekend workshop covering this development, though these are not attempting to train students to work online.

Anthony and Goss (2003) stated that they held the opinion that online work was only suitable for experienced F2F counsellors. Around the same time one of my trainees emphasised:

> If I hadn't been working for some time with clients in a F2F set-
> ting, I really don't think I could have been grounded enough to
> cope with the extra dimensions and pressures of [working] online.
> (Jones & Stokes, 2009)

However, in the future, I would see initial training introducing blended learning that covers F2F, telephone, and online work. The reasons for my change of heart are that despite my own Luddite tendencies, I know that more and more counsellors are very at home with technology, and also that the world is changing and initial training courses need to adapt. Hopefully, the online elements or modules will take place online. This advance would parallel the counselling that happens with many clients—they blend F2F with online and/or telephone sessions to suit their life and work styles. There is much to be worked out before this becomes a reality, but it is being discussed in several institutions and professional organisations.

A further development may well be the increase in the number of workshops that are offered to online counsellors for CPD purposes.

Currently, professional organisations do not demand that online practitioners demonstrate CPD activities specifically related to that part of their work. As well as updating our practice, CPD is an opportunity to network and reduce feelings of isolation (Bor & Stokes, 2011). The latter can be particularly present in an online counsellor's life. S/he may be surrounded by F2F colleagues, none of whom understand the issues of online working, and indeed may be still dismissive of it.

Online supervision

I mentioned online supervision above in relation to working with clients during online counselling training. There are a growing number of online courses for trained online counsellors who wish to become online supervisors. These range from short workshops through to diploma level courses.

So, are the training institutions simply endeavouring to create a burgeoning industry for online training? I don't think so—at least I hope not.

There is a debate around the necessity of having an online supervisor of online clients. My position is that whilst not absolutely essential, it is extremely helpful, as it is often easier to uncover parallel processes, online transference, etc., when working in the same medium. I certainly would not want to receive supervision of online clients from someone who had never worked online.

Online supervision can be useful for F2F counsellors who are, for example, geographically isolated or who would like a supervisor with a particular specialism. Again, the profession may, in time, move to embracing a blended model of supervision—F2F, telephone, and online. I am reminded of one supervisee with whom I currently work who has adopted this approach for her F2F practice. I used to see her entirely F2F, but that became impossible on a regular basis because of a house move. So she comes to my consulting room about twice a year, and the rest of the time we "meet" by telephone or by using Skype. Very occasionally we also conduct our supervision by email.

Some practitioners argue that all supervision is best carried out F2F, but I have never heard a convincing argument as to why this should be so. If we have for years accepted that we can mix the medium for supervision so that the majority of supervision of telephone work has always been carried out F2F, why cannot the process be reversed? Perhaps as a profession we are suspicious of change—a strange place to be for one that bases all its work on the notion that humans are capable of change!

I agree that there are some contractual concerns that have to be addressed, but that is a different matter. These concerns centre on areas of time and money in many instances. So does an hour of live text equal an hour of F2F supervision, as people may be slower in typing than speaking? How do you equate time, and therefore fee payable, in email supervision? While accepting that there isn't a simple answer here, it is no different from working this out with F2F client work.

At the time of writing, my organisation has just finished our first externally validated diploma in therapeutic online supervision. In many ways, it has been breaking new ground, as very little has been written about online supervision, so students have been presenting sessions on various aspects of the practice and possible new models. Happily, Anthony and Nagel are publishing an edited book shortly. My hope is that all online training organisations will offer diploma level courses soon, and that researchers become involved in this arena so that we can build up a body of knowledge together.

In conclusion, while I do not believe that online counselling and supervision training is either superior or inferior to F2F training, I do contend that if counsellors are going to work in this medium, they need to train and experience it online if they are going to offer a highly professional and ethical service to their clients.

The role of new media in therapy training

Chris Blackmore and Digby Tantam

Psychotherapy theory and e-learning

Electronic approaches to theoretical learning ("e-learning") have grown hugely over the last twenty years, but their impact on the field of psychotherapy education has not been great, perhaps because there has been a perception that psychotherapy training can't be done over the Internet, and that the only acceptable methods of training are face-to-face ones. Although online therapy is still in its infancy, there is a growing literature on the practice of online therapy, with studies showing significant improvements for those engaging with it (Griffiths &

Cooper, 2003); in contrast, studies examining the role which e-learning might play in psychotherapy training are still few and far between. There are several crucial questions which need to be answered about the role of new media in therapy training: How accessible is e-learning in psychotherapy to potential trainees?

- How do e-learning and face-to-face learning in psychotherapy compare?
- How acceptable is e-learning to trainees, for example, does it encourage or inhibit some of the crucial components of psychotherapy training such as collaborative learning, self-disclosure, personal development, and emotional processes?
- What issues are raised by online training?
- How quality of training can be assured?
- What kind of emotional change does e-learning facilitate? What are the impacts on trainees' mental health and wellbeing?

Accessibility

In 2000, Professors Emmy van Deurzen and Digby Tantam at the University of Sheffield and European colleagues undertook a survey of European psychotherapy training (SEPT) which found that access to psychotherapy for those who are in most need is restricted in many European countries by distance from a training centre, family care responsibilities (which affected almost one in five of female respondents) and educational background (which affected men more than women) (Tantam et al., 2001a, 2001b). e-learning showed obvious potential for facilitating psychotherapy teaching and training, as it would curtail the need to relocate and allow those with family and work commitments to fit their studies around other activities.

There was no European Register of Psychotherapists at the time (this was a project that van Deurzen and Tantam were working on with the European Association of Psychotherapy that was not yet finalised) and it was therefore impractical to arrange local psychotherapy supervision, placements, or therapy for students—and there was not online supervision or therapy provision available, although there is now (see Case Study Two). Many experienced psychotherapists at the time were also suspicious of online teaching and training, believing that psychotherapy was a personal experience that required face-to-face encounter, and that this was also true of training. The project team therefore decided to focus on developing theoretical teaching online. Some countries did incorporate this into their training programmes, but not all.

The SEPTIMUS project (Strengthening European Psychotherapy Through Innovative Methods and Unification of Standards) involved establishing a one-year online psychotherapy training course in eight partner countries (Austria, Czech Republic, Ireland, Italy, Poland, Portugal, Romania, and UK) (Blackmore, Tantam, & van Deurzen, 2008). The online components were modules of theoretical material which were integrated into each partner's existing clinical training in different ways, as the training requirements differ across European countries. Topics included "Well-being and Mental Health", "Existential and Human Issues", and "Conflict and Reconciliation".

Each module consisted of ten weeks of online material, with an associated bespoke virtual learning environment including discussion forums, chat rooms, and relevant hyperlinks. The programme was devised to accord with the European Certificate of Psychotherapy (ECP, 2013).

Evaluations on application data of 167 learners were conducted and showed that over fifty per cent of e-learners had been previously prevented from accessing psychotherapy education, the most common factors being distance from training centre (fifty-eight per cent), finance

Figure 1. The SEPTIMUS islands.

Well-Being Island

Unit 1
Well-Being and Mental Health

Figure 2. Entry point to "Well-being and mental health" module.

(fifty-three per cent), lack of practical experience (thirty-three per cent), childcare responsibilities (nineteen per cent) and lack of qualifications (nineteen per cent). Of enrolled students, over forty per cent had children living with them or other family responsibilities, and over eighty-five per cent were working twenty hours per week or above. The drop-out rate was twenty-four per cent, and when students dropping-out and those completing were compared, there was no significant difference in gender, age, frequency with which training institute could be visited, distance from training institute, disability, English language skills, IT skills, domestic responsibilities, or current working time per week. For both those dropping out and completing, the proportion of students prevented from accessing psychotherapy education previously was similar, and the most common barrier was "distance from the training centre".

Comparison with F2F learning

Data were also collected on sixty students registered with three of the partner institutions for face-to-face (only) psychotherapy training, and compared with e-learners from across the partnership. At the time of starting their studies, e-learners could visit their training institutes less often than face-to-face students, were more likely to own a computer, used the Internet more frequently, and rated their IT skills higher. e-learners reported higher satisfaction with the course material and tutors than face-to-face learners; e-learners spent more time on the course materials than face-to-face learners, but less time interacting with tutors. Other differences noted between the two groups were not statistically significant.

This research suggests that not only is e-learning highly attractive to students who would otherwise be unable to engage in a psychotherapy training (due to geographical isolation and family/work commitments), the drop-out rates are not particularly high. Students who do enrol on e-learning courses report satisfaction levels which are comparable to face-to-face courses, and in the SEPTIMUS course, some important aspects of the learners' experience were rated more highly than on similar face-to-face courses. e-learning in psychotherapy training appears to be highly acceptable to students.

Acceptability to students

Given these encouraging findings, further research projects built on the SEPTIMUS course to establish full Masters level programmes in Psychotherapy in the Czech Republic, Romania, Sweden and the UK (Developing European Education in Psychotherapy—DEEP) (Blackmore et al., 2008) and to transfer this innovation to two new partner countries, Belgium and France (Continuing Education in Psychotherapy—CEP), including translations of material into French and Dutch (Ibid.). In this latter project, the partners (P1–4) gathered student data on levels of collaborative learning and online activity; satisfaction with modules; module mark; and student well-being/mental health levels.

To look at collaborative learning, students completed the COLLES (Constructivist On-Line Learning Environment Survey) scale (Taylor & Maor, 2000) at the mid-point of each module. This provided feedback on student self-rated levels of perceptions of both their preferred and actual online classroom environment, relating to relevance, reflective thinking, interactivity, tutor support, peer support, and interpretation. Scores on this scale were taken to be indicative of collaborative learning—a desirable mode of learning for psychotherapy students training to work therapeutically in a collaborative way with clients. e-learners' activity levels were calculated from VLE (Virtual Learning Environment) database records, showing that the more active students were, the more highly they rated their collaborative learning experience. Also the more emphasis placed on interactivity according to partners' pedagogical approach, the higher levels of collaborative learning seen in students.

Student satisfaction levels were calculated by asking students about their experience in a post-module questionnaire. Satisfaction levels were high, and confirmed the previous finding, in that the more collaborative approach to learning, the higher the satisfaction levels observed. The drop-out rate was relatively low, and students were often surprised by how engaging and even intimate the experience of studying online was. Regarding academic performance and module marks, all the indications are, from the various research projects undertaken, that there are no differences in academic achievement in terms of module marks between e-learners and attending students.

Online training tutors and therapists

As Stokes mentions above, there are some important differences between face-to-face and online work, and some specific skills which online therapists and tutors need to acquire in order to work safely and ethically. Accordingly, throughout the SEPTIMUS/DEEP developments, an emphasis was placed on providing new tutors with an appropriate induction to the practices and culture of online work. Whilst these programmes focused primarily on training people who would go on to tutor online, some of them also subsequently offered therapy online, and there was, in practice, very little difference in training staff who would go on to be e-tutors or e-therapists.

Training new staff began with an initial face-to-face training day in a computer lab, focused on getting people online and familiarised with the learning environment. Very often, new tutors and therapists came to this with significant anxieties about the types of connections they would be able to make with students and clients, and so enabling them to work through this anxiety with support was vital. The face-to-face session was augmented with an electronic manual, and associated videos—since then, the increasing availability of screencasting technologies has greatly enhanced the trainer's ability to convey procedural information clearly and succinctly, and to make it available for repeated viewing. Once modules had begun, tutors and project partners found that regular (weekly, then fortnightly) online chat room sessions and ongoing discussion forums were valuable channels whereby staff could share experiences, anxieties, and success stories.

It soon emerged through these feedback sessions that when training online tutors and therapists, those involved quickly need to develop a confidence in how to interact online, and an awareness of how their interactions were likely to be perceived. They also needed to know how to minimise hierarchies, respect difference, identify alienation (and deal with it early), prioritise experience over qualifications, and create a culture of openness and disclosure. In short, teaching a tutorial group online closely resembles facilitating group processes in an online context—a kind of applied group analysis.

To ensure that new tutors and therapists felt supported and sufficiently confident in this new way of "being-in-the-world/online", some supplementary procedures were used such as shadowing a more experienced tutor, and gathering mid-term evaluations (which could inform and direct subsequent interactions). An important overarching principle in online work was established—although there was the opportunity for private messaging and email contact with the person leading the training or therapy group, discussion in the group was encouraged, by (re)directing members to post their questions to the forum. Benefits of this were several-fold, but principally involved limiting the repetition of information (different group members asking a tutor or therapist the same question), and encouraging the development of a learning community whereby learners would take responsibility for their own and each other's development. The most successful groups seemed to be those where the online interactions reached a "critical mass" and forum postings blossomed into long, intense dialogues, replete with diversions, revelations, challenges, realisations, and transformative moments.

Quality assurance

The original SEPTIMUS course was developed in accordance with the European Certificate of Psychotherapy, and the programme arising in the UK from the SEPTIMUS, DEEP, and CEP projects, the MSc in Psychotherapy Studies, has been subject to all the usual quality assurance procedures via the University of Sheffield and, from 2012 onwards, the New School of Psychotherapy and Counselling (validated by Middlesex University). So the theoretical materials and virtual learning environment (VLE) have been approved as suitable for masters level study. Whilst not a clinical training course, the course does nevertheless reflect the need for a basic set of psychotherapy competences (regardless of modality). The course content covers the basic science relevant to psychotherapy including insights from behavioural science, theology, anthropology, philosophy, psychology, and sociology. Such variety is made possible by a collaborative teaching team and by incorporating contributions from students themselves.

There remain some issues about authenticity and originality of student work—the Internet has made it increasingly possible to "cut and paste" coursework together form online sources. The online submission and plagiarism detection service "Turnitin" is one way of combating this, and it has been used successfully to encourage academic literacy and discourage plagiarism.

The issue of identity, and whether a student is who they claim to be, can also be problematic. VLEs can adopt secure sign-in procedures requiring unique username and password entry. Whilst it is possible for a student to share these details, or for them to be stolen and misused, the tutors may well be able to pick up a difference in linguistic style in a chat room, forum posting, or essay. With increasing use of video, it will be possible to require students to be visually identified. Issues of provenance of purely written material online are no different to those for attending students—whilst plagiarism is more difficult with the advent of plagiarism-detection software, it remains a possibility that a student can have someone else write an essay for them, and submit this as if it were their own original work. Indeed, there are companies who will do just that, for a fee (*The Guardian*, 2012).

Emotional change

Data on emotional change was gathered from mental health/ wellbeing measures, via a linguistic analysis, and from feedback from tutors.

a. Mental health/wellbeing measures

This was measured by having students complete a battery of measures before and after modules, and measures relating to education achievement at the mid-point of modules. Measures included:

- PHQ-9: Depression scale of the Patient Health Questionnaire (Kroenke, Spitzer, & Williams, 2001)
- GAD-7: Scale of Generalized Anxiety Disorder (Spitzer, Kroenke, Williams, & Löwe, 2006)
- WEMWBS: The Warwick-Edinburgh Mental Well-being Scale (Tennant et al., 2007)
- SWLS: Satisfaction with Life Scale (Diener, Emmons, Larsen, & Griffin, 1985)
- SIWB: Spirituality Index of Well-Being Scale (Daaleman & Frey, 2004)
- SAIL: Spiritual Attitude and Involvement List (Meezenbroek et al., 2012).

By looking at individual partner data, the following conclusions were possible from T-tests:

- After completing the existential module, P1 students were more anxious/depressed, and expressed higher levels of spirituality
- After completing the conflict module, P1 students were somewhat more anxious
- After completing the existential module, P3 students expressed higher levels of well-being
- Other change scores not statistically significant.

Given established levels of satisfaction with tutor and peer interactions, these findings suggest that it was the content of modules, such as a close examination of conflict, or consideration of issues such as anxiety, death, meaning, and freedom, which left students experiencing some of these emotions after the module had ended.

When data were aggregated across all partners for all modules, no significant group changes from pre- to post-module outcome measures were found. So the pre-post comparisons did not detect change overall, but inspecting individual change scores enabled the identification of individuals for whom there were significant emotional events or journeys over the course of a module. For example, students struggling to engage in modules showed negative pre- to post-scores, possibly indicating a disparity between optimism and enthusiasm at the start of a learning experience, and disappointment, disillusionment, or fatigue at the end of it. These individual differences were most observable on the WEMWBS and GAD-7 measures.

b. Linguistic analysis

An analysis of the type of language being used online by learners in two of the modules was also undertaken, using the Linguistic Inquiry and Word Count (LIWC) text analysis software program (Pennebaker, Chung, Ireland, Gonzales, & Booth, 2007). The Conflict module evoked more negative emotions and anger than the Existential Issues module (and this confirms the experience of tutors). Negative emotion language:

- increased when self-rated levels of "interpretation" (collaborative learning) increased (measured halfway through existential module)
- increased when activity levels increased (measured throughout existential and conflict modules)
- increased when levels of spiritual well-being increased (from pre- to post-conflict module).

Use of the personal pronoun "I":

- decreased when activity levels increased (measured throughout existential module)
- increased when module marks increased (measured at the end of the existential module)
- increased when scores on WEMWBS and SAIL increased (from pre- to post-conflict module), that is, increased with increasing well-being and spirituality
- decreased when scores on PHW and SIWB increased (from pre- to post-conflict module), that is, decreased with increasing depression and spiritual well-being.

The processes uncovered were complex, and sometimes one module's findings were contradicted by another's. But clearly, the modules are provoking significant changes in the levels of emotional language being used by students.

c. Tutor feedback

From the early days of the SEPTIMUS programme, tutors were consistently feeding back a level of surprise at how engaged their students were. Contrary to some staff members' expectations, online learning did not provide a distant, dry, formulaic experience. On the contrary, and as suggested by the satisfaction data, students seemed energised by their interactions with the course materials, peers, and tutors. Through comparison with different tutoring styles, and the analysis given above, it became apparent that many students felt able to be open and honest with one another, in ways they found more difficult face-to-face, particularly when discussing difficult, personal material. This was perhaps due to the absence of what Sartre calls "the look", whereby "the absence of the look may enable a person to talk about their problems to another person on the Internet although they would feel too ashamed to talk in the flesh" (Tantam, 2006).

Significantly, the online context is an affordance for (and seems to require) a flattened hierarchy, presumably because the trappings of power—which are so often embodied—do not easily translate online. Tutors found that they needed to pay particular attention to the existence of conflict, which would sometimes erupt due to simple misunderstandings and which could prove difficult to resolve online, with the absence of the non-verbal cues which are important markers of a person's internal emotional state. Given that tutors were usually experienced psychotherapists, they were able to decide when and how to intervene in group interactions, with the result that many students were able to engage in significant emotional development during their time on the programme, and this development resembled, in many ways, a therapeutic journey towards greater understanding of their own and others' emotional processes. The therapeutic outcomes of e-learning were found to be similar to those experienced in psychotherapy (whether that was face-to-face or online). This led one of the partners to a consideration of how best to deliver therapy online.

The virtual therapy office

The conception of the virtual therapy office began in 2006. By that year, a substantial number of therapists were using email, phone calls, or even instant messaging to provide therapy. The idea of the VTO was to provide similar facilities within an environment that had the look of an office, and that duplicated procedures that would be familiar in a face-to-face setting: a waiting room, diaries for making bookings, a variety of means of communication (Skype, Google hangouts, text-based chat, and so on) plus group meeting availability using forums. All of this would have to take place in a secure environment, safe from hacking and other breaches of confidentiality. The original plan was to combine the site with a "rant and rave" site (SOaNAR—"Stressed out and Need a Rant"), an agony aunt site (Ask the Oracle), a social media site (that idea has been dropped in the face of the multitude of well-designed sites already available), and a site providing information about therapy, with the opportunity to have one-off sessions (something provided elsewhere, for example in France, by the journal *Psychologies*). It has taken the subsequent years to build just three of these sites, and two years to beta-test and then to undertake usability testing of the VTO. This was originally written in ASP for a Windows environment, but had to be rebuilt in PHP for a Linux environment for various technical reasons. It had to be moved, too, to a faster server with a better tradition of upgrading its software to incorporate the latest security fixes.

To a large extent, the project aim has been fulfilled. The site has been hosting online psychotherapy supervision for two years, and has been largely glitch-free for the last six months. Many unexpected issues have been dealt with—the different properties of browsers, the requirement for a fixed IP address that means that people cannot participate on trains (it was not expected that they would want to), and the tendency for buttons to appear in very different places, and sometimes even be hidden, on different types of screen. There were conceptual objections, too, although there was less distrust of technology being used in therapy than expected. In fact, over the two years of beta-testing, more and more students have signed up, and supervisors, too, have increasingly reported that they have enjoyed the experience. A high level of IT support has to be available at the beginning of a new supervision but, despite this, a survey showed that users' experiences were much more positive than some of the emails asking for immediate help might suggest.

Supervisees at the New School of Psychotherapy and Counselling who had experience of both online and face-to-face supervision were invited to complete a Google survey and compare the two methods (Figure 3) as part of an audit of online supervision using the VTO environment. They were also asked what they wanted from online supervision (Figure 4). Seventeen students completed the survey.

As can be seen from the figure, satisfaction with online supervision was less than, but close to, that with face-to-face supervision. There was least difference in the satisfaction with online supervision as a learning experience.

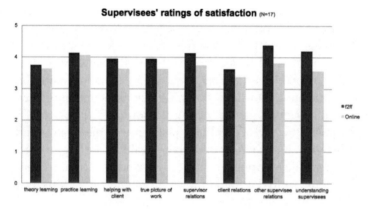

Figure 3. Rate your satisfaction with supervision from 1 (very poor) to 5 (very good).

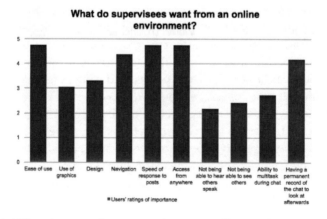

Figure 4. What do supervisees want from an online environment?

Supervisees thought that ease of use, having access from anywhere, and having a permanent record of the supervision were the most important requirements for online supervision.

Therapy has been carried out at a distance for a long time. Freud's Little Hans case was entirely conducted by correspondence, for example. Therapists have, for a long time, used phone calls to keep in touch with clients during periods of absence, and emails probably began to be used similarly as soon as they became available. An online counselling service at Cornell University, "Ask Uncle Ezra" was founded in 1986. New methods of texting, telephony, and videotelephony do not, in fact, add much to these methods, other than convenience and ease of use. What has changed is the penetration of social media into our everyday world, making these methods of communication much more familiar. Relationships are not just conducted face-to-face anymore, but by mobile calls and texts, by Skype or Google hangout, and through the numerous social media sites. Social media is especially popular because one can have a home page, with links to pictures or videos. The home page has a look and feel that brings people, and their friends, back to it and creates an emotional flavour around it (see Figure 5).

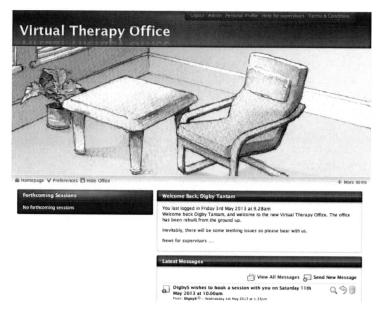

Figure 5. The virtual therapy office.

Therapists rightly devote much care and attention to the space in which therapy is conducted. It must of course be warm, safe, and private. But there must also be good ways of being in touch with the therapist with urgent messages, appointments must be made or changed through a reliable method, and the waiting room, in which clients spend a significant amount of their time, must allow time to pass peacefully. Many therapists feel that their room projects their personality, and pay attention to the decor. Many patients will walk into their therapist's room, and even in the therapist's absence, get an impression of their therapist's personality and their care. The virtual therapy office was designed to simulate an online office, with furniture that could be chosen by the therapist and would provide something of this ambience (see Figure 5).

Other key requirements are to give clients, and therapists, a choice of means of communication. Text-based communication suits some more than voice-based, whilst others prefer the latter. Video calls are often disappointing because bandwidth rarely allows voice and body to sync, but also because people are less likely to make their voices emotional if they believe that their facial expressions can be read. Eye contact is also disrupted by the time delay and it does not have the special value that it has in a face-to-face setting. In some ways, an obviously unreal form of communication may be easier for clients to accommodate. This may be one reason that immersive environments, such as Second Life, have not proved as successful as expected.

Most of us use nonverbal cues to disambiguate our speech, and quite often, too, to reduce its emotional sting. More care than usual needs to be taken to ensure that negativity does not creep into, or be thought to have crept into, online communications, and therapists will often need to be more active than in face to face communications, if only to ensure that statements that could be read negatively but may not be intended to be are disambiguated.

Silence in a face-to-face setting never means non-participation, or at least never if the silent member is hearing, understanding, and reacting nonverbally. The silent member online is not a participant. They may indeed feel alone—or may perhaps have gone to open the door or make a cup of tea. But it is easy for online silence to be missed in group work online—the way that the VTO is most often used. The therapist or supervisor may have to periodically scan for silent members (most chat rooms have a list of participants and may even, like the VTO, show the time since that member last contributed), and ask silent members directly about their reactions to the chat so far.

Foulkes (1948) described the most effective kind of group as being a microcosm of society. The limits of society possible online far exceed those usually available to attend a face-to-face group. It is not just that there may be a more various mix of ethnicities, cultures, genders, attitudes, and beliefs by throwing an online experience open to the world (with the proviso that variations in time zones do, in practice, limit which places people can attend from for any particular online experience). It is also that people are attending from very different environments, circumstances, and levels of privation, security, or danger.

Foulkes' remark applied to online group therapy or supervision, but online individual therapy may also be more inclusive than face-to-face therapy. As demonstrated by the survey work undertaken in SEPT, there are countries where face-to-face therapy continues to be available only in the very largest cities, or where people are ashamed to be seen going to a therapist. There are some conditions that lead people to suspect that they will be humiliated if they do go to a therapist: self-harm and eating disorders are examples. People with these conditions have been using online self-help via discussion forums for a long time.

A number of issues have emerged around online therapy:

- Emergencies—what to do when someone is (or appears to be) in crisis online
- Contact outside the therapy environment
- Client's facilitated access to recordings of sessions
- Deceit: same patient each time, actual gender, age, address, and GP?
- Confidentiality
- Jurisdiction and licensing
- Could it ever really be therapy?
- Where is therapy taking place? For example, it is illegal to provide e-therapy to a Californian citizen without an appropriate California licence, even if you are based in the UK (Maheu, 2003).

The following are some of the necessary steps involved in the process of implementing an e-therapy service:

- assess the client (and be assessed by them)
- determine the appropriate method of e-therapy and the mix of e-therapy and personal therapy
- determine an appropriate and agreed method of reimbursement
- undertake appropriate training and professional preparation

- decide which sources of referrals to accept
- provide information to educate potential clients about the therapy
- have an adequate procedure for obtaining consent.

The efficacy of e-therapy is equivalent to that of face-to-face therapy (Barak, Hen, Boniel-Nissim, & Shapira, 2008), with post-traumatic stress disorder and panic and anxiety disorders proving especially suited to online treatment. In particular, the structured nature of cognitive-behavioural input seems to work well online—programmes such as "Fear Fighter" (2013) and "Beating the Blues" (2013) are examples of larger online therapeutic initiatives. Other benefits can be summarised as follows:

- Useful materials, for example, assessment forms, protocols, guide-lines can be made available to clients online
- More information about therapist, for example, cost, experience, user rating, therapist's availability, can be accessed by clients before choosing
- An increasing array of tools can be used for tracking the progress of e-therapy, monitoring quality of experience, etc.
- Use of the Internet opens up the option of blended treatment, for example, a mixture of face-to-face and online sessions.

Conclusion

The online context has great potential for both e-learning and e-therapy, and there are even some potential advantages over traditional teaching and therapy methods.

First, the Internet greatly widens participation for those living in remote areas or those with work/family commitments. This has impli-cations not only for access to therapy and clinical training, but for cli-nicians' continuing professional development, which increasingly has to fit in around work and other commitments. Psychotherapy has also begun to be offered as a subject in the MOOC (Massive Open Online Course) format (MOOC-list, 2013) and whilst this may not be a suitable vehicle for therapy or clinical training, MOOCs can certainly play a role in CPD, and in attracting potential students to training.

Second, the medium lends itself to intensely stimulating and engag-ing discussions, either synchronous (e.g., chat room, virtual classroom) or asynchronous (e.g., discussion forum), which can help clients and students to open up and discuss difficult or personal issues. Some of the characteristics of online interactions can make these dialogues even more intimate online than in a face-to-face setting, with the added advantage of enabling contact with therapists, tutors, or students from different countries and cultures. Just as the therapist has a central role in facilitating dialogue online with individual or groups of clients, so the input of the tutor is crucial in facilitating group processes that enables this kind of intimacy and connectivity to flourish (van Deurzen, Blackmore, & Tantam, 2006).

Third, both online therapy and e-learning based around the Internet can take advantage of the huge amount of resources now available online, from wikis to discussion forums to webpages to videos, all available for viewing, sharing, and discussing via increasing connection speeds and an increasing array of mobile devices.

At present, it is still the case that a clinical training requires placement in a face-to-face counselling or psychotherapy context, and face-to-face clinical supervision. But with advancing technologies, particularly in video capabilities, clinical supervision by distance is more and more feasible, meaning that trainees could in theory be in a clinical placement in any location and still be able to receive the necessary level of supervision and support online. And if online therapy continues to increase in popularity, there may, before long, be a call for training specific to this modality, with students engaging in their training, personal therapy, clinical practice, and supervision entirely online. However fast the speed of change turns out to be, it seems highly likely that the role of new media in psychotherapy will only grow in importance.

Commentator one: Kate Thompson

This chapter provides a convincing case for the development of e-learning in psychotherapy training and, with some sensible caveats, in online supervision and therapy. The three authors are pioneers in the technical and practical applications for online work. Their expertise includes online training for therapists for both online and face-to-face work and providing therapy and supervision online.

I have taught online courses for psychotherapists and therapeutic writing facilitators. These employed a variety of the methods the authors describe, both synchronous and asynchronous forms and the

VTO. I have also used Skype and email for both therapy and supervision (as a journal therapist I find text-based methods particularly suited to the modality). I am therefore already a convert to these new forms of teaching and therapy which, as the authors say, "will only grow in importance".

Widening participation in and access to education and therapy is one of the great gifts of the Internet age. I particularly appreciate the richness of teaching or supervising groups whose members come from many different countries and cultures (sometimes living through some of the defining events of our age in real time, which adds depth to existential training). This truly allows the group to be a microcosm of global society. In synchronous chat rooms an extra dimension and challenge is provided as non-native speakers of English strive for clearer and more explicit forms of linguistic communication and everyone learns to ask for further clarification.

I teach the practice of group therapy online. In each class the students find their online group demonstrating and displaying all the characteristics of group process; their group thus embodies their learning in a disembodied sphere.

Commentator two: Susan Iacovou

This text provides the reader with intriguing insights into the efficacy of both online psychotherapy training and online therapy. The authors' conclusions as to the tremendous potential of this context are founded upon an impressive research base. Hopefully this will do much to counter the deeply held suspicions of many tutors and therapists as to the compatibility of online settings and psychotherapy related activities.

Having facilitated many online classes in psychotherapy—and completed some of my own training online—I concur with the authors' view that the potential for emotional connection and growth is as great, if not greater, in this setting than in traditional environments. The quietness of written communication compared to "noisy" face-to-face sessions (where the message is complicated by the reaction of others and by the communicator's appearance, tone of voice, accent, non-verbal behaviour, etc.) offers the participants the freedom to grapple with concepts, ideas, and feelings at a deeply personal level.

This chapter challenges the assumption that face-to-face communication is somehow the most informative, fulfilling, and complete way of interacting, either as trainer and trainee or as therapist and client. In doing so, it encourages us to approach web-based learning and web-based counselling with more openness and curiosity. In my experience, those new to the online environment experience some initial trepidation, but this is quickly replaced by an appreciation of the richness and complexity of the relationships it facilitates.

Accessibility may have been the main driving force behind the development of psychotherapy training and therapy online, but ultimately this format delivers far more than convenience and flexibility.

Notes

1. Association for Counselling and Therapy Online http://www.acto-uk. org
2. www.ismho.org/online_therapy_training.asp
3. http://www.onlinetrainingforcounsellors.co.uk
4. Accreditation of Prior Experiential Learning, and Accreditation of Prior Learning.

References

Working with the next generation: training for online counselling

Anthony, K. (2009). *Guidelines for Online counselling and Psychotherapy* (3rd ed.). Rugby: BACP.

Anthony, K., & Goss, S. (Eds.) (2003). Technology. In: *Counselling and Therapy: A Practitioner's Guide*. Basingstoke: Palgrave Macmillan.

BBC Radio 4 (25 June 2013). *The Life Scientific*: Jim Al-Khalili interviewing Elizabeth Stokoe.

Bor, R., & Stokes, A. (2011). *Setting up in Independent Practice: A Handbook for Counsellors, Therapists and Psychologists*. Basingstoke: Palgrave.

Bor, R., Gill, S., & Stokes, A. (2011). *Therapy for Beginners: How to Get the Best Out of Counselling*. London: Sheldon Press.

Evans, J. (2009). *Online Counselling and Guidance Skills*. London: Sage.

Goss, S., Anthony, A., & Nagel, D. (2012). The wider uses of technologies in therapy. In: *Sage Handbook of Counselling and Therapy* (3rd edition). London: Sage.

Inskipp, F. (1996). *Skills Training for Counselling*. London: Cassell.

Jones, G., & Stokes, A. (2009). *Online Counselling: A Handbook for Practitioners*. Basingstoke: Palgrave.

Page, S. (1999). *The Shadow and the Counsellor*. London: Routledge. Stokoe at www.lboro.ac.uk/research/view/spring-2012

The role of new media in therapy training

Barak, A., Hen, L., Boniel-Nissim, M., & Shapira, N. (2008). A comprehensive review and a meta-Analysis of the effectiveness of internet-based psychotherapeutic interventions. *Journal of Technology in Human Services, 26*: 109–160.

Beating the Blues (2013). Available from: http://www.beatingtheblues.co.uk [Accessed 5 June 2013].

Blackmore, C., Tantam, D., & van Deurzen, E. (2008). Evaluation of e-learning outcomes: experience from an online psychotherapy education programme. *Open Learning: The Journal of Open and Distance Learning, 23*: 185–201.

Daaleman, T., & Frey, B. (2004). The Spirituality Index of Well-Being: A new instrument for health-related quality-of-life research. *Annals of Family Medicine, 2*: 499–503.

Diener, E., Emmons, R., Larsen, R., & Griffin, S. (1985). The satisfaction with life scale. *Journal of personality assessment, 49*: 71–75.

ECP—European Certificate for Psychotherapy (2013). Available from: http://www.europsyche.org/contents/13489/european-certificate-for-psychotherapy-ecp [Accessed 6 June 2013].

Fear Fighter (2013). Available from: http://www.fearfighter.com/ [Accessed 5 June 2013].

Foulkes, S. H. (1948). *Introduction to Group-analytic Psychotherapy*. London: Heinemann. Reprinted London: Karnac, 1983.

Griffiths, M., & Cooper, G. (2003). Online therapy: implications for problem gamblers and clinicians. *British Journal of Guidance & Counselling, 31*: 113–135.

Kroenke, K., Spitzer, R., & Williams, J. (2001). The PHQ-9: Validity of a brief depression severity measure. *Journal of General Internal Medicine, 16*: 606–613.

Maheu, M. M. (2003). The online clinical practice management model. *Psychotherapy Theory, Research, Practice, Training, 40*: 20–32.

Meezenbroek, E., Garssen, B., Van den Berg, M., Tuytel, G., Van Dierendonck, D., Visser, A., & Schaufeli, W. (2012). Measuring spirituality as a universal human experience: development of the Spiritual Attitude and Involvement List (SAIL). *Journal of psychosocial oncology, 30*: 141–67.

MOOC list (2013). Available from: http://www.mooc-list.com/tags/psychotherapy [Accessed 4 June 2013].

Pennebaker, J., Chung, C., Ireland, M., Gonzales, A., & Booth, R. (2007). The development and psychometric properties of LIWC 2007. *Development*: 1–22.

Spitzer, R., Kroenke, K., Williams, J., & Löwe, B. (2006). A brief measure for assessing generalized anxiety disorder: the GAD-7. *Archives of internal medicine, 166*: 1092–1097. doi:10.1001/archinte.166.10.1092.

Tantam, D. (2006). Opportunities and risks in e-therapy. *Advances in Psychiatric Treatment, 12*: 368–374.

Tantam, D, van Deurzen, E., McHale, E, Pritz, A., Szafran, W., Zerbetto, R., & Osterloh, K. (2001a). The Survey of European Psychotherapy Training. 1. Information provided in the national reports. *International Journal of Psychotherapy, 6*: 142–144.

Tantam, D, van Deurzen, E., McHale, E, Pritz., A., Szafran, W., Zerbetto, R., & Osterloh, K. (2001b). The Survey of European Psychotherapy Training 2: Questionnaire data. *European Journal of Psychotherapy, Counselling & Health, 4*: 379–395.

Taylor, P. & Maor, D. (2000). Assessing the efficacy of online teaching with the Constructivist On-Line Learning Environment Survey. In: A. Herrmann & M. M. Kulski (Eds.), *Flexible Futures in Tertiary Teaching*. Proceedings of the 9th Annual Teaching Learning Forum, 2–4 February 2000. Perth: Curtin University of Technology.

Tennant, R., Hiller, L., Fishwick, R., Platt, S., Joseph, S., Weich, S., Parkinson, J., et al. (2007). The Warwick-Edinburgh Mental Well-being Scale (WEMWBS): development and UK validation. *Health and quality of life outcomes, 5*: 63.

The Guardian (2012). Who writes your essays? [online]. Available from: http://www.guardian.co.uk/education/mortarboard/2012/feb/06/essay-writing-for-students [Accessed 4 June 2013].

van Deurzen, E., Blackmore, C., & Tantam, D. (2006). Distance and intimacy in internet psychotherapy training. *International Journal of Psychotherapy, 10*.

PART II

THERAPY IN PRACTICE

CHAPTER FOUR

The therapeutic alliance online

Kate Dunn

Case study

Sam was an only child who had left school at eighteen with three A-levels and begun working full time in a landscape-gardening business. His parents had separated when he was thirteen after his dad lost his job as a postal worker, partly due to his extreme mood swings and heavy drinking, which then worsened. Sam maintained contact with his dad but saw him only infrequently. During his A-levels his dad was diagnosed with liver cancer. At first he seemed to respond to treatment but then suddenly developed an infection and died within three months of diagnosis. Sam was deeply shocked; his mum refused to talk about it, having remarried a couple of years after she separated from his dad.

Although he enjoyed his job, Sam often felt frustrated; he had particularly enjoyed studying English at school and had written short stories and articles for the school magazine, which he missed doing. He had begun a relationship with a girl he had met at a party and they had kept in touch mainly online, spending occasional weekends together. She was about to study for a PGCE and encouraged Sam to apply for university. With his girlfriend's encouragement and support, he was successful in gaining a place about eighty miles from home and three hours' drive from where his girlfriend was studying. He settled in quite quickly and threw himself into life at university, living in halls in his first year and then moving into a shared house with three friends in early summer.

During his second year at university, he was devastated to receive a letter from his mum, informing him that she was suffering from advanced ovarian cancer and that treatment was proving largely ineffective. She reassured him that she was being well looked after by his stepdad and that he must "continue working hard to make a new and different future for himself". He felt lost, frightened, and confused but said nothing to his housemates or friends. He began drinking heavily, missing lectures and seminars and failing to meet course deadlines. He became irritable and withdrawn, avoiding his friends and often failing to respond to his girlfriend's messages and calls. A concerned tutor urged him to visit the university counselling service. At first he refused (within his family, feelings were never talked about) but whilst online he spotted a website link to the university's e-counselling service, where he discovered he could speak to a therapist weekly by email without them ever having to meet. This reminded him of the way he and his girlfriend had often maintained their relationship, both when they first met and again, since coming to university. He decided, hesitantly at first, to find out more and completed the online application form.

He received an immediate response and soon found himself engaging in a weekly exchange of emails with a therapist, where he began to write about feelings he would never have previously articulated; he explored his family relationships, engaging with his losses and simultaneously expressing his fears about the future. His therapist helped him to identify links between these areas of his life and his current feelings and behaviour. The emails took on great significance for him and he found himself urgently checking his inbox each Thursday and feeling a sense of relief to find each new communication. After a short period of time, he realised he was feeling calmer, more able to engage again with his university work and less frightened and angry. He also found that he was opening up more to his girlfriend and friends in person and feeling more supported, less alone, and less frightened.

Sam's circumstances replicate those of many young adults, for whom computerised technology has been central to their lives from infancy. This has impacted widely: on educational experiences and opportunities, leisure activities, personal relationships, all forms of communication, social interactions, creativity, access to global information, and much more. Far from being in awe of the speed of digital progress, Sam views it as a "given". He belongs to what is sometimes called the Facebook generation, whose identity is significantly shaped and expressed online. His smartphone is always close at hand and in his studies, as well as in other areas of life, he uses an extensive array of hardware and software to enhance his learning, generate information, and construct ideas.

Many of the emotional challenges he faces as he progresses from adolescence into adulthood are common across generations and cultures, but Sam's approach and attitude to seeking help may also reflect his contemporary lifestyle. Might there be opportunities to provide support for Sam in innovative ways that take into account the technological age in which he lives? His upbringing took place within a family where feelings were not openly shared. As a young male, the likelihood of him visiting a therapist in person is considerably less, and risk of suicide is up to three times greater, than if he were female, as evidenced by a report by the Royal College of Psychiatrists (2011). He is struggling to make sense of turmoil in his life and in danger of sabotaging his opportunities whilst feeling isolated, angry, and alone. In 2007, Dr Moira Walker reviewed the provision of mental health treatment online and wrote: "It is vital to access those silently suffering often extreme distress who desperately need services that do not exist and who rarely find a voice through research projects" (p. 60). Prior to the introduction of the e-counselling provision at Sam's university, he might have remained one of those "silently suffering". Much is written about the dangers and shortcomings of online relationships but perhaps we can consider their possibilities, too.

Students and online counselling

I meet many students like Sam in the university where I work. Perhaps online counselling is a more natural therapeutic approach for students than for other client groups; their lives have been immersed in online activity from an early age and they have clearly expressed themselves fluently in computer-mediated formats in order to attain their university place. When they seek answers to problems, the first place they look is online.

In 2007, having undergone training in delivering online therapy, I developed an email counselling provision for students as an alternative to the long-established face-to-face (F2F) service. I was cautious; might this approach feel like a "poor relation" to my usual work? How would I engage with individual students? How could we create an alliance "just" through exchanging emails?

The online service was first proposed as a practical way of extending equal access to counselling for all students, regardless of individual obstacles such as timetabling problems, physical constraints in attending sessions or perhaps being away from the university on placement. In reality, we have found that students who apply for e-counselling are less likely to do so for practical reasons; it is more likely to result from feelings of shame or embarrassment which inhibit them from applying for F2F help. For some students like Sam, e-counselling has provided an essential lifeline at what may be a critical moment in time. Furthermore, the factor that emerged as being of greatest significance for participants in online therapy is the special nature and quality of the *relationship* at the centre of the experience.[1] This was not, perhaps, what I had predicted at the outset.

The therapeutic relationship online

Research studies relating to the efficacy of the online therapeutic relationship are still limited in number and scope. However, encouraging evidence is emerging that suggests that alliances in online text-based therapy show similar ratings to F2F studies (Hanley & Reynolds, 2009). Given that it is widely agreed that the single most important factor determining the effectiveness of *any* therapeutic intervention is the quality of the relationship or alliance between therapist and client, this feels significant. Furthermore, it is emerging that there are elements of online therapeutic relationships that may be qualitatively different from F2F alliances and perhaps uniquely facilitative. This chapter will explore these elements, and illustrate them in action by considering how they impacted on Sam's experiences within his own online counselling.

Some online therapeutic interventions set out to *replace* the counsellor with software especially programmed to respond "appropriately and empathically" to the input of the client. The earliest of these was created by Weizenbaum in 1966 with his computerised therapist "ELIZA". This tongue-in-cheek experiment, designed to demonstrate the limitations of artificial intelligence using a computer program to convincingly replicate the responses of a person-centred practitioner (!), was so effective that some participants continued to seek opportunities to talk to ELIZA even after it was disclosed to them that they were communicating with a computer rather than a real person. Critically, it seems that there was a particular quality about this "unseen therapist", despite her artificiality, that felt different from the "seen", even in this primitive form. Although here I am exploring engagement between two *real* people but mediated through technology, it is helpful to remember the impact of ELIZA.

Early debates about whether or not it was actually possible to engage therapeutically online suggested that such approaches should attempt to reproduce all elements of F2F relationship. Murphy and Mitchell (1998) expressed concern about the lack of visual cues and physical presence, and advocated a need for "compensatory skills" to make up for this. However, others, such as Fenichel et al. (2002), suggested it might be a mistake to take this stance and that it could be more realistic and thought-provoking for online therapists to explore creatively those existing and unique factors of online interaction that might be both qualitatively different and simultaneously beneficial for those involved. Schultze (2006) echoed this idea, encouraging practitioners to explore special qualities that may characterise computer-mediated forms of communication of any kind, rather than to seek to develop specific, ever-more sophisticated hardware and software.

The relationship in action

At the university, we decided initially to offer e-counselling by email only: an "asynchronous" approach (involving a time delay of hours or days between communications), rather than a "synchronous" approach (involving a direct live audio or video link between participants). This decision was taken pragmatically, based on the ethical need to ensure security and confidentiality, which we felt more able to address if the provision was delivered asynchronously. (Training programmes in online counselling stress the vital importance of establishing clear frameworks, articulating them through careful contracting and implementation of robust protocols.) We wondered whether asynchronicity might reduce the quality of the therapeutic alliance in terms of immediacy and authenticity. The actual experience reported by many participants has demonstrated this to be a false premise. From the outset, the striking power of the relationships that emerged in these email exchanges surprised both therapists and students alike and was specifically commented upon by almost all involved. Observations on this were so striking that I decided to conduct research to attempt to identify more clearly some of the phenomena impacting on these online relationships.

Students who had participated in our e-counselling provision and university counsellors offering similar services elsewhere volunteered to be interviewed about their experiences. Data were gathered which sought to identify those factors which had most led to the positive relationships many had spontaneously reported. Full details of this study have been published (Dunn, 2012) and I will describe here, both in the context of Sam's story and also more generally, the major factors that emerged as having significance.

Questions which underlie the online therapeutic relationship

Central to much online communication is the *unseen* nature of the "meeting". This can prompt a phenomenon that has been described as a "disinhibition effect" (Suler, 2004). Presence online is communicated solely by the text or images that appear on the screen, initiating an urgent drive in many participants to disclose detailed information about themselves and their situation rapidly and as fully as possible. This phenomenon can be illustrated by asking a number of philosophical and also practical questions.

Who am I?

When communicating a sense of self online and asynchronously, many report conserving very carefully how they will be perceived by the person receiving and responding to their communication. Anonymity is a powerful feature of disinhibition; it can empower people and free them from the constraints of embarrassment and shame that may silence them in other settings. (At the same time, of course, we should not forget that there may be risks within this freedom of expression, too. Cyber-bullying and even cyberwars are widely reported and demonstrate the negative potential in such "freedoms".)

Participants in online communication report valuing the opportunity to convey aspects of themselves that they may have previously kept hidden or perhaps not even considered before. Indeed, they sometimes choose to explore fantasies as well as realities in this respect, expressing these not only in words but also using sound, video, avatars, and other symbols or metaphors. For Sam, "Who am I?" was the question at the heart of a search for his young adult identity in a world far removed from his family setting. "Who am I?" also prompted new curiosity about his background and the influence of his parents and upbringing; it gave him a safe space to express both his love for his family members and his anger concerning some of the things that had happened between them alongside his fears for the person he might become. Sam often felt that assumptions were made about him, based on how he spoke, dressed, and conveyed himself physically; communicating a sense of himself that was unaffected by such things felt liberating. He shared concerns in his counselling about his father's mental health that he had never previously articulated. I was able to send him links to reliable sources of information where he could explore his concerns and we were able to discuss his fears in this context.

Who are you? Who is in charge of this?

Not only does the personal identity that the client chooses to portray take on special significance, but also the identity he apportions to his therapist. The unseen nature of their relationship enables the client to imagine his therapist however he might wish him to be, to apply to him a persona that feels helpful for him *at that time*. If this reflects a rather idealised image, might that be empowering at first for the usually inhibited and fearful client? This phenomenon is reported as being especially significant for clients who are usually suspicious of the motives of others, who may have been let down previously by figures of authority, or who may have experienced earlier unsuccessful therapeutic encounters. One role of the online therapist may be, slowly and gradually, to challenge this phenomenon, having initially acknowledged its usefulness and purpose.

In Sam's case, his reluctance to talk aloud about feelings arose partly from a lack of experience, but also from a background that stigmatised emotional difficulties and could prompt feelings of disempowerment when engaging with "experts" or authority figures. Clients in online therapeutic relationships regularly report feeling greater equality and autonomy, and more frequently identify feeling an internal locus of control than F2F clients. Trust is a necessary component of any successful therapeutic encounter and Fletcher-Tomenius and Vossler (2009) suggest that trust may actually be enhanced by anonymity. For Sam, to experience feelings of trust in such a relationship was empowering.

Transference and countertransference phenomena feature powerfully within online interactions (maybe the potential is heightened by the unitary clues when communication is by text alone) and these phenomena are often more openly and explicitly discussed within the therapy. Without the other cues (body language, etc.) that exist in F2F meeting, there is more need and, indeed, freedom to *describe* inner responses and to request information from the other about the same.

Where are we?

When two people engage in communication online, where do they each perceive the meeting point to be? Sam chose to write his emails privately in his student accommodation, at a time of his choosing (usually late at night), where he felt secure and unobserved. When he finally pressed the "send" button, he imagined his email travelling through cyberspace and visualised its destination as somewhere neutral and separate from locations that were linked in his mind with stress, pressure, and upsets. (It is important to note that "black hole" experiences may arise if communications fail to elicit a response at the expected time. These can be disturbing and this should be acknowledged by both parties. Contracting information should include reference to this phenomenon and suggest ways of avoiding it.)

Sometimes Sam may have felt that the interaction was taking place inside his head; previously he had kept such inner dialogue to himself and it may have reassured him to be able to connect his therapy back to this safe place. This inner location may represent "transitional space" (to use Winnicott's terminology). In time, he found he began to communicate more openly and out loud about his feelings. Healy (1996) describes this effect beautifully when he says: "It has been suggested that the Internet represents a kind of 'middle landscape' that allows individuals to exercise their impulses for both separation and connectedness". Fink (1999) refers to "telepresence" or "the feeling (or illusion) of being in someone's presence without sharing any immediate physical space" (Rochlen, Zack, & Speyer, 2004). Sam recognised this feeling too, having taken initial tentative steps towards beginning a relationship with his girlfriend in a similar way, before developing their relationship in person.

What can I say?

Disinhibition may create a refreshing sense of freedom. Within some family settings, such as Sam's, emotional disclosures may be viewed as embarrassing and emasculating. At the time of seeking help, Sam's repression of these feelings was making him feel profoundly angry, depressed, and leading to withdrawal from his usual activities. Freedom to own and articulate emotions, without fear of witnessing a judgmental response in the listener can be very powerful, and can bring surprisingly rapid relief. (This was something described repeatedly by participants in my research). Many find that their first emails initiate a kind of outpouring of extreme feelings and accounts of deeply traumatic events (often using little punctuation and formal sentence structure). Sam's first email described in stark detail the rapid deterioration in his father's health and what it had been like to visit him in hospital just before his death—something he had not been able to share with anyone before. James Pennebaker, has extensively explored the therapeutic value of writing about traumatic events, a process which he has shown to provide rapid and significant benefits for those who engage in it, not only emotionally and psychologically, but also physically.

We feared that asynchronicity might impair the immediacy and authenticity of the relationship, but the evidence suggested otherwise. The explanation for this may best be found in the expression "time to think", used repeatedly by those reflecting on the positive qualities of their e-counselling relationships. Having this facility was identified as significant more consistently than any other factor within the online relationship. For many, the fear that daunts them most when considering F2F therapy is that they will either not know what to say "in the moment", or that they will "say something stupid". Sam was strongly influenced by this, having grown up believing emotional expression to be a sign of weakness. Having a greater sense of control over what is said and when, such as is afforded by asynchronous online counselling, has been described as transformational. Not only can the content be reconsidered or revised before sending, it can also be deleted; there is always the opportunity to change or review the content until the "send" button is engaged.

How do we go about this—what are the "rules" of our relationship?

Therapists aim to establish and work within careful boundaries with their clients, contracting about when and where to meet, addressing matters of confidentiality, striving at all times to protect the interests and safely of the client. This applies no less to the online therapeutic encounter. Through training, practitioners learn about features unique to online work that are critical when implementing safe and ethical practice. It is not within the scope of this chapter to describe these in detail; nonetheless, they play an important role in the creation and development of the relationship. Online therapists will have originally trained in many different modalities and they adapt these within their online approach. Some particular elements of this process have been identified in the research as being significant in the development of the online relationship. An online therapist, especially when working asynchronously, is more active than many F2F therapists; after all, you cannot simply respond with "aah ….", "hmm ….", "uhuh …."! Many clients, like Sam, welcome this more equitable dynamic where they can always expect a full and detailed response. As all information is delivered electronically, initial contracting information must be explicit and full; this is welcomed by cautious and perhaps wary clients. Here, the initial information he received encouraged Sam to continue.

The actual structure of the exchanges evolves uniquely for every therapist/client pairing. Creative use of text, font colours, punctuation, emoticons, and much more can communicate surprisingly rich feelings. The use of imagery, perhaps through shared, extended metaphors or through the attachment of pictorial or audio-based files, for example, can generate a profound sense of connection. The medium also affords the therapist "time to think" where mentalisation processes may perhaps be encouraged and modelled. Sam, as a writer, welcomed this opportunity to communicate and share imagery and began developing a new vocabulary for feelings that felt both validating and helpful in understanding responses of others.

What happens when we finish?

Endings are central to relationships—therapists pay great care and attention to this critical element of their work. What remains of a relationship after it has ended is unique in every case. The relationship will be remembered for many reasons, shaped and determined by factors relating to each individual, the dynamics between them and an enormous array of influences from the outside world. Within the online relationship, whether synchronous or asynchronous, there is an opportunity for every word (or image) that has been exchanged to be stored, kept "on the record". Although this may be a daunting prospect, at first, for the therapist, clients report it as instilling a meaningful and significant quality to their therapeutic relationship. They describe returning to transcripts, sometimes months or years later, and gaining new insights from re-reading the exchanges. They are reassured by the record; they can use it as a monitor of change. It is also a tangible and permanent link to a relationship that may have occurred at a critical moment in time.

For Sam, endings, grief, and loss were central to his situation at the time of seeking help and the opportunity to explore these and then manage the ending with his therapist in a thoughtful and considered way, retaining a concrete record of the events to which he can return at different times in the future, was an essential therapeutic element of the relationship.

* * *

After a therapeutic engagement ends, practitioners hope that an essence of the relationship will endure. We hope that, as a result of the engagement, our clients may move forwards in their lives in ways that may have a positive impact both on reflections on past experiences and also on present and future events. Sam's online counselling relationship gave him a chance to explore new forms of expression, particularly relating to previously hidden inner feelings and thoughts. He recognised that this had a significant effect on many aspects of his life, not just his online world. He experienced a transition through his online therapeutic relationship to a greater openness and confidence in other relationships and this mirrored major transitions taking place in his life more generally at that time. Sam chose to end his online therapy without meeting his therapist; others choose to engage in further sessions in person, a further powerful transitional step.

Online therapeutic relationships differ in very many ways from F2F relationships. Whilst this chapter has dealt with an example involving asynchronous communication, many of the features described here can and will apply similarly to synchronous approaches, although these may vary in essence with each different use of technology. Many elements of the F2F relationship can never be reproduced online, but I hope that this exploration of some of the unique and special qualities that arise alternatively in this context may encourage more practitioners to consider online work and to enter the technological arena professionally as well as personally. This may challenge traditional thinking about the nature of communication but so long as human beings remain at the heart of the process, the motivation for true relationship will surely endure.

Commentator one: Heward Wilkinson

In this chapter, Kate Dunn has skilfully and sensitively mapped subtle features of the Internet-based therapeutic relationship in a particular form, that of email to email exchange. It would not be impossible to reconstruct other modes or forms by transformation from this one but this is a clear and valuable start. Kate talks with much subtlety about how the email to email exchange can, especially for the present generation for whom it is second nature and almost a reflex (but we may note that many of the previous generation have adapted creatively also), enable an extremely and sometimes unexpectedly rapid depth of disclosure. Obviously this phenomenon is also vividly evident in both political and erotic uses of the Internet, which are changing mores fundamentally "as we write".

"As we write", is precisely the point! Kate indicates this here and there, and I wish to allude to it more fundamentally. As she indicates, there is the rich paradox of a permanent but yet generative record, not needing supplementation by the dubious and undialogical mechanism of "notes". This paradoxical combination of permanence with generativity is the prerogative of "writing" since the god Theuth in Egypt (as, for instance, Socrates wrestles with him in Plato's *Phaedrus*), and is at the heart of what, since Derrida, is known as "deconstruction". And here is another delicious paradox: that it has leapt fully clad into four-dimensional life in our use of the Internet for this carefully boundaried, yet so unexpectedly powerful, kind of dialogue, which the serendipitous modern creation/discovery of the Internet has made possible! So, in fact, it was perhaps not inappropriate that Tim Berners Lee was recognised by the British Olympics Lead-In in 2012 before Peter Higgs, though on a classical understanding we would be placing Professor Higgs far higher! These are the implicit issues Kate Dunn's very subtle piece evokes.

Commentator two: Martin Pollecoff

It's in the nature of Web 2.0 and Psychotherapy 2.0 that clients access services in the way that works for them rather than the way in which it has been traditionally offered by the therapist.

Whether its twenty-four hour online banking, a next-day delivery from Amazon, or email therapy, each new offering gains a fresh tranche of clients, converts who would never have had any interest in the traditional offering. Ms. Dunn's work steps right out of the meme of the consulting room and the fifty-minute hour complete with its by-the-hour fees. And this send sends a signal that it's no longer the clients who have to change to fit in with our way of working. The challenge for us therapists is that we have to be creative and step out to meet the "new clients". For those of us who believe that wider access to therapeutic services is vital, the advances featured in this chapter come as a breath of fresh air.

Here, unlike in the consulting room situation, the client has control of the medium. Both the therapist and the client remain imaginary to each other, in that they are dealing with someone they have never met and may never meet. There is not even the sound of a voice, only story, style, and grammar, and yet, transference is there—freed of notions of time and space. The work occurs in this wonderfully disinhibited "middle landscape", a perfect place for us to state and share feelings that could never previously have been uttered. And when you think about it, for a young person, there is something magical and sustaining in knowing that you travel with a wise ally, one who is never more than a text message away.

Note

1. A pilot scheme was run for the first two years and students provided feedback about many aspects of the service in questionnaires sent to them at the conclusion of their online therapy.

References

Dunn, K. (2012). A qualitative investigation into the online counselling relationship: To meet or not to meet, that is the question. *Counselling and Psychotherapy Research, 12:* 316–326.

Fenichel, M., Suler, J., Barak, A., Zelvin, E., Jones, G., Munro, K., Meunier, V., & Walker-Schmucker, W. (2002). *Myths and realities of online clinical work. Observations on the phenomena of online behaviour, experience and therapeutic relationships.* A 3rd year report from ISMHO's Clinical Case Study Group. Retrieved 4 October 2006 from http://www.fenichel.com/myths/.

Fink, J. (1999). *How to Use Computers and Cyberspace in the Clinical Practice of Psychotherapy.* Northvale, N.J.: Aronson.

Fletcher-Tomenius, L., & Vossler, A. (2009). Trust in online therapeutic relationships: The therapist's experience. *Counselling Psychology Review,* 24: 24–34.

Hanley, T., & Reynolds, D. J. (2009). Counselling psychology and the Internet: A review of the quantitative research into online outcomes and alliances within text-based therapy. *Counselling Psychology Review,* 24: 4–12.

Healy, D. (1996). Cyberspace and place: The Internet as middle landscape on the electronic frontier. In: D. Porter (Ed), *Internet Culture* (pp. 55–68). New York: Routledge.

Murphy, L. J., & Mitchell, D. L. (1998). When writing helps to heal: Email as therapy. *British Journal of Guidance and Counselling,* 26: 21–32.

Pennebaker, J. W. (1997). *Opening Up: The Healing Power of Expressing Emotions.* New York: Guilford Press.

Rochlen, A. B., Zack, J. S., & Speyer, C. (2004). Online therapy: Review of relevant definitions, debates and current empirical support. *Journal of Clinical Psychology,* 60: 269–283.

Royal College of Psychiatrists (2011). Mental health of students in higher education. Retrieved 7 April 2013 from http://www.rcpsych.ac.uk.

Schultze, N. -G. (2006). Success factors in Internet-based psychological counselling. *Cyberpsychology and Behavior,* 9: 623–626.

Suler, J. (2004). The online disinhibition effect. In: *The psychology of cyberspace.* Retrieved 11 October 2006 from http://users.rider.edu/ suler/ psycyber/disinhibit/.

Walker, M. Dr (2007). *Mental health treatment online.* Digital Inclusion Team commissioned report.

Weizenbaum, J. (1976). *Computer Power and Human Reason.* New York: Freeman.

CHAPTER FIVE

Challenges and dilemmas in the online consulting room

Alexandra Chalfont and Martin Pollecoff

Thiis enjoyable chapter provides the reader with an opportunity to enjoy some examples of practice and the dilemmas that sometimes arise. Some are in case study style, others are allegorical tales. The styles are intentionally very different, as readers too are very different, and the challenges and dilemmas posed by these accounts are examples of the challenges and dilemmas that we may come across in our own clinical practice.

Same old, with new angles

Alexandra Chalfont

(All the cases presented here are just snippets drawn together from various clients, and are fictionalised and fully anonymised.)

I am only beginning to offer therapy as a stand-alone "product". Not quite a techno-luddite (in fact, often an early-adopter), like many colleagues I am not yet fully versed in the application of technology for therapy. Working online with clients I usually see in the therapy room has become fairly habitual, but an exclusively online therapeutic relationship has so far happened only twice.

People come to work therapeutically with much the same issues with living as ever they did. The difference is that, over the past few years, technology has gained an increasingly central role in the way these issues have affected their lives; sometimes it has even crossed a boundary and entered the therapy room. In the following, I will not aim to describe therapeutic process; rather, I will give just a few common examples of how the role of technology in people's lives has become increasingly noticeable in my own practice, and will invite us to consider how we might need to pay attention to this trend.

The physical boundaries we put in place in our practice have become more permeable. In general, those of us in private practice create our own boundary rules, encompassing issues from physical contact to how we present the therapeutic space.

I know colleagues who maintain starkly empty rooms, without even water to hand. My approach is less purist: my room is comparatively crowded. It has space to move around, but also books, plants, filing cabinets, decorative objects, whiteboard, and the inevitable PC and peripherals. Swivel armchairs allow us to change angle as we think and communicate and we have water to hand. All this comprises the outer boundary. The space between us, our relationship, and the work itself hold attention, focus, and relational space. It is in this space that the language is spoken, psyches interact, experience is expressed and examined, possibilities explored and experimentally enacted.

There is little else that can encroach on the inner boundary of this work. Or so it used to be. Although my devices are switched off and silent and I ask clients to switch off their phones, this is where design has found its limits.

Clients bring phones into therapy for various purposes. One client "needs" to list thoughts and experiences between sessions on his mobile, and likes to refer to these during the session. This tells me something about his way of being in the world, his relationship with memory and recording experience, and offers another way of working together as he shapes and re-shapes his living.

Sometimes clients have felt the need to show me texts or emails for affirmation or recognition of something that felt existentially vital, especially where they feel deeply uncertain about what is true and what not. This was the case for Stacey, and I touch on her dilemma later.

For Joanna, the issue was one in a long line of events leading to breakdown of trust in her marriage.

> Joanna and her husband were struggling to maintain their relationship, although both said they wanted to make a go of it. Joanna could not accept her husband's assertion that he had lost all interest in sex.
>
> One day she came in for a couple's session. She sat down, arms tightly folded across her chest and her lips pursed. Her husband, who had come from work, arrived a few moments later, hurried and apologising. The atmosphere was tense, and I gently invited both to say what was going on for them in that moment.
>
> Joanna immediately responded, leaning forward and pointing her outstretched arm at her husband. Her voice raised, she said that, on returning from visiting family, she was devastated to discover a text he had sent to another woman. (The mobile in question was her husband's second phone and one she had his permission to use). Her husband declared that the text had been totally innocent. Joanna waved the phone in his face. Her already highly tuned internal lie detector was activated. She shouted that he should not take her for a fool, and she was clever enough to learn how to find and retrieve texts he thought he had deleted. He paled visibly, and before he could intervene she confronted him with a number of texts that showed that he had corresponded with, and booked, a prostitute while she was away.
>
> She urged me to look at the texts to prove what she was saying. I declined, bringing the session to focus on the present moment, what was going on for them both, and how we needed to address this in terms of their relationship.

For me, one of the challenges was to not accept this invitation to act as arbitrator or judge. My concern was to maintain the safety of the therapeutic space for both parties as we developed our work.

I also learned something new. At that time I did not know that something I had thought deleted was actually still accessible. This revelation has made me consider very carefully working online in any way that can be retrieved.

As Eric Schmidt says: "The option to 'delete' data is largely an illusion—lost files, deleted emails and erased text messages can be recovered with minimal effort". (p. 897)

He goes on to advise:

> "Since information wants to be free, don't write anything down you don't want read back to you in court or printed on the front page of a newspaper, as the saying goes. In the future this adage will broaden to include not just what you say and write, but the websites you visit, who you include in our online network, what you 'like,' and what others who are connected to you do, say and share." (p. 915)

Joanna had somehow learned how to retrieve "deleted" information. Another client, Stacey, had been lagging a little behind in her knowledge.

> Stacey had accepted her husband's assurance that his three-year affair was over, and that he wanted their marriage to heal and continue. In spite of this, she found herself feeling suspicious.
>
> She looked at her husband's phone, and found that he had continued texting his lover with intimate messages and arranging to see her.
>
> The following day, Stacey confronted her husband, who maintained that she was mistaken and showed her that there were no messages of the kind on his phone. She was puzzled, but inclined to believe him.
>
> The story repeated itself the following week, and Stacey's husband again showed her there were no messages, and said that her imagination was in overdrive. He was so convincing, and she so willing to accept his version, that Stacey began to doubt her own sanity.
>
> At this point a friend suggested that a techie she knew could look at the phone. This duly happened and, in fact, the "missing" texts were retrieved.
>
> Stacey now chose to go down the age-old route of hiring a private detective, who verified that her husband was continuing his affair.

It was at this stage that she came to therapy to untangle her own feelings, behaviours, beliefs, and wishes and to find a way forward.

In both cases there was much else involved in the story; for example, the husbands' readiness to have their wives use the phones was in itself a focus of work. Towards the end of therapy, one couple decided to separate, whilst the other successfully began to rebuild their marriage on new terms and understandings.

Safety, in its various meanings, is a central ethical concern in psychotherapy. Safety of private information is an important concern with any device we might be using. It is incumbent upon the therapist to find the most reliable encrypted systems for online work, and potential clients also need to be aware of the limitations on privacy when using, for example, text, email, or Skype conversations.

I commonly use email to arrange appointments. My therapy contract with a client also invites them to use email as a way to "dump" thoughts and feelings and have them held by me. I will read them and keep them to inform our next session either implicitly or explicitly, but not reply unless specifically requested to do so. I now have a clause in the written agreement that invites the clients to inform themselves about the level of privacy inherent in any online communication they might use in therapy, and to accept responsibility.

But what about when a client uses email to talk with others about their therapy and/or issues? Kevin did this several times.

> Kevin's father had just died. Kevin had described how he had hated his father for most of his life, and had talked about this with his partner. Now he was suffering intense grief mixed with all his difficult feelings about this challenging relationship.
>
> He decided that he wanted to go to the funeral, and asked his partner to come and support him. The arrangements would have been quite complicated, as they would have had to take three days off intense work schedules to travel the distance. His partner refused to go, and refused to believe his grief, saying she could not understand it in light of the hate he had always professed. Kevin felt powerless. Our next session was scheduled for immediately after the funeral. At this stage he found some relief in writing down

his emotions and thoughts as stream of consciousness and sending them to me to "park".

As his feelings intensified with the approach of the funeral date, and with his partner still refusing to go and to accept that he was not dissimulating, he decided to write another email.

This time I was surprised to see that the email was addressed not only to me, but also to a couple of close relatives and a friend. In it he poured out not only his confusion and grief, but also recounted in detail his suffering under the "cruelty" of his partner's attitude. He presented himself as a victim, begging them for their advice.

He had also copied this email to his partner.

He received one reply, copied to all. It was a supportive, non-judgemental and generalised expression of sympathy.

I wrote back to him without copying anyone in, simply acknowledging his feelings and pointing to our next session, as we had agreed I would do.

I was disconcerted and worried. Our therapeutic boundary had been violated, but I felt it was not the time to address this with him. It was also not the moment to address how he had put his partner in a powerless position and presented her as a perpetrator.

It was the moment to explore how writing that email had helped him—or not. All the other issues, including drawing relatives in to the same environmental space as his therapist, could wait. In the event, this proved to be a helpful decision for our continuing therapeutic work.

Although I had previously been aware that clients might show emails to others, or even forward them to others, I had not taken into account that they might write to others and to me in the *same* email.

I now point out to new clients that our correspondence should only be between ourselves unless specifically agreed otherwise for any reason. I now realised, with full impact, just how public therapy communications can be, and how much I still needed to learn, and be aware of, in this brave new online world.

In spite of caveats, in general using email communication as an adjunct to face-to-face therapy has been very useful, and has often given me additional useful information about my clients. Take Ellen, for example.

Ellen had been a high-flyer at work, and was devoted to her job. Company restructuring had meant redundancy in middle age, and she became listless and began to lose hope for her future. This is when she began therapy.

We would confirm our face-to-face sessions by email, and occasionally Ellen would also report her progress or concerns in these emails. This I found acceptable. "Report" is quite an apposite word here, for Ellen's email style was corporate. I felt this matched quite well the way she initially saw our relationship as a business arrangement, from which she expected certain results. Over time, her attitude to our therapeutic work changed radically, becoming far more open, more casual in use of language, intimate and revealing in content. Her writing style followed suite, but remained several notches more formal in register.

As our work began to focus increasingly on her personal and familial relationships, she described the lack of understanding between herself and her brother. Instead of supporting Ellen in this difficult situation, her brother was becoming increasingly bellicose in telephone conversations, and judgmental of Ellen for not yet having found a new job and in not "pulling herself together".

Ellen began forwarding their email exchanges to me. She could not understand why her brother "refused" to speak in an "adult and reasonable" way. She asked what she might do to improve communication.

Both she and her brother wrote lucidly and clearly. There the comparison ended. Her brother's style was full of invective and charged with emotion. Ellen's style was straight out of her corporate environment, carefully crafted to avoid expressions of emotion and divergence from the subject line. Her linear thinking was exemplified to perfection.

I felt that our therapeutic relationship was now deep and strong enough for a direct approach. In our sessions we compared both styles of writing in the exchanges with her brother. One of the exercises was to notice words that expressed emotion. Her brother's texts became peppered with yellow marker, while her own remained pristine. We discussed what this meant for the relationship, and also for Ellen's relationship with emotion and feelings. Suddenly she broke down and, for the first time, admitted to herself her lifelong dissociation from many feelings, and her connection particularly with anger, which she constantly suppressed.

These emails proved to be rich terrain for Ellen's therapy. She gradually modified her writing style and allowed herself to get in touch with feelings. She began to recognise how she had responded to life events to protect herself. Although the relationship with her brother is still challenging, she is now able to recognise where the difficulties stem from. She is beginning to understand how things developed, to feel empathy for both her brother and herself, and to be able to express this far more readily. Developing empathy with herself and exploring possibilities for future relationships that might have a very different quality about them has been, thus far, a deeply liberating experience for Ellen.

Whilst Ellen played out very little of her personal and emotional life online, there seems to be a general tendency for many people to do the opposite, Facebook and Twitter being cases in point.

I have now made my Facebook page private, and do not even write anything on it any more. Some years ago, a short time after I became aware of Facebook, I made the mistake of accepting a client request to "friend". To this day I have not had the heart to "unfriend" this erstwhile client, and in this case that feels all right. For all new clients nowadays I specify that we will not link via Facebook. This feels like a tricky area, as with LinkedIn I work rather differently. Here I draw a boundary of at least six months after close of therapy, but see no reason after that to refuse a request to link up. This is something I feel I may modify in the future, and I accept that many colleagues might have tighter boundaries in this respect.

How clients deal with each other on Facebook can also spill into the therapy room as significant material. As, for example, in the case of Penny and Liam.

Liam began therapy when he felt his new marriage to Penny, who was fourteen years his junior, was in danger of disintegrating after the following events.

Liam's Facebook page was full of his previous life, including ex-girlfriends and ex-wife. Often the text that went with the images was full of warm, not to say hot, appreciation of these exes.

Liam and Penny had been together for eighteen months, and married for six. Whenever they had a tiff, Penny would express her displeasure about Liam's apparent attachment to past romances, as presented on Facebook. Tiffs became arguments, which escalated to rows. Penny began to demand that Liam remove pictures of his ex-girlfriends and any mention of his ex-wife. She was very upset that he had not yet put up an album of their own wedding photos.

Eventually this grew into demands that he break off all contact with people who knew these exes, and that online he refer only to his "new" life with her. He gave in and removed a few of the less significant people. Old friends contacted him and expressed puzzlement, and Liam began to feel he was losing all autonomy. He finally dug in his heels, and told Penny she would have to accept that he had a past and wanted to be able to express it.

Penny's resentment grew, and after one particularly volatile row, she went onto the Facebook page and "unfriended" her spouse. Such a public declaration of their marital difficulties shocked friends and left Liam gasping, and he wonders at the moment whether to stay in the marriage at all.

Perhaps Penny had clicked "unfriend" in a moment of pique. As with writing a letter and parking rather than sending it, it is often recommended that we leave emotional emails unsent for a while. Google now allows you to delay sending emails by five seconds, so that even after you have pressed "send", you can retrieve the missive within those precious five seconds.

Unfortunately, as therapists conducting email therapy we might tend to the other extreme of caution. Some of us spend inordinate amounts of time composing and editing our emails to clients, and not sending them until they feel just right. These are honourable intentions, which can quickly lead to a depleted bank balance if we find we spend twice the amount of paid time (or more!) on writing, leaving little space in our day to take on new clients. This can happen particularly if we get carried away in modelling the client, matching style, type of vocabulary, tone, etc. For me it feels a mistake to try to create rapport if it means removing oneself more and more from one's own authenticity.

Of course, as humans and as therapists we may be comfortable in several different linguistic registers and styles, and able to be congruent and authentic in various identities, or (in dialogical terminology),

I-positions. Where this is the case, it will add diversity and richness to our experience of our work, and enable us to be a good enough match for more people.

Using different language styles and registers can point to the different identities we may inhabit. Many people find that their various identities in the physical world find more room for expression online.

> Client Jeremy is a successful lawyer by day, respected and dedicated. Some weekends and evenings he changes out of his suit, dons very different clothing, snorts cocaine, and with his partner visits country houses to enjoy S&M parties. On returning he changes into his other main identity of respectable city lawyer. He does not present in therapy because of any problem with these two identities, but because he is becoming very stressed in trying to balance his life now that he has a third identity as a new father. He has also gone virtual with all three of these identities and joined "communities" online that resonate with each physical identity. In order to keep them separate and safe, he has assumed a number of new names and new email addresses.

Jeremy is matching his physical identities with his virtual ones. Others may create identities that exist only online, and as Schmidt says:

> In many ways, their virtual identities will come to supersede all others, as the trails they leave remain engraved online in perpetuity. (p. 110)

Jeremy will have not one, but at least three, virtual profiles. Schmidt again:

> Your online identity in the future is unlikely to be a simple Facebook page; instead it will be a constellation of profiles, from every online activity, that will be verified and perhaps even regulated by the government. (p. 532)

Once again, we need to be aware of big brother (government and commerce) holding the strings; we need to notice where, and to what extent, our freedoms might be invaded, and be prepared to fight for our privacy where necessary.

Tommy found himself fighting his father in order to preserve not merely his online identity, but his very identity as a human being.

Tommy was repeating his first year university exams, and had to pass to continue. He had been depressed. He felt that he was on the wrong course; felt shy and very isolated, and felt he didn't fit in with anyone. Although very intelligent, he was about to give up.

The one thing that kept him alive at this stage was his link to the World Wide Web. Tommy was the original Internet geek. He had formed a group of close friends across the globe, with their own social code, gaming groups, and esoteric techie conversations. These people knew each other better than anyone else knew them, and in this environment they were high functioning.

Tommy's father despaired as he watched his son almost incarcerate himself in his room, refuse to go out and socialise, and above all, not do well at university. Regularly during this time he would put his head round the door and yell if he found Tommy gaming instead of cramming. These occasions multiplied, the yelling got louder. One day his patience, strained at the best of times, snapped, and he disconnected Tommy's Internet link. Furious, Tommy rushed towards his father with murder in his heart. The two men struggled, and gained control of themselves just in time to avert anything serious happening.

They quickly arranged a joint therapy session. The father expressed his deep concern that his son seemed anti-social, "not normal", and shared his fear that Tommy was throwing away his education and life chances.

The son assured him that he was working hard and aimed to pass the exams.

What the father was unable to understand was that by removing Tommy's Internet link he was doing him more damage than he could imagine. Tommy's social community was online. That was where his friends were. That's where his connection was at its peak, that's where he functioned fully in his own experience. Take that away (his only piece of autonomy, to boot), and you took away his life. It was not an understatement to say his life was now in danger.

Eventually his father accepted Tommy's otherness, and recognised that his need for gaming was his way of relaxing between sessions of learning. Tommy passed his exam, changed course to something that suited his talents, and met his first love.

Some might say that Tommy was addicted. I would disagree, and say that Tommy simply found the environment that best allowed his identity to flourish at a particular time in his life. He has since gone on to form other identities, and (through his romantic relationship) has become a far more social, rounded human being in the physical world.

Someone who might be described as addicted (and very readily so in the USA) is Harry.

Harry had just become a father, and his partner was completely engrossed by the baby. Harry had already turned to finding sex elsewhere during his partner's pregnancy when she felt unresponsive, and had started an affair.

Alongside the affair, he began to visit porn sites and pay for online sex ever more often.

"Caught out" (as he put it) by his partner, he promised to stop the affair and the online porn. Although the affair ended, what seemed to have become an obsession with porn continued, and the couple separated.

Desperate to win back his partner, Harry increased his commitment to therapy, and began to face aspects of his life and personality that he had never looked at before in any depth.

The couple decided to go to a residential course—he to one for online porn addicts, she for relatives of addicts. The experience of being in a group, of hearing the stories of the other men and sharing their behaviour and feelings had a normalising effect. He now no longer felt quite the evil creature that most of his family and friends seemed to think he was.

He continued with therapy with yet more commitment and made good progress, but his partner was unable to come to terms with his infidelity and the couple finally separated again.

In Harry's case, as for so many people, the easy availability of an addictive substance (online porn) had led to the breakdown of a relationship and a broken home for his baby. For him, virtual connectivity had negative consequences in this case, and his online identity almost led to the disintegration of his physical identity for a time.

As a therapist, how can I ever know who I am working with, whether in the room or online? Everything in the end is on trust. The technology industry will probably help us identify whether potential clients are who they say they are. But we will not necessarily know what other identities they might have, unless they choose also to bring these to therapy and unless the trust built in the therapeutic relationship enables them to bring all parts of themselves.

Some people would not come to therapy, preferring to remain totally anonymous, and now they have the option to visit online therapy groups that allow anonymity. Some colleagues might be comfortable with working in this way, too, as do Samaritans and other services. I choose to work with people who identify themselves, and I let them know who I am, in spite of the problems of Internet security, and the increasing danger of having our identities hacked.

Online identity will become such a powerful currency that we will even see the rise of a new black market where people can buy real or invented identities.

Being aware of developments in online connectivity and communication is just one aspect of our need to be aware of social developments and change in general. Virtual media is inevitably a major influence in the way future lives and societies are being shaped. How far we choose to go in adopting the new media for our own work is, thank goodness, still a matter of personal choice.

Love—West London Style—May 2013

Martin Pollecoff

"You have zero privacy anyway. Get over it."

Scott McNealy, CEO of Sun Microsystems,
Wired, 26 January 1999

There is nothing new about looking for love, nor is there anything novel about infidelity—it's eternal.

Love, sex, relationships—are part of what Adolf Bastian describes as "elementary ideas[1]—they are common to all humanity", but the "courting" that takes place is overlaid with cultural peculiarities.

So one generation's courting habits will be different from the next generation's way and it will vary from culture to culture but couples have always needed two types of environments within which to meet. The public—the light—in which they find themselves attracted to each other—and the private—the dark—where intimacies can be exchanged, vulnerabilities exposed, and relationships consummated (I like that word "consummated": it means "brought to completion", which says something about our intentions).

In my grandfather's day, public meetings took place either through introduction or on a Sunday promenade for which people would put on their best clothes and simply go for a walk or listen to a band in the park. It was where you could see and perhaps talk to girls. Today that promenade may be taken online.

Here we are multiplying the size of the field and also multiplying the risk of being hurt or confused.

What is new—West London style is the social backdrop against which all this takes place and the Media via which these transactions take place.

My clients are not Freud's. Men and women, gay and heterosexual, worry about their work—their careers—as well as relationships and children. Even the best are made redundant, and the use of email, cell phones, and all the gewgaws of new media, ensure that they are at work 24/7.

I am now used to cellphones going off during sessions, clients anxiously examining texts, and even the command—"I have to take this!", which normally preceeds a conversation between us about—"Must you?" or "When do you get time that is just yours?"

But new media does not exist in a social vacuum. Another peculiarity of practicing in West London is that few people are from here, rather we are flotsam—we float up here. At eighteen, I made the journey from Birmingham, which was both a relief—to be away from home—and frightening because I was away from home. Loneliness was the propellant that compelled me to create relationships and it was the anonymity of the city that allowed me to talk to strangers.

My clients have come from further afield and tend to be hybrids—Russian-English, Korean-Australian, French-Syrian, all of whom have found home in W2. Careers rather than relationship bring them here but that means that they are seldom surrounded by family or old friends. All find that once they have left university, meeting new people is hard and takes time, their scarcest commodity.

Yes, you can always meet people at work but relationships in the office, once de rigueur, take place hidden away from HR, the new corporate superego—judge, jury, and executioner.

Brian's a city trader. He was having an affair with a work colleague and he began this story with the old "A team" adage: "I love it when a plan comes together."

So Brian wants to split up with this woman but she had too much on him. If the affair comes to light, he will lose his substantial bonus, which is held against good behaviour. And he may lose his job.

So: these two lovers go to a pub. His phone is on the blink so he asks to use hers then, the idiot, "accidently" drops her cell phone into his pint of beer. He feels terrible and making loud apologies, leaps up and runs to the toilet promising to rescue it with the aid of the hot air hand dryer; which he does, but not before finishing off the poor thing by running it under the cold-tap.

The next morning she was surprised and delighted when a brand-new, top-of-the-range 64 Gigabit, £699, iPhone 5, gets delivered to her desk. As he put it, "All is well that ends well": and of course, he was relieved that all his incriminating texts had been safely washed away.

The City really is no country for old men. Brian is forty-five, ancient for a trader and the bank is as ruthless as he is. On paper he is a winner but he feels that somewhere he has lost, and, right now, is some other Machiavelli running Brian under the tap?

He fears that the life he has known is extinguishing and so we gently probe his vulnerabilities and from this disowned material we work to recognise the Ariadne's thread from which he will shape his own resurrection.

Those texts are lethal. I cannot tell you how many new clients begin their stories with "My partner found this text on my phone". Or, "My partner went to have a shower and I took a look at his phone".

They belong to the world of the deeply private—they use language that may be appropriate in the dark but bring hurt and shame when a third party reads them. If you shine a torch into the darkness suddenly all you can see is that which is illuminated—everything beyond the penumbra becomes pitch black and may as well not exist. This deep, deep material goes to the heart of vulnerability and when it is suddenly illuminated, the result is traumatic.

There are parts of the self that are reserved for lovers. We reveal such parts to act as ransom—insurance against abandonment. Words that are so private, they do not even sit comfortably in therapy.

And yet these messages left on phones, in much the same way that love letters were tied in bundles and hidden for rereading and reassurance that we are loved and desired. In the dark, ideas and feelings can slowly gestate. We need privacy within which to grow relationships. At school we learned that plant roots were geotropic, pushing themselves down into the ground whilst the plant itself grew upwards following the light. We need to grow in both directions in order to flourish.

Lucy describes herself as a "millennial".

It's a term she uses a lot to describe how she feels about herself and her friends. Born in the late eighties she was brought up with new media, only it's not "new" to Lucy. When she was a toddler she delighted her parents by being able to use the video set even though she had once experimented by inserting a jam sandwich where the cartridge went. She could not remember a time when there wasn't a computer in the house. She chatted to school friends online and she recalls the day she joined Facebook like it was a graduation day. On her eighteenth birthday she has 472 Facebook friends.

Lucy's issue is that when the virtual world collides with the corporeal one, life gets tough. She feels that everything she does is public and that she has nothing for herself. Nothing private that is. On weekends she goes out with a shoal of friends. They cruise from bar to bar, texting others, arranging meet-ups, and bumping into other shoals. Sometimes she has a one-night stand but she dreads it being announced on Facebook or someone actually saying that she is "going out" with X or X changing his status on Facebook to "in Relationship" (with Lucy). It's that light being turned onto her private world that she dreads. And there is always the threat of being trashed on the net—that some camera-phone picture of her will appear on one of those spiteful revenge sites where old boyfriends put up souvenir phone shots of the ex with his cock in her mouth and that is way, way, too much light being shone on anyone. And Lucy knows that those shots will be there when she is a grandmother—they are digital tattoos.

Lucy is wary of sex. She feels that she has to really perform—her sex tutors have been on the Internet sites which feature celebrity porn—Paris Hilton, Kim Kardashien, Pamela Anderson, she has seen how the stars have sex. And she wonders—can she match up?

In TV dramas you see people ripping up unwanted photos or burning them, but the web is not like that, you can't take down anything published. The Internet was designed to maintain communication and data against the threat of war damage. Data published on one site is quickly cannibalised by others, your past is with you for ever—there are no second chances. No redemption—your only choice is to "get over it". In cyber-space no one can hear you scream.

We fail a lot in life especially when we are young—we have to practise to get good at something. If we do not allow ourselves to fail how can we learn to succeed? And so for Lucy and others, therapy is a place in which they can practice relationship and try ideas out—far away from the imagined glare of film lights.

Our work is timeless, it's about a young person's reluctance to embrace the adult world. Native Americans refer to our strengths as "medicine". It's the power that will keep us well and that we can use to fight away sickness. Lucy is funny, she can laugh at herself—she has "laughter medicine".

At times the two of us might as well be aboriginals, an old man and a young woman sitting in a cave laughing at the shadows cast by the fire, two people creating more and more grotesque and ridiculous scenarios of shame and embarrassment, giggling and roaring like drunken hoot-owls, for laughter has always driven fears away.

For some the virtual world is their world, and their identity is ever shifting.

> Bernard always pays cash. He says he is Brazilian/German, a handsome young man who works out religiously every day. "I am not after bulk," he says, "only tone and shape". He has two phones and two websites because Bernard takes his work as a male prostitute seriously. "I think I have five years left … max. I do not want to be doing this at thirty."
>
> One phone is for his alter-ego "Rita", a pre-operative transsexual with her own web page. "Transsexuals get the best money and I earn it—it takes me two hours each time to dress, to shave and make up as Rita.
>
> Some complain because I don't have breasts but I tell them I am saving for the op. No one has ever refused".
>
> He has another site as Danny—Danny is butch and dominant. "If the Samsung rings it's for 'Danny' so I answer it in a low voice. But if this phone rings, it's Rita and I just purr."

He talks with gratitude about the brothers who raised him in the orphanage (and "No" they did not abuse him). He was fostered several times but he was never special to the mothers that took him in, and he has little idea about the mother who gave him to the care of the Church.

Bernard has had thousands of lovers but no relationships. What he says is that he would like simply to be ordinary—a small house, away from London, with a little garden—find a partner. "Perhaps I will paint". But there is no partner and no friends and the life he's led is too vivid for intimacy. That world is nuanced and detailed—his is one in which colours are the brightest, and ecstasy is expected—he is by trade and history a part-object, one that may be taken away for a few days but never taken home. He lives the narcissistic porn life and Bernard fears that he has had 'too many tongues in his mouth to ever settle down'. He talks as if he is in control of his life but sometimes the party-drugs push Bernard over his edge, and he has a "meltdown" which can last weeks.

Some months back, I arrived home, just as he was ringing my doorbell. I greeted him, and locked my bike to the railings. Bernard looked shocked. "You cycle in London ... but that is so dangerous."

I like Bernard and I do care about him. And I appreciated that he had grown to care about me, cared about my safety. He had said that I mattered and that if I were to be hurt he would hurt too. Something had moved for both of us.

I don't think Bernard is his real name. It's the one he gave me and it's the one I use but I figure him more as a Fabio or a Marcos. Maybe Bernard is just another character in this virtual world of his.

Who knows what might happen. I'm an optimist. Perhaps he will be true to his word and someday, before he is thirty, Bernard will simply take down the sites—drop the phones in the canal, shed Rita, Danny, and even Bernard—put on a new skin and simply walk away—retire to somewhere like St Albans, find a partner and take up painting.

Commentator one: Steve Johnson

A common theme in these scenarios seems to be the role of technology in illicit sexual relationships. This, and Martin's delightful analogy of "a bundle of love letters", set me thinking: is this really new? Or has it always been thus? Won't we humans always use nascent "technology" to further our sexual urges (particularly those illicit ones!) and then bring these new problems into therapy as a challenge for the modern-thinking therapist? I like to think that there was once a therapist somewhere listening to a stone age man concerned that his wife had stumbled across his cave paintings of "the other woman".

New media has an established role in modern living. Clearly, there is a generation emerging for whom love letters are as much a part of history as are cave paintings. As therapists, we need to recognise this and be prepared to help our clients to cope with the consequences.

But we also need to embrace technology and use it to our advantage while, of course, being mindful of some of the potential pitfalls. Alexandra points out, for example, how easy it now is to retrieve records, even those thought to have been deleted, from hard drives. How safe are your client records? And, in another example, I am reminded how easy it would be when responding to emails to hit the "Reply All" button. It wouldn't be the first time we have helped a therapist out of that particular hole!

Commentator two: Ian Gilmore

Although the two delicious little romps that constitute this chapter seem quite different in tone, they nonetheless reflect different perspectives on what amounts to the same activity: online psychotherapy. And what, we may enquire, is so very different about online psychotherapy compared to its more traditional antecedent: person-to-person psychotherapy, apart perhaps from the absence of that most traditional of landmarks, the chaise-longue?

It is here that we have to make the most critical of distinctions: namely that between the central task or activity and the various mechanisms through which it is delivered. The core task is of course psychotherapy, but that is where our quest for easy answers comes to a grinding halt, for before we can determine the precise nature of, to quote our two previous contributors, the "new media," we surely need to determine first the nature of the old media; without determining this distinction, we can determine no other.

To my way of thinking, the traditional in-person edition of psychotherapy represents an engagement with three principle discourses: an experiential, a relational, and a hermeneutic one. So now we may ask whether this is what online therapy proposes to accomplish, and my answer is in the affirmative, for just as in traditional person-to-person psychotherapy, online therapy serves to assist its clients to discern a sense of meaning (hermeneutics) from their life experiences, and it seeks to do so largely through the relational medium of a meeting between a therapist and one or more client(s).

Therefore, we may conclude that the only difference between online and in-person psychotherapy is the various mechanisms through which they are conducted. Both contributors paint a picture through recourse to several vignettes of how the new medium affects the psychotherapeutic "service delivery system", but the crucial point is surely that the efficacy of these various mechanisms is to be evaluated through recourse to precisely the same principles and values that are reflected in our profession's existing ethical formulations. The requirements for robust training and supervision remain the same, and although the various new media will throw up different shadows to be considered, the light will remain firmly focussed on safe accountable practice that is clearly geared to the needs of its clientele.

Note

1. Campbell, Joseph. *The Masks of God: Primitive Mythology*, p. 32. London: Secker & Warburg: 1960. "Jung's idea of the 'archetypes' is one of the leading theories, today, in the field of our subject. It is a development of the earlier theory of Adolf Bastian …"

Reference

Same old, with new angles

All quotations are from

Cohen, J., & Schmidt, E. (2013). *The New Digital Age: Reshaping the Future of People, Nations and Business* (Kindle edition). London: John Murray.

CHAPTER SIX

Lost in translation—meeting the challenges of language and regional customs when working online, cross-border, without visual cues

Divine Charura

"It is surely now, more than ever, necessary for us as practitioners to work together in ways that will develop our conceptualisations and understandings of what is the most useful relationship for people in distress."

—Haugh & Paul, 2008, p. 37

Through language formulation, subjective experiences are communicated in our daily encounters in life. The same is true also for the therapeutic relationship. However, in communicating through language in face-to-face therapy, and more so when working via new media, there are many levels where subjective communication processes increase the potential of intended meanings being lost. In this chapter there will therefore be a central focus on the complexities of the client's and therapists' subjective experience. Some reflection on theory and practice between client and therapist will be explored. As the chapter progresses focus will shift to the challenges of regional differences in language and customs when working without the visual clues. Towards the end, an exploration of ways of minimising the possibilities of interventions being ineffective, misunderstood, or of both client and therapist misinterpreting each other, will be discussed.

In order to highlight some challenges and complexities of working via new media, a case study will be presented and explored. Having gained consent to use this case study, some pseudodetails are used and the name Chris is a pseudonym to protect the client's identity.

> Chris is a twenty-eight-year-old client that I worked with for over six months. He initially contacted me stating that his GP had suggested that therapy may be helpful as he was experiencing low mood and stress from his postgraduate medical studies. In our first session I explored with him his reason for referral. He stated that he had increasingly found it stressful being away from home, especially following the recent death of his father. He also stated that the medical postgraduate work he had was "getting on top of him". We contracted for an initial twelve once-weekly hourly sessions, to which he attended. Towards the end of these sessions in our review, Chris stated he had found the sessions very helpful. He, however, requested to continue therapy but stated that as he had completed his studies, he was going back home [Ireland]. From there he would go to Syria where he would be working with an international organisation. He requested whether I could continue to be his psychotherapist for another twelve sessions. He stated he had considered other therapists, but felt he wanted to continue with me. Initially I was hesitant to work through digital media [Skype and email] but following supervision, and consultation, I agreed. We worked together for the next three months and communicated through Skype or email once a week. These sessions, he reported, were very useful for him.
>
> They were also challenging sessions, particularly with regards to using new media, for example, at moments in which our communication, meaning to each other was "lost in translation"—times when we both misinterpreted what the other meant.

I will draw on this case study to illuminate ideas I will raise in this chapter.

Before any further exploration I would like to draw you, the reader, to some stark questions that I asked myself at the start of my therapy engagement with Chris via new media. These were the root cause of my initial hesitation to this way of working and I think it may be helpful for you, too, to consider them and to reflect on your own responses. Being aware that, apart from psychotherapeutic skills the only tool I had in working through new media was the use of language, my focus shifted to my awareness of these questions.

Table 1a. Exploratory questions to challenges of working via new media.

1. What ethical framework is there to working online: i.e., with regards to confidentiality, safety of content that is discussed with the client?
2. In regards to the concept of presence and immediacy: in the absence of visual clues, how could I use language to keep the client in contact, aware of my process and presence?
3. How would the core conditions of empathy, unconditional positive regard, and congruence be communicated via language within new media?
4. What part would language play in establishing and maintaining a therapeutic relationship?
5. How would the lack of visual cues, body language, and paralinguistics affect the therapeutic relationship?

The questions in Table 1a are all central to communication and language within the therapeutic encounter. They are also challenges when considering working via digital media. My intention is not to answer them for individuals but rather to enable a reflective process to occur when exploring ideas within this chapter. In order to help clarify some of the concepts, it is important to consider psychotherapy before the emergence of new media.

In the beginning was non-digital psychotherapy: why change?

It is well noted within psychological literature that nearly all therapies emerge from the four forces of psychology namely psychoanalysis, behavioural, humanistic, and transpersonal psychology (Haugh & Paul, 2008). Evolving from these forces of psychology, there are now over 400 different approaches to therapy (Corsini & Wedding, 2008). In my analysis of these different therapies I have noted that nearly all give theoretical postulations about facets of practice which related to working face-to-face with clients in their immediate presence. In other words, from the beginning, it has always been non-digital therapy.

Although this does not discount the new media it raises an important question. Why then depart from ways of working which have served some clients well for many decades?

As a starting point, I believe it is best to state the factors related to positive outcome within the therapeutic process. I have noted the quote at the start of this chapter by Haugh and Paul (2008), which highlights the importance of us as psychotherapists and counsellors shifting our focus more to what works for clients. Although research highlights the unequivocal efficacy of face-to-face therapy, there is now a plethora of research also showing evidence of clients benefiting highly from new media ways of working (Jackson, 2013; Walker, 2007). The benefits of digital technology for both clients and counsellors are well noted and it is hypothesised that in the future online therapy is likely to overtake the volume of clients that access face-to-face therapy (Jackson, 2013; Walker, 2007). This inevitably raises questions and adds the challenge of facets of communication being lost in translation from when experiences develop internally to when they are shared through language. This is where the possibilities and realities of naming subjective *experience* through meaning being lost in translation begin. The term "experience" in this chapter denotes "all that is going on within the envelope of the organism at any given moment which is potentially available to awareness" (Rogers, 1959, p. 197).

Levels of being lost in translation: challenges of symbolisation of subjective experience through language in formulation and exploration of meaning

The developmental subjective experience of the individual client and the endeavour to communicate his/her experiences through language is a complex process. Through neuroscience we now understand that language is central to survival in terms of communicating basic to complex needs, exploring/giving meaning to experiences, feelings, imagination, communicating emotions, and so on (Barden & Williams, 2007). Vontress (2011) highlighted that through language the essence of life's experiences is communicated. This therefore puts language at the centre of human psychological and social development.

Many experienced therapists will concur that words and language do not equate to the accurate symbolisation of an individual's experience. Even for clients who I have worked with who considered themselves extremely emotionally or linguistically eloquent, there are clear moments when they struggle to put their internal experience into words. In other words, their experience is not accurately symbolised through the process of translating their internal experience into words. Through working with a diverse range of clients in therapy I note that there are moments when clients can spend a whole session, weeks, or even months in therapy attempting to explore an experience, feeling, or emotion. However, each time they vocalise it, the words, phrases, or language they use do not appear to be accurately reflecting what they are experiencing or feeling.

In our work together, Chris spent at least seven sessions exploring his experience of "grief", a word he had heard so often in his work as a doctor. However, when he experienced it himself, he found the word did not match the intensity of the "pain" and confusion he was experiencing. It is clear that the therapist's endeavours to respond with empathic reflections are attempts within the therapeutic relationship to redeem what is being lost in translation. This is evident when the clients attempt to translate their experience into words (Spinelli, 2005; Worsley, 2008). I concur that the empathic responses endeavour to draw from the client's internal frame of reference and to check accurate symbolisation of experience. Through empathic responses the client is informed that the therapist understands his/her internal experience (Haugh & Paul, 2008; Rogers, 1959).

Barden and Williams (2007) cut to the heart of the matter when they suggested that what is lost in translation is the client's intersubjective reality. They hypothesised that in the process of communication there is a fragmentation between the experience of self and the vocalisation of language. On one level this translation of experience into words allows individuals to communicate their experience. However, on the other hand, it does not permit the client's experience to be fully shared (Barden & Williams, 2007). As a therapist I therefore understand the complexity of language within the therapeutic encounter. It is also important to be aware that as words become more interconnected it may become more complex to understand the client's subjective experience.

Drawing on the case study, although Chris often stated how there were no words (language) to describe the pain, sorrow, hurt he felt on the loss of his father. There were also moments when he used language and words like "pain" to try to explain it, and still we both noticed that the exact meaning of his experience was lost in translation en route from explaining his experience. The first potential of meaning being lost in translation is, therefore, through the process of expressing experience through language/words.

Eugene Gendlin, a renowned writer in the field of philosophy, psychotherapy, and psychology, highlighted that what we experience and name as our feelings is an inward flow he termed "felt meaning", which, he stated, is much broader in its rawest form (Gendlin, 1997, p. 11). He further stated that when individuals become unable to symbolise or give interpretation to this felt experience then they are lost and can seek to regain this connection to the felt sense through the therapeutic encounter. When working through new media therapists read text, or hear the client's experience through his/her attempt to put subjective experience into words. Gendlin (1997) argues that there is a complexity in this process, as what clients attempt to symbolise through language can be interpreted into endless meanings. In applying this idea to this chapter, the challenge therefore becomes the interpretation of the language that the therapist hears, sees, or reads (via telephone, Skype, email, or on other information technology platforms). This, then, presents a second level at which meaning may be lost in translation, that is, through the use of language by the client and the resultant plethora of levels of interpretation of meaning by the therapist.

To further explore this idea I am drawn to philosophical thought and the concept of hermeneutics. Hermeneutics is the philosophy of the interpretation of meaning. Vedder (1998) highlighted the relevance of hermeneutics when exploring attempts to understand language. Richard Worsley (2012), a prolific writer within the psychotherapy arena, expounded on this philosophical idea. He clarified that the interpretation of meaning when drawing on hermeneutics is different from psychodynamic interpretation of meaning. In hermeneutics there is an appreciation of the richness of personal language and what is expressed, as the client's narrative has multiple meanings. This characteristic of having multiple meanings is described as polysemic (Worsley, 2012). In other words, when I am working within new media and read a client's email, or other text forms in which his/her experience is noted, then I should approach this as a polysemic narrative. Within hermeneutics, the process of exploring the client's experience, and linking the multiple meanings together, is termed the hermeneutic circle. Meaning is thus gained through dialogue and tentatively asking questions (Severson, 2012; Worsely, 2012).

Whilst reading for this chapter I noted that taking a hermeneutic stance presents an opportunity when working through digital media. That is, it emancipates us from being fixated on the client's experience as having only one meaning. A different perspective is offered by Severson (2012), who offers a critique of the concept of hermeneutics as a dyad of self and other in which the focus is on interpretation of text/narrative. Severson argues, through the philosophy of Emmanuel Levinas, that the hermeneutic encounter is less about interpretation and more about the condition of being-in-the world (Severson, 2012).

I can take an example from the case study presented in this chapter, where Chris stated to me that he was stressed. On hearing this, or reading his email with this content, I may have initially derived, from what he was naming as stress, my own internal mass of a personal felt sense which I call stress. If I explore this from a hermeneutic stance however, my interpretation of the language relating to stress (or my experience of being-in-the-world when I am stressed) could result in Chris's own meaning being lost. The therapeutic challenge, therefore, is to be open to the fact that my felt sense of what I call stress would be very different to what Chris may be symbolising as stress. Upon adopting a hermeneutic stance and exploring the polysemic narratives that Chris often emailed, which I read as text, we were both able to go beyond the words. (I was able to go beyond my own interpretation of stress and we were freer to explore Chris' experience and meaning.) When we explored the possible meanings of the language he used, and the narrative he told about his changing emotions of stress, love, and sadness for his father, we were in what is termed a hermeneutic circle (Severson, 2012; Worsely, 2012). This hermeneutic circle exploration was made possible through tentatively checking each other's meaning over multiple sessions and over time. As it is only through time that experience and meaning can be explored, it is important to also note that it is through time that meaning can also be lost in translation. Time is therefore an important actor to explore when working within new media.

Time and language: loss of meaning when working via new media

Through the exploration of clients' experience in the hermeneutic circle it is highly possible that meaning may be lost in translation because, without the visual clues, all clients and therapists can mostly go with is language used in the description and exploration of the narrative. Moreover, when working via email, as I did with Chris, there is a delayed response to connecting with the client's felt sense and his immediate experiencing. This is often due to having to wait for responses from each other rather than working through experiencing in the present moment. One of the challenges I faced through new media, in particular email, text, and other modes of working, was responding during different time zones to the clients. This results in a complexity in the use of language that deals with the immediacy of the client's experience. An example is when Chris sent me an email (email Six) in which he stated:

> ... I feel very stressed and am beginning to wonder if I made the right decision to leave so soon after Dad's death. Although there are people around me and the work is supposed to make me feel fulfilled as I am helping others who are currently facing war, hunger, pain and multiple losses, I feel alone, isolated and unfulfilled. I am in serious pain. ... I feel out of place most times ... I'm like a jackdaw among peacocks ... ☹

In getting such an email, many themes come into play. Amongst these are ones I have already explored, including the various levels at which the meaning may be lost in translation, which, as noted above, may happen at the following levels:

1. Internally for Chris when trying to explain his subjective experience of feelings of pain and putting them in words (language).
2. In my interpretation as a different other (using my own experience of these feelings) and understanding of what the words *stressed, unfulfilled, alone, pain* meant for Chris at the time of writing?
3. Furthermore, in considering the polysemic nature of his narrative (the many possible meanings of the language used) meaning may be lost as we may both have different meanings.
4. The metaphor which Chris used—*I'm like a jackdaw among peacocks*—is another level at which the meaning of his experience may be lost in translation. What does this metaphor mean in relation to his experience? (I noted the use of the emoticon too in his email. What does it mean about his internal felt experience to himself and to me?)

The fifth point I will now explore focuses on the impact of time and how language used in responding to the client can often result in the client's felt experience being lost in translation; that is, if language is not carefully chosen to reflect the acknowledgement that the response could possibly be out of sync not only with the client's experience but with the timing too. In order to understand this I draw on the work of the great French author Paul Ricoeur. He hypothesised, in his hermeneutical discussion on narrative identity, the complexity, when we consider time, of reading text and of interpretation of meaning through language. Ricoeurnian thought notes time on two levels. Cosmic time (scientific time) and phenomenological time (that is, time as subjectively experienced) (Ricoeur, 1985). Worsely (2012) expounded on this concept and stated that from a phenomenological stance, when time is considered as past, present, and future, there is an interrelational concept. The ability to draw subjective experience from events that occurred at a particular time is only available from the individual (Worsely, 2012). In other words, the client's subjective experience draws meaning in relation to his ability to recall experience in relation to a particular time.

When working in new media, the therapist therefore faces a challenge. The client's experience and meaning, which he accesses through use of language, is not only textually, or audio-graphically encoded (when using email/letter, video-phone, i.e., Skype or phone). (In moments when Chris and I used Skype, there was often a delay in receiving each other's responses. Even a few second's delay when working through Skype impacts on the "immediacy" and "presence" conditions of the therapeutic relationship). Another point relating to time is that on receipt of an email, the words and language are received and read in the therapist's present time. A challenge, therefore, of working through some new media modes is that the client's experience and language, when received or read by the therapist, is in the here and now. However, because of cosmic time differences the experience lacks immediacy. It therefore means that the therapist should also be aware of the client's language if she is responding to feelings and experiences which the client would have written from a phenomenological stance (the client's here and now).

To elaborate on this idea using the case example, I would highlight that by the time I responded to Chris' email, although sometimes his feelings were still present when I accessed his emails two days later, at other times they had changed. It was therefore important for me to carefully consider the language I used in order to avoid it being out of Chris' phenomenological/present experience. In other words, the

Table 1b. Therapist's response exercise to client's language, meaning and phenomenological experience.

Client's language	Meaning	Time frame and language	Language response exercise
i. *I feel very stressed, … I feel alone, isolated and unfulfilled …*	What meaning do you derive from these sentences?	Present at time of writing. In other words in Chris's phenomenological experience it is in the here and now but when I got the email it was past for him but became present for me.	What response would you give? (Consider your words, language carefully) Consider also that at the point of responding, his feelings may be still the same.
ii. *… and am beginning to wonder if I made the right decision to leave so soon after Dad's death*	What meaning do you derive from this experience of Chris wondering if he made the right decision of leaving to work abroad *so soon* after his father's death?	Complexity here is that … *beginning to wonder*, considers a span of time. Furthermore, there is a question posed in communicating his subjective experience to his father's death which was in the past (eight months ago) but feelings of bereavement are still very much in the present for Chris as he used the words *so soon after Dad's death*.	What response would you give? Consider your language, especially the possibilities of what may be lost in translation for him and for you. Also consider time and its impact, as already discussed, on how it may mean that we lose meaning in translation.
iii. *I'm like a jackdaw among peacocks …*	What does this metaphor mean? Does it have anything to do with his culture?	What does the emoticon ⊗ —say about how Chris was feeling at the time of sending email?	How would you respond?

therapist's response and use of language should be tentatively selected in order to buffer against it being lost in translation. Adlington (2010) advises that therapists should be aware that when they respond, clients may no longer be in crisis, as they were when they initially made contact. It is therefore important to use language that enables clients to re-engage with their process. The box below is an exercise to help the reader reflect on the complexities of how meaning may be lost in translation on the different levels and also due to time complexities. Consider email Six noted earlier.

It may already be evident that in your attempts to respond to the questions in Table 1b that more questions than answers emerge for you. When I shared this with the colleagues I work with, the conversations nearly always ended up being about how each therapist may respond differently and choose different words, depending on his or her modality, the client-therapist relationship, and the client's culture. These conversations further illuminated for me the relationship between language, customs, and regional differences. Furthermore the complexities of the absence of visual clues when working across new media became an issue that some colleagues challenged me on. The next section will therefore explore the challenges of language and customs cross-border, without the visual clues.

Challenges of regional differences in language and customs cross-border without the visual clues

Lago and Wright (2006) raised an interesting point that through working online, because of lack of visual clues, we miss between seventy-five and eighty per cent of the expressed communication. As a result they noted that we are only really working at twenty per cent communication potential. Before exploring the challenges this limitation presents, as well as those of regional differences in language and customs cross-border without the visual clues, it is important to acknowledge the benefits of working with visual clues. In my experience, drawing from the case study presented, even when Chris was silent I paid specific attention to his body language and paralinguistics. He would often have tears rolling down his face, or would blush, or cover his eyes with his hands when he found it hard to speak. In the therapeutic encounter I could draw on this body language as clues to what Chris was experiencing, which we then brought into the therapeutic frame. In other words the visual clues were a language that we could draw on to explore meaning of our immediate experience/experiencing.

Neuroscientific perspectives offer some fundamental strengths of visual clues within the therapeutic relationship which are linked to the ability of us as humans to respond to others when we view their body language (Decety & Ickes, 2009; Hollan, 2012). Mirror neurons—which are a network of neurons that become activated upon observation of the other's body language—are central to evaluation and adjustment of each other's behaviour moment by moment (Hollan, 2012; Kogler & Stueber, 2000). Hollan (2012) gave an example in which he stated that when individuals see rapid breathing, a flushed face, or squinted eyes they know that the person is angry without even thinking about it, and that we continue to make different emotional assessments of the other through the visual clues we get from body language. As a result, our ability to be empathic is highly dependent on these mirror neurons, which enable us to have a sense of what it may be like to be experiencing that emotion (Hollan, 2012). In the absence of visual clues how, then, do we develop and share through language our empathic responses in a culturally and therapeutically engaging way?

In considering responses to this question I started drawing some ideas from Vontress (2011), who highlighted the differences that may exist among different cultures and customs in body language and communicating. This includes dress, the ways people greet each other and speak, gender norms, and eye contact and what it may mean. Lago (2011) and Hollan (2012) agree that body language differs widely across cultures. This acknowledgement of the importance of visual clues in helping therapists see the client's bodily response moment by moment and the appreciation of variances depending on different cultures has resulted in a plethora of cross-cultural studies of empathy and culturally tailored empathy as an essential ingredient in the therapeutic relationship (Hollan, 2012; Lago & Charura 2013; Lepowsky, 2011). When visual clues are absent in working with clients in new media, we may therefore miss another level of what clients may be communicating. This means that we have to have a way of compensating for this. Given the inevitability of regional differences in language when working via new media it is important to ensure that therapists' interactions via language are culturally sensitive, experientially appropriate, congruent, and empathic for the client.

Transcultural and anti-discriminatory perspectives

Barden and Williams (2007) hypothesised that what an individual is able to articulate through language is often accepted by others or by the therapist as the real experience and what is left unsaid can suffer alienation. Hence being unable to put subjective felt experience into language often results in others or therapists attempting to make sense of it, concluding or filling in the space with language. It may also result in experiences which may actually be outside the frame of reference of the individual. Again, their meaning is lost in translation. To add to the complexity is the fact that different regions and cultures use language differently. Vontress (2011) highlighted how different individuals may have various elisions characteristic of their region. He stated how different groups may pronounce words or phrases in a way that is different. There may be variance in dropping or gliding over sounds and endings when pronouncing certain words which is symbolic of regional or cultural divides. Vontress (2011) further warns against therapists being aware of how they respond or check understanding; if this is not done sensitively it can leave clients feeling some annoyance, asking themselves "What's wrong with the way I said it?"

Drawing from the case example, there were moments when I said something in a telephone conversation or in response to an email, and Chris responded with ... "I did not quite mean that, Divine." This evidenced what I would term a *flow of meaning rupture*. This could be described as being when the therapist's response triggers a client's need to correct the therapist or to politely inform the therapist that s/he meant something different. In fact it signifies the clients' awareness that his/her experience was lost in translation. When working in new media it is extremely important for therapists, therefore, to choose their language carefully and to acknowledge the flow of meaning rupture in order to repair it. I would often respond with something like "Thank you for correcting me Chris, would you kindly say a little bit more to enable me to understand". This often enabled Chris to go deeper into his experience and respond to me further.

Another issue which has been noted in practice and literature, which applies to both spoken and written language when considering challenges of regional differences when working in new media without the visual clues, is therapists' perceptions of what is correct vernacular. An example is noted by Beaman (1994), who argued that therapists must be sensitive to their clients' use of language. He further reiterated the concept of what is termed "black", which was transgenerationally transmitted through the slave trade and subsequently developed into Creole and then Black English. He argues that it is not a misuse of Standard English but rather a language that reflects unique historical and cultural aspects of individuals' identities. Although this is one example, the point that this raises relates to other examples from cross-regional English dialects in the UK, which clearly show wide variances in accents and pronunciations.

It is important when working through new media without the visual clues to appreciate that some clients, particularly from ethnic or minority groups, may speak using language that is understood in their circles which may be difficult for the therapist who is unfamiliar with it to understand. Vontress (2011) gave an example of how clients from different social classes may use language different from that of middle-class therapists. It is clear that within transcultural literature there is consensus in warning therapists to beware of inadvertent discriminatory practice in the way they communicate with clients (Beaman, 1994; Vontress, 2011). This also relates to the way therapists speak and email with clients.

Barden and Williams (2007) argued that there is a danger of authenticating or rejecting people through our interpretation of language without even understanding their lived experience. It is important for therapists to develop what I term *transcultural linguistic sensitivity and competencies*. This concept is not about therapists being fluent in speaking the client's language but rather being sensitive to the language that they use in working with clients. It is also about sensitivity and competencies in exploring meaning, or in their empathic responses to a wide range of culturally different clients. For example in my work with Chris, when I did not understand aspects of his email, I would select my words and response carefully. An example taken from a part of one email to him is

> ... having received your last email Chris, I spent a lengthy period of time reading it and I have also spent time thinking about how I can respond to you in a way that is helpful. I am being very sensitive in my response and have spent time thinking and wondering whether I captured everything you were sharing with me. When you stated you feel very isolated and lonely I sensed that you used

these words to share a deep sense of being disconnected from others even though you stated they are all friendly and welcoming … however, I am not sure if I am getting this fully right …? With regards to wondering whether you had left too soon after your father's … death, I have been sitting here thinking, and occasionally looking outside the window thinking how I might respond to this heartfelt process … it is clear to me that …

My email response was intended to relay to Chris my sensitivity to the feelings which he had shared. I attempted to use language which describes my process openly (including giving him a visual image of my process of looking outside whilst thinking). I also shared and owned that I may not be getting it right, which presented him with the opportunity to explore further and correct me if I did not understand.

Further challenges on regional differences: transcultural theoretical perspectives

There is a plethora of literature which may help therapists to work in ways that ensure that we are working towards transcultural linguistic sensitivity and competency. D'Adenne and Mahtani (1999) noted that a priority when working with clients, is to find a common language and to select and adjust our mode of speech sensitively to our client's needs. They further stated that through the use of language, therapists can understand and request feedback from clients as to whether communication is effective, and this enables therapists to be competent practitioners.

For some clients, English might be a foreign language and hence they might not feel confident exploring their experiences, feelings, or emotions in that foreign language. In my experience, when working with clients whose first language is not English, special attentiveness should be paid to the sophistication of interpretation of the metaphors or somatic language that clients use (Charura, 2011). For example, a client may use cultural metaphors that when translated directly into English mean "my head feels hot". In fact what the client really means is s/he feels confused. The same complexity occurs when language that is not available in the client's mother tongue is used. As in many other languages, there are no direct equivalents of some words. For example, in the Zimbabwean Shona language, where there are no direct translation terms for depression or anxiety. The closest interpretation would be "thinking too much". Another example is the label *shenjing shuairuo* (neurasthenia) 神经衰弱 in China, which translates as weakness or exhaustion of the nerves/nervous system. This is the equivalent of what is often termed a nervous breakdown (Lee et al., 2000; Kishore, Reddaiah, Kapoor, & Gill, 1996; Nations, Camino, & Walker, 1988; Patel et al., 2001; Reynolds & Swartz, 1993). Such complication of language shows the sophisticated challenges of the regional differences terrain. Due to regional differences, when communicating via new media, some clients may not be able to relate to some words or phrases in a way which matches their knowledge and experience of mental ill health or dis-ease. Hence it is always important, when we are not sure, to check.

Proctor (2002) considers language to be associated with issues of power and oppression in therapy. She argues that the use of jargon and specialised language can be a catalyst to impressions being formed of a practitioner's superiority of knowledge and expertise. Using some labelling words in mental health language, or even when using professional translators (Raval & Smith, 2003), in order to identify, or name, specific mental health distress/dis-ease may in fact not be in line with one's cultural experience. This inadvertently maintains and validates expert positions which can be oppressive and lead to inaccurate information when working cross-culturally via new media. For therapists, it is therefore important to be aware of using language in ways that enable the client to feel able to explore words and language phrases with which they may not be familiar.

Working with populations of refugees and asylum seekers, I am also aware that some may not even be able to access phones, computers, or the Internet. As a result it is important to be mindful that there are marginalised populations who may not have access to new media modes. Having noted this, however, it is important to be aware of the further importance of sensitive, competent use of language when working in new media in order to limit the possibilities of losing client-therapist meaning in translation.

Importance of language now there is new media

Throughout this book, and this chapter, there have been different explorations of the usefulness of new media within the therapeutic arena. It is important, however, to note that despite the different levels noted as being possible ones at which the essence of the client's or therapists meaning may be lost, there are many noted benefits which support the use of new media. One already noted, and presented through the case study, is that of working across vast geographical regions.

One of the benefits is that where a client continues to have access to the text, s/he can revisit the contents of the session and explore the meaning. As already noted, that narrative has a polysemic meaning; there is therefore a possibility that meaning can change over time. Wright (2002) noted how an advantage of writing is that clients can re-read their own accounts, thoughts, and feelings, and the responses too. Payne (2000) writes on the importance of narrative ideas, highlighting the benefit of this re-authoring phenomenon. Wright (2002) furthermore noted other advantages, such as the possibilities of text being less shaming; the pace and focus is within the client's control. She also suggested that some people gain clarity about their thinking and communication through writing. Lago (2004) offered similar ideas in a chapter in which he highlighted uses of personal writing by international students. He noted writing as therapeutic, enabling individuals to work things through.

Lago and Wright (2006) highlighted useful points about adopting use of the hour, which enables boundaries to be maintained in parallel with face-to-face therapy timings. Furthermore, they advocate time being spent on careful composition of the content of concerns that need addressing. They also highlighted the need for boundaries, by informing clients that their messages would be responded to at a specific time each week. As a result they highly advocate that therapists develop and become wordsmiths. To add to the complexity, this writing, they suggest, should convey the attitudinal qualities of congruence, unconditional positive regard, and empathy.

On a different note, Adlington (2010) highlighted the importance of building rapport in cyberspace through use of language. He suggested ways in which therapists work effectively with clients through language without the visual clues. He noted basic skills such as matching the client's language. For example, where a client starts an email with "Hiya" or with "Dear so-and-so", that the therapist matches the client's use of language by responding with a parallel reply which also starts with "Hiya" or with "Dear so-and-so" respectively. It is therefore important to use language which enables the client to relate to the response.

Conclusion

There is therefore no doubt that language is central to the therapeutic encounter and in this chapter the complexities of the use of language have been noted. The different levels at which meaning may be "lost in translation" have been highlighted. The attempt to symbolise subjective experience through language is the first hurdle of "lost in translation". Second, dialogue, between therapist and client—as the client expresses his/her felt sense and feelings, and the therapist attempts to make sense of them—presents another hurdle at which meaning may be lost in translation. A third hurdle is when the therapist and client respond to each other and the essence of the meaning of these responses can also be lost in translation. Metaphors also add to the complexity. Last, the impact of time on responses between therapist and client add another level where meaning may be lost in translation. These factors highlight the complexity of the terrain that, as psychotherapists, we have to work, because even before we consider accent, regional differences, or visual cues it appears that there is a double jeopardy of losing the meaning of the client's real experience.

There has also been a further exploration of theory on the functional use of language and how culture/regional differences influence the structure and functional use of meaning. It is of paramount importance to note that despite the multiple challenges that digital ways of working present in relation to language, there are many benefits. The research and practice presented has shown this to be a method of working highly worth accepting and embracing. Therapists need to become transculturally and linguistically sensitive, and to be open to repairing flow of meaning ruptures. Our conceptualisations and understandings of what contributes to being lost in translation and to what is most useful and helpful within the therapeutic relationship when working in digital media, will become the driving force of our practice.

Commentator one: Aaron Balick

Divine Charura's chapter offers a penetrating investigation into the very nature of language and therapeutic process. As he so clearly and broadly references, these are issues that are long familiar to psychotherapy, long before psychotherapists began to encounter the further issues provoked by new media. I was particularly enthralled with the subjects in the title centring on the notions of "translation" and "cross-border" communication. How are these elements, so central to traditional psychotherapy, altered by new media?

Much of Divine's work with his client "Chris" occurs over email, a method of communication known as "asynchronous" because of the way in which therapist and client are not speaking at the same time (as they would be on Skype). The issue of asynchrony adds a whole new level to the hermeneutic challenge that Divine suggests is paramount when it comes to sharing language. Daily language use is problematic enough; the use of asynchronous text without the wider context of voice and body language, let alone a live presence, provokes a serious challenge. Being mindful of these challenges is the thrust of Divine's chapter. Paradoxically, it creates a situation in which the therapist has to do more work outside the context of the client, searching inwardly for meaning whilst at the same time trying to presume the mind of his client.

The remedy for this, for Divine, is to share his thinking with the client. In this way the client's meaning is consumed through the therapist's difference, and then fed back, allowing the client to elaborate. It seems to me that the history of the "in real life" therapist/client relationship further enables this, but begs the question of doing such therapy outside the context of this history. The relationship to transcultural and anti-discriminatory work is obviously vital here, but seemingly the challenges are even tougher than in the context of real life, as "cross-border" includes asynchronous timing and a relative lack of other interpersonal cues that we are used to in the traditional setting.

Divine's grid (Table 1b) strikes me as ideal. That is, when working with multiple clients over email, are therapists really going to have the time to devote a hermeneutic enquiry of this depth into each of their client's emails? While my instinctive answer is "No", it does remind me of working with early trainees, particularly on the application of theory to practice. They invariably ask "How am I supposed to keep all that in mind during the therapeutic hour?" I usually respond, "It comes with practice. For now, just try your best to be present, and apply theory afterwards." They find that, with practice, it does certainly come. In the world of new media, both novices and seasoned therapists alike will need to practice in order to learn to adapt to the new context. It may become second nature, but it won't be traditional psychotherapy.

Commentator two: Alexandra Chalfont

Divine Charura focuses mainly on the challenges we all have in expressing our felt experience through language, and in interpreting the meaning of another's linguistic expression. Understanding each other's meaning, even in straightforward email conversations, is often fraught with difficulty.

Metaphor is our most common human way of expressing experience and feeling, and also tends to be the most commonly misunderstood form of communication. Culturally specific metaphors may have inaccessible meanings for the therapist, and may take much care, attention, time, and several exchanges to be deciphered. On the other hand, individual client-generated metaphors can yield rich information when explored carefully, and can be worked with in many different and helpful ways.

Together with attention to language and meaning, what remains of vital importance in this online work is "belief in the relationship". Divine reveals his deeply humanistic way of working, in which he opens himself in vulnerable sensitivity towards his clients suffering.

In Chris' case, Divine had created a place of trust in the face-to-face sessions before the email therapy started. Thus some of the implications about the ethics of online work are somewhat pre-empted by his client's experience of a therapist who is wholly there for him. He already trusts that in their dialogue Divine will give him his complete attention, and that he is dedicated to joining him quietly in his personal hermeneutic endeavour.

Despite such benefits, email therapy also harbours other challenges, including those of asynchronous communication; the client may already have gone to quite a different place in his process by the time he receives a reply to a previous email, so that the therapist intervention may be redundant or even unhelpful.

Far from being an easy or quick option, email therapy may sometimes involve even more time engagement than in-person therapy. To be done well, it requires the therapist to become a highly skilled wordsmith and able to craft texts which respond empathically and curiously to the various voices, register, tone, and meaning of the client's narrative, opening the space for therapeutic progress.

> There are, it may be, so many kinds of voices in the world, and none of them is without signification. Therefore if I know not the

meaning of the voice, I shall be unto him that speaketh a barbarian, and he that speaketh shall be a barbarian unto me. I Corinthians, 14:10–11.

References

Adlington, J. (2010). Rapport in cyberspace. *Therapy Today, 21.*

Barden, N., & Williams, T. (2007). *Words and Symbols: Communication in Therapy.* Maidenhead: Open University Press.

Beaman, D. (1994). Black English and the therapeutic relationship. *Journal of Mental Health Counselling, 16.*

Charura, D. (2011). The effects of an African Heritage. In: C. Lago (Ed.), *The Handbook of Transcultural Counselling & Psychotherapy.* Maidenhead: Open University Press.

Corsini, R. J., & Wedding, D. (2008). *Current Psychotherapies* (8th ed.). Belmont, CA: Thompson Wadsworth.

D'Adenne, P., & Mahtani, A. (1999). *Trancultural Counselling in Action* (2nd ed.). London: Sage.

Decety, J., & Ickes, W. (2009). *The Social Neuroscience of Empathy.* Cambridge, MA: MIT Press.

Gendlin, E. T. (1997). *Experiencing and the Creation of Meaning: A Philosophical and Psychological Approach to the Subjective.* Evanston, IL: Northwest University Press.

Haugh, S., & Paul, S. (2008). The Therapy is the relationship? *Therapy today, 19.*

Hollan, D. W. (2012). Emerging issues in the cross-cultural study of empathy. *Emotion Review, 4*(1): 70–78.

Jackson, C. (2013). E-therapy, equality and access. Available: http://therapytoday.net/article/show/3541/. Retrieved 20 October 2013.

Kishore, J., Reddaiah, V., Kapoor, V., & Gill, J. (1996). Characteristics of mental morbidity in a rural primary health centre of Haryana. *Indian Journal of Psychiatry, 38*: 137–142.

Kogler, H. H., & Stueber, K. R. (Eds.) (2000). *Empathy and Agency: The Problem of Understanding in the Human Sciences.* Boulder, CO: Westview.

Lago, C. (Ed.) (2011). *The Handbook of Transcultural Counselling & Psychotherapy.* Maidenhead: Open University Press.

Lago, C., & Charura, D. (2013). Culturally tailoring client centred therapy. In: L. M. Hooper, *Culturally Competent Counseling and Psychotherapy: From Research and Theory to Action.* Thousand Oaks, CA: Sage.

Lago, C. O. (2004). When I write, I think: Some uses of personal writing by international students. In: G. Bolton, S. Howlettt, C. Lago, & J. K.

Wright, *Writing Cures: An Introductory Handbook of Writing in Counselling and Therapy*. London: Brunner-Routledge.

Lago, C. O. & Wright, J. K. (2006). Email supervision. In: K. Tudor & M. Worral (Eds.), *Freedom to Practice (11): Person Centred Perspectives on Supervision*. Ross; PCCS Books.

Lee, S., Yu, H., Wing, Y., Chan, C., Lee, A., & Lee, D. T. S. (2000). Psychiatric morbidity and illness experience of primary care patients with chronic fatigue in Hong Kong. *American Journal of Psych, 157*: 380–384.

Lepowsky, M. (2011). The boundaries of personhood, the problem of empathy, and "the native's point of view" in the Outer Islands. In: D. W. Hollan & C. J. Throop (Eds.), *The Anthropology of Empathy: Experiencing the Lives of Others in Pacific Societies* (pp. 43–65). New York, NY: Berghahn Books.

Nations, M., Camino, L., & Walker, F. (1988). Nerves: folk idiom for anxiety and depression? *Society, Science and Medicine, 26*: 1245–1259.

Patel, V., Abas, M., Broadhead, J., Todd, C., & Reeler, A. (2001). Depression in developing countries: lessons from Zimbabwe. *British Medical Journal, 322*: 482–484.

Payne, M. (2000). *Narrative Therapy*. London, Sage.

Proctor, G. (2002). *The Dynamics of Power in Counselling and Psychotherapy: Ethics, Politics and Practice*. Ross-On-Wye: PCCS Books.

Raval, H., & Smith, J. (2003). Therapist's experiences of working with language and interpreters. *International Journal of Mental Health, 32*: 6–31.

Reynolds, J., & Swartz, L. (1993). Professional constructions of a "lay" illness; "nerves in a rural coloured" community in South Africa. *Society, Science and Medicine, 36*: 657–663.

Ricoeur, P. (1985). *Time and Narrative (Vol. 3)* (Trans. K. Blamey & D. Pessauer). London and Chicago: University of Chicago Press.

Rogers, C. R. (1959). A theory of therapy, personality and interpersonal relationships as developed in the client centered framework. In: S. Koch (Ed.), *Psychology: A Study of Science*. (Vol. 3) (pp. 184–256). New York: McGraw-Hill.

Severson, E. R. (2012). Beyond hermeneutics: Levinas, language and psychology. *Journal of Theoretical and Philosophical Psychology, 32*: 251–269.

Spinelli, E. (2005). *The Interpreted World: An Introduction to Phenomenological Psychology* (2nd ed). London: Sage.

Vedder, B. (1998). Schleiermacher. In: S. Critchley & W. R. Schroeder (Eds.), *A Companion to Continental Philosophy* (pp. 417–423). Oxford: Blackwell.

Vontress, C. E. (2011). Social class influences on counselling. *Counselling and Human Development, 44*.

Walker, M. (2007). Mental Health Treatment online: A report commissioned by the Digital Inclusion Team, City of London. Bournemouth University, Centre for Social Work and Social Policy.

Worsley, R. (2008). The ground of our relating: Martin Buber's "I and Thou". In: S. Haugh & S. Paul (Eds.), *The Therapeutic Relationship: Perspectives and Themes*. Ross-on-Wye: PCCS Books.

Worsley, R. (2012). Narratives and lively metaphors: Hermeneutics as a way of listening. *Person-Centred & Experiential Psychotherapies, 11*: 304–320.

Wright, J. K. (2002). Online counselling: Learning from writing therapy. *British Journal of Guidance and Counselling, 30*: 285–298.

CHAPTER SEVEN

Avatars—opening the virtual doors of therapy

Kate Anthony and DeeAnna Nagel

Alice, a single mother in her late forties with a daughter at university, has sought a therapist to help her with her increasing sense of loneliness and her dependence on channels of communication with strangers via the Internet. Already an avid user of Facebook and other social networking sites, she has found she has lost whole weekends to gaming in World of Warcraft, an online multi-user team game in virtual reality. One of her online companions in the game encouraged her to join Second Life, a virtual world where one can build houses, run businesses and socialise with others. Having been immersed in Second Life for several months now, she finds that she is consumed with a sense of loneliness and despair that she finds difficult to describe. She finds she doubts if anything has meaning and sometimes feels her life has none apart from the relationships she has formed online. She has even stopped writing the short stories she enjoys writing so much in favour of spending time in online environments.

Lucy, a psychodynamic therapist local to Alice, offering face-to-face sessions as well as some email work, received Alice's enquiry via her encrypted form at her website. The form indicates mild depression and anxiety and, in Lucy's opinion, a tendency to escape into fantasy worlds. Lucy knows little about the culture of cyberspace beyond her own Facebook page and a brief foray into Twitter, which she heard could help her market her services. She is the first to admit, however, that she is not entirely comfortable with technology and is seeking continuing professional development training in working with text (emails and chat) and video to inform her about the nuances in offering that in the future. In the meantime, she feels confident in offering Alice face-to-face sessions on a weekly basis for an initial contract of ten sessions before review.

Lucy and Alice met for fifty minutes each week. They discussed Alice's feeling of emptiness now that her daughter is away at college. They talked about her job and her dream of writing a mystery novel. Alice would occasionally bring in bits and pieces of her short stories to share in therapy because she would often use her own life to portray a certain scene or create a character in the story. For instance, her most recent mystery was set in the East End of London in the sixties and in describing the house and the local markets, she had pulled from her memories of her own childhood. She thought that by sharing those few paragraphs with her therapist, it might help her therapist understand her better.

Lucy would often take Alice's lead and guide her toward her past—particular moments or feelings—especially those lonely feelings Alice would repeatedly describe. Lucy also noticed a thread of lonely characters in Alice's stories. Alice would often summarise her latest blog story and, between the short summaries and the snippets that Alice would bring in and read, Lucy would often find herself overwhelmed by the loneliness Alice carried with her. For months Alice and Lucy talked about the lonely feeling. Alice had no recollection of abuse or particular neglect at the hands of her family. She was molested by a neighbour across the street when she was eleven, and while she and Lucy talked about the significant impact this had on her life in many ways, Alice just could not identify the lonely feeling she had as being connected in any way to that event.

Shortly before Alice and Lucy's review session, the topic of Lucy's own online experiences came up in the session, which Alice felt compelled to ask about, as sometimes Lucy looked rather blank as Alice described her Second Life.

Lucy explained to Alice she mainly used her computer for word processing, although she did enjoy keeping up with friends and family on Facebook. "Oh. So you must think I am really strange going on and on all these months about my avatar and Second Life stuff." Suddenly Alice felt unheard and out of place. For the first time since she started seeing Lucy she felt exposed. Lucy said, "Alice we have talked about many things since you began therapy, including your game issues." Alice was quiet. Lucy did not quite know what to make of the silence. She could not understand Alice's reaction. Lucy sat with Alice in the silence. Alice's eyes teared up. Lucy finally asked, "What are you feeling, Alice?" Alice looked away and stared out the window, tears now streaming down her face. She replied with a tone completely void of affect, "You don't get me … all these weeks I have been talking about all my stuff, but a lot about my other reality. I even told you about my avatar. I thought it was odd that you didn't latch onto that piece. I mean, I thought it was perfect—that I was willing to share with you this avatar—my persona, a part of me that I created online—I told you her name even." Alice began to speak with a wavering and loud tone, "Do you remember? Her name is Wendy and she is eleven years old. Well, anyway, you probably didn't say anything because you don't even know what an avatar is do you? I figured you were the therapist. You are supposed to know things better than me. So I just assumed we would circle back to Wendy. But we never did. Now I know why. You think she is just part of a silly game I play, don't you? To you, she has no purpose in here. But guess what, Lucy? She is real. She is real to me!"

Virtual worlds are computer-simulated environments where one can create an avatar—a computerised representation of the self. Many people take the opportunity to create an ideal self, such as a strong warrior or heavily sexualised woman. In the classic historical version of the uses of virtual worlds, they are for socialising and gaming. Increasingly, however, they are used for business purposes—both for selling wares in a virtual currency; for training purposes for companies, such as honing interview skills; and for education purposes such as virtual conferences. The creation of the environment is as limitless as the imagination—for the Online Therapy Institute, we have Second Life offices with virtual laptops, break-out rooms, a board room with virtual doughnuts and coffee, a virtual therapy room, and a garden and gazebo. In addition, we have what is known as a SkyBox—a space that is more private than the rest of the environment as it can only be accessed by invitation, in that it "floats" above the rest of the world. We use our SkyBox as a teaching space, with slide projector, lectern, and conference style seating. We even have a resident virtual cat, Reva, who lurks around purring to greet visitors and keep them company while they explore.

Second Life is the best known of the virtual worlds, but there are many which are specifically designed for therapeutic use, including implementing the ethical considerations that are essential in working virtually, such as ensuring all communication is encrypted (which Second Life does not). Examples are ReactionGrid and InWorldSolutions for creating avatars and therapeutic spaces to explore issues with clients, alongside others such as ProReal which uses simple non-identity avatars for the client to attribute roles to (father, sister, son, etc.), which they can manipulate in a virtual metaphorical world with virtual road blocks, ravines, mountains to climb, etc.

Traditionally, avatar therapy and therapeutic virtual environments have been treated with as much resistance as other forms of online therapy have been in the last fifteen years, which, themselves, have only just become more mainstream. The concept, however, has been around since the early 2000s (Goss & Anthony 2002, for example), and has been used widely in the treatment of anxiety and phobias in particular (Parsons & Rizzo, 2008). Other successful treatments that take advantage of virtual environments are for social skills groups in schools (Sappio, 2013) and for exploring autism (Liveo, 2012).

There are many reasons why a person would turn to a virtual world to exist in a different way. Not least of these is because of disability—the documentary film Login2Life (Nagel & Anthony, 2011) examines the case of Alice Krueger whose disability from MS is the reason she set up Virtual Ability Island—a virtual space within Second Life where those with a limited physical existence offline can dance and socialise much as those of us without those constraints do. This vital element of the use of virtual spaces to improve lives is good enough reason for us not to dismiss them as areas only of interest to the few or the geeky. These spaces transform lives.

Aside from the therapeutic effects of existing in virtual words to address disability, there are the psychological effects that need considering. Take our client Alice, for example—was it boredom that led her to try out World of Warcraft? A desire to escape, as her therapist clearly concluded at intake? A need to express herself in a way that she felt was her true being rather than the social construct that her roles as ex-wife and mother offered? After all, she can create any being she wishes to be, whether male or female, creature or human, animate object or beam of light. What parts of the psyche kick in when we create our ideal self? As we stated in a recent article (Anthony & Nagel, 2013):

> The parts of the psyche that rise to prominence in behaviour when online may look very unfamiliar in face-to-face societal norms. In many cases, this leads to confusion at best and psychological damage at worst, and as mental health practitioners it is our remit to recognise those facets that emerge and facilitate the client's management of them.

To address this—and indeed to understand the changes in society that have occurred in light of technology, we need to discuss the culture of cyberspace itself. In Anthony and Nagel, with Louw (2012), we argue that cyberspace transcends culture while being its own culture. It is not enough to consider our offline life as separate from our online life—both tell us, as professionals, a lot about our client if we can assist them in teasing out what it is that makes them the person they are—and why those facets of the self they are discovering are causing them distress.

One of the central facets of having an online existence—and particularly pertinent to having a virtual world existence—is the concept of disinhibition (Suler, 2004). Without a face, and often without a voice, feeling unconfined by social norms means that behaviour online is often closer to how we would behave if society allowed us to. There are obvious negative behaviours associated with this—the trolling, cyberbullying, or cyberinfidelity that leads to breakdown of offline relationships, creating huge damage to lives, are but three examples. These, alongside less obvious manifestations such as slander and libel on Twitter, are the ones we tend to hear about on the national or international news and that result in court cases, suicides, and murder. These facets are something every practitioner needs to know about to be able to empathise with the client who brings these new issues to sessions.

But what of the side of the Internet and virtual living that the media tend not to tell us about? What of our new ability to have access to and gently explore, therapeutically, with a skilled and trained therapist or other mental health practitioner, the usually hidden parts of ourselves that would actually lead to better mental health? Why don't we, as a profession, embrace these new tools that show us the real, unconstrained client asking for assistance from a soul-depth that only recreation of the self as avatar can represent? Avatars and work in virtual worlds has the potential to give us the "person behind the defences", which Buber (cited in Clarkson, 1990) would argue is the point at which true therapeutic change can occur.

Let's revisit to see how Alice is doing. Alice has recreated her alter ego, Wendy—the eleven-year-old girl who was abused by the man across the street. Wendy can't exist in the offline world—she is grown up now and the chance for any therapeutic help she may have received during or immediately after the abuse is long gone. But for Alice, these issues haven't gone away—they are entrenched in her psychological makeup and have resurfaced as an adult. Lucy heard the references to Wendy, but dismissed them as a game because she had no concept of how her client was actually living—that is, virtually. The only way Lucy could continue to work ethically with Alice was to address her shortcomings in understanding cyberculture and be authentic with her client in not only vocalising this but also humbly asking for education.

> "Oh Alice. I am truly sorry. I was working off the emotions you were bringing into our sessions and I admit I did overlook your mentions of Wendy. You are right. I don't understand because I don't know about this other reality you have spoken of. I should have asked more questions and allowed you to lead us to what is obviously important. Would you be willing to show me and guide me to this place you talk about?"
>
> Alice wondered for a moment if she should even come back. She felt, in a word, invalidated. Ironically, she learned about feelings of invalidation from Lucy. But when Lucy admitted her mistake, Alice sensed that Lucy was speaking from a place of humility and recognised her own naivety. She asked Lucy, "Do you want to meet Wendy?" Lucy replied that she would be honoured to meet Wendy. Alice said she would bring her laptop to the next session. Lucy explained that she did not have an Internet connection at the office and Alice assured her that would be fine because she would bring her air card (a device enabling Internet access anywhere). "Okay

Alice. Thank you for being willing to bring me up to speed so we can continue our work together. I think it might be helpful if I take a look at Second Life before our next session. I clearly have some catching up to do."

It is often something as simple as seeing clients in a new light, as being their own experts on their own lives, that creates a major paradigm shift for the therapist. This recognition of our ability to be open to innovations and new ways of working can lead to an explosion of possibilities—not just considering the way that technology has transformed our ways of communicating with each other, but also the possibility of whole new therapeutic theories—entrenched in our traditional orientations, but translated and developed to evolve with our changing society.

Alice has taken a facet of her life that she instinctively, if not consciously, knew was something that needed naming, validating, and coming to terms with. Where this may have taken years in a therapist's consulting room, by being empowered and using what she considered her lonely time to work on being Wendy and reframing her situation, she is able to heal the inner child and take care of the self in the present day. Where in the therapist's office she may have remained inhibited, the freedom of the anonymity, twenty-four-hour access, and perceived distance of what she was doing remained positive—her own way to therapeutic healing, in much the same way as clients find their own support, diagnosis, and treatment online (and have been doing so for a long while, so we as a profession should stop being threatened by technology and embrace it!). Where both Alice and Lucy struggled in the process was in trying to fit Alice's time in virtual worlds into the constraints of societal norms as we traditionally understand them: by treating Alice's time online as separate from her time offline, it became what Rosen (2012) would call an iDisorder. By bringing the therapeutic sessions into the virtual world to meet the client where she was living online, the work was able to shift and continue.

At their next in-office session, Alice talked about her mystery writing. She said that her latest story involved "the house across the street. You know, the one Wendy showed you in Second Life." Alice asked why she chose that house as the house in her mystery story and she said, "Well, the house that Wendy created in Second Life is the house I was molested in when I was eleven. Since that house has bad memories for me, it makes sense that it would be the perfect place for a murder in my next story. A young girl is murdered there." Lucy asked if there was any significance between Wendy creating the house in Second Life and Alice writing about the house as the scene of a murder and Alice replied, "I don't think so."

Within seconds, Alice was clenching her fists, rocking and shaking with her eyes closed. Lucy reminded Alice where she was and that she was safe, and asked her, "What do you see?" Alice replied, "It is not what I see, I mean, I have seen this house, well I mean, I don't know, I was just there, in the house. Wendy took me there inside ... you know, in Second Life, but now I am there again, I mean it is me, or Wendy, oh I don't know. And he is there, and he is hovering, oh I just know I am going to die. I think I will just die if he touches me, oh my God." Lucy contains Alice's emotions and brings her back fully into the present. Alice is co-conscious and aware of what just happened. Alice whispered, "Soul murder ... that's what happened to me. I have been searching for my soul ... he took it. Wendy is the me before the murder. She is free and light and ..." Lucy said gently "And you can be free and light again, Alice."

"I mean, my parents didn't show me a lot of attention. They read the paper a lot. But I never felt like they meant to hurt me. I knew there was something—I don't know, it is hard to explain. I have always remembered what happened. But today, I remembered it differently. I remembered how I felt—that it was wrenching, that it left me emotionally empty and I have been so lonely searching for myself all these years. And Wendy, she is so innocent."

Lucy offered to meet Wendy in Second Life for the next session. "Alice, why don't you think about how you would have liked things to be different?" "Well, I would have liked to have not been molested." Lucy sat on the edge of her chair and proclaimed, "And so it is."

"What do you mean, Lucy?"

"Let's let Wendy show us a different ending to this story. She can take us in the house. You will be safe because I will be there and besides, this did not happen to Wendy."

"But Wendy is a part of me", Alice said.

"And Wendy has something to share with you Alice, so let's see what she can reveal to you."

Avatar therapy and the use of virtual environments for exploration of the self is a very dynamic way of working. The case of Alice is but one example of the possibilities, offered as an illustration of how we can treat mild anxiety and depression. However, as stated earlier, the limits are really only in our imaginations. The work of Leff (Leff, Williams, Huckvale, Arbuthnot, & Leff, 2013) is exemplary on how auditory hallucinations can be brought to life through avatars and brought into treatment to take power over the voices heard. The concept of Virtual Reality Immersion Therapy (VRIT) has proved one of the primary treatments for post-traumatic stress disorder. Even physical disabilities such as Parkinson's disease are not only coped with while living an online virtual life, but also are seemingly treatable (Au, 2013) due to practicing motor skills in a virtual life in which physicality doesn't exist.

> Seven days later, Wendy and Lucy met in the meadow in Second Life. The meadow was full of poppies and daisies all abloom. Wendy talked with Lucy about how wonderful things have been. "You remember I told you I have a best friend? Her name is Maggie. She is my age and guess what? She lives right across the street!" Lucy and Wendy "teleported" back to Wendy's house (the term used for moving between locations in Second Life). Wendy walked across the street and Lucy followed. "Maggie isn't home right now but I just wanted you to see! Go in! Maggie and I have the most fun ever here! This is one of my favourite places in the whole wide world!" Lucy enters the house full of pastel colours. Cupcakes and cookies lined the kitchen counter and a huge doll house was set up in the living room. There were balloons everywhere. "What are the balloons for Wendy?" Wendy replied, "Oh, we had my birthday party earlier today! I am twelve now!"
>
> Alice, sitting at home, led by Wendy's unwavering quest for fun and harmony, felt reborn in that moment. Her soul was alive again and the trauma she had experienced washed away as if it never happened. The feelings of loneliness that had engulfed her as she searched for herself were gone. Wendy had been able to reframe the entire experience for Alice, turning her eleventh year into something to celebrate instead of to regret.
>
> Lucy and Alice continued to work together and processed these events over the next couple of sessions. Alice's driven desire to be

inworld (the term used for being present in Second Life) and online passed over time and when she did go into Second Life, she would allow Wendy to show her all of those safe and fun places they shared. Whenever Alice felt unsure or unsafe, Wendy was there to show her life and remind her of the incredible soul work that was accomplished in a virtual world.

The uses of technology, and particularly the more innovative ones such as virtual worlds, are nothing more than new ways of thinking, communicating, and working. As Jung put it in 1938:

> Everyone carries a shadow, and the less it is embodied in the individual's conscious life, the blacker and denser it is. ... if it is repressed and isolated from consciousness, it never gets corrected.

Avatar therapy and the use of virtual worlds to explore how best to correct that black dense shadow that Jung identified all those years ago is just one more way to facilitate "the long-hoped-for and expected triumph of consciousness over the unconscious" (Jung, 1940).

Technology is not to be feared, it is to be embraced and used wisely to respect all we already know about the human psychological condition. In this way, we better serve our profession and, most importantly, our clients.

Author's note: a full version of Alice and Lucy's story was published in *Therapeutic Innovations in Light of Technology*, Issue One (Nagel & Anthony, 2010).

Commentator one: Martin Pollecoff

In this fascinating care history the virtual world of Second Life enters the virtual world of the consulting room. Therapists may argue that their work is super-realistic but the consulting room has always been a theatre in which things can be said that cannot possibly be uttered in the wider world of social reality.

The therapist/client relationship is virtual—paradoxically, that's the point. Our work is as boundaried and rule-based as Kabuki theatre, yet it's these very formalities that allow for authenticity and change. Just as the anonymity of Second Life encourages disinhibition, so do the formality and ethical boundaries of the consulting room.

Alice presents with feelings of meaninglessness and isolation. Her writings are attempts to be known. Lucy looks down on fantasy and dismisses Alice's "game issues" but the unconscious is at work here and that's a process we can all trust.

It's the plot of this tale. From the beginning, we readers know this is a clash that is bound to happen, and it comes in one of those transferential moments when the unconscious breaks through and the client's unwanted condition makes itself wonderfully and horribly real within the therapeutic relationship—life bursts into the room and we move sharply from theory-driven interpretation to raw experience.

Lucy steps up, she has her Parsival moment, relinquishes her practitioner role, and leans on her own humanity—she apologises. Alice, in fighting for the respect that she is due, discovers that she has something worth fighting for.

Early therapists were often anthropologists by background or fascination. The authors remind us that the virtual world is also a culture and one that demands our respect.

Commentator two: Alexandra Chalfont

No life-world is actually hermetically sealed, and therapy can be a space where other worlds safely enter, once recognised and allowed.

This case history seems to illustrate the theory that clients often already have a notion at some level about what might help them heal. What a therapist needs to demonstrate is openness to every nuance of the client narrative and a sensitivity that can explore its many aspects.

Here Lucy, the therapist, has missed clues both in the stories that her client Alice writes, where she draws on her childhood experience, and in her "other reality", where her online avatar is an eleven-year old girl, the same age as she was just before being molested by a neighbour.

When Lucy's lack of insight is revealed, she admits her mistake from a place of genuine humility. Despite her own distress at not being understood, Alice accepts Lucy's remorse and steers her therapist towards working with her in a more helpful way by acknowledging and exploring this virtual life.

As children we allow our imaginations to flourish and assume all kinds of roles, characters, and personae in our games and pretend-worlds, and these fulfil various functions for our creativity, adaptability, and learning. As adults, options are more limited for the different parts of ourselves that need attention and space to manifest in our life-world. Online virtual worlds allow us to inhabit spaces of our dreams, of our shadow, of our creativity. Our avatars in these worlds may satisfy our needs safely, get stuck, or lead to more troubled experiences.

Sharing these worlds in the therapy room can open doors to fruitful creative play, as it happily does in this case example, where all worlds are real within their own subjective perimeters.

References

Anthony, K., & Nagel, D. (2013). Appreciating cyberculture and the virtual self within. *Self & Society, 40.*

Au, W. (2013). "Woman with Parkinson's reports significant physical recovery after using Second Life". http://nwn.blogs.com/nwn/2013/02/second-life-possible-parkinsons-therapy.html

Clarkson, P. (1990). "A multiplicity of psychotherapeutic relationships". *British Journal of Psychotherapy, 7:* 148–163.

Goss, S., & Anthony, K. (2002). Virtual counsellors—whatever next?. *Counselling Journal, 13:* 14–15. http://www.issuu.com/onlinetherapyinstitute/docs/titliss10?mode=window&page Number=24

Jung, C. G. (1938). "Psychology and Religion." In: *C. W. 11: Psychology and Religion: West and East* (p. 131). Princeton, NJ: Princeton University Press.

Jung, C. G. (1940). "The Psychology of the Child Archetype". In: *C. W. 9, Part I: The Archetypes and the Collective Unconscious* (p. 284). London: Routledge.

Leff, J., Williams, G., Huckvale, M. A., Arbuthnot, M., &, Leff, A. P. (2013). Computer-assisted therapy for medication-resistant auditory hallucinations: proof-of-concept study. *British Journal of Psychiatry, 202:* 428–433.

Liveo, S. (2012). "Exploring autism with avatars". http://www.nj.com/politics/index.ssf/2012/11/exlporing_autism_with_avatars.html

Nagel, D., & Anthony, K. (2010). Alice in Virtual Land. *Therapeutic Innovations in Light of Technology,:* Vol 1, Issue 1: 16–27. http://www.ncbi.nlm.nih.gov/pubmed/23429202

Nagel, D., & Anthony, K. (2011). Login2Life: Expanding the cyberculture POV. *Therapeutic Innovations in Light of Technology, 2:* 47–51. http://issuu.com/onlinetherapyinstitute/docs/tiltiss8?mode=window&page Number=47

Nagel, D. M., & Anthony, K., with Louw, G. (2012). Cyberspace as culture: A new paradigm for therapists and coaches. *Therapeutic Innovations in Light of Technology, 2:* 24–36.

Parsons, T. D., & Rizzo, A. A. (2008). Affective outcomes of virtual reality exposure therapy for anxiety and specific phobias: A meta-analysis. *Journal of Behavioural Therapy and Experimental Psychiatry, 39*: 250–261. Epub July 25 2007. http://www.ncbi.nlm.nih.gov/pubmed/17720136

Rosen, L. (2012). *iDisorder: Understanding Our Obsession with Technology and Overcoming its Hold on Us*. Basingstoke, Palgrave Macmillan.

Sappio, E. (2013). Social Skills Groups in the Virtual World. *Therapeutic Innovations in Light of Technology, 3*: 32–35.

Suler, J. (2004). The online disinhibition effect. *CyberPsychology and Behavior, 7*: 321–326.

CHAPTER EIGHT

Establishing an online practice

Philippa Weitz

Note: As a question of style I shall use **text** or SMS to refer to mobile phone messages, **emails** for emails, and **chat** for Internet Relay Chat (IRC) such as VSee or other written messages.

Setting up an online practice doesn't seem very challenging at first glance; just a matter of having a computer, sound, a webcam, and the Internet. Oh, how I wish life was so straightforward! Many of us are used to using these items on a daily basis but whilst the digital age provides opportunities in abundance, there's much we need to consider before setting out on this particular path in a professional therapeutic capacity. I'm going to start with a case study that I'd like you to think about over the course of the chapter. Jackie has done just what she shouldn't have done and has plunged into working online without thinking some crucial factors. One particular factor actually means she shouldn't have elected to work with this client in this way. I'd like you to think over the following question whilst you read the case study that follows.

Q: If you were to raise one concern about why Clara should not be working with Jackie online, what would your central concern be?

Case study

Jackie, twenty-seven, lives in Germany with her partner Peggy, and has been working with a psychodynamic therapist, Clara, for around three months, on a weekly basis, via Skype. Jackie's work takes her to Los Angeles (USA), where she was mugged about six months ago.

Clara qualified in 2002, but has not had any formal training in working online as she considered that her IT skills were good enough; she started working online around eight months ago.

Jackie's job is very high-powered and her working days are long and unpredictable. Whilst travelling, Jackie uses Facebook to keep in touch with all her friends and family. Because of Jackie's job they do not spend much time together but talk every day via Skype, usually in the evening. Jackie has been suffering from panic attacks for about five months, mainly at night and mainly when she is away from home, which she finds very distressing and does not understand. It was this problem that encouraged her to look for help.

Jackie chose Clara as a therapist because when she Googled her she liked what she read and felt that Clara would understand and have the skills required to work with her. In her professional profile, on both her website and LinkedIn, Clara mentioned her specialist post-qualification training in working with anxiety.

Jackie and Clara have just had their thirteenth session, which has been spent looking at issues in Jackie's past relating to her mother: Jackie views her mother as frightening and violent at times. The previous five sessions had been very intense, with Jackie showing feelings of anger, sometimes towards her mother, sometimes towards Clara. Session thirteen was online, when Jackie was in California. Jackie feels very vulnerable and angry with her mother, as she blames her for her current problems; without warning she cuts off the session, before the end, in a fit a rage. In the middle of the following night she posts a comment on her Facebook wall to her mother in a very public way; she describes her recent therapy session in a very negative way, and includes Clara's name.

Q: Ignoring the central concern about jurisdiction, what might be important factors to think about in the therapeutic relationship?

Q: What contracting issues might Clara, as therapist, need to clarify before she starts working with client Jackie?

Returning to Jackie, she began having panic attacks that she found distressing and couldn't explain. She turned to the Internet to research these, and confused herself more. She equally Googled a number of therapists before making her choice of therapist. This is the common pathway for a member of the public investigating how to find a therapist. Whether we are digital natives or digital immigrants (Buckingham, 2013), it is likely that if your clients are younger than you, they will live their lives "joined at the hip" with technology. I will return to Jackie later in the chapter; the context, method of working, and issues arising in the course of therapy, and, of course, the therapeutic alliance itself, are all issues that will be discussed in this chapter.

Given that this is a chapter and not a book there are some key expectations underpinning it:

- You will already have a professional qualification to work face-to-face (F2F).
- This chapter sets out to provide information to help you develop your online practice efficiently, professionally, and legally. It does not try to tell you how to set up and organise your practice and the business elements of your practice: you need to have this knowledge already before launching an online practice. Running a business is hard enough, and setting up and running a private practice requires implementing those same principles of running any business, but we have the extra dimension of being in the caring profession to consider, if we are to be successful. These issues have been fully covered in books on setting up and managing a practice, for example, Weitz (2006), McMahon, Wilding, and Palmer (2005) or Bor and Stokes (2011).
- Equally, in parallel with the above of course, the qualified practitioner will have thought about all the professional practitioner issues such as confidentiality, security, ethical guidelines, both within your training and through on-going supervision and CPD.
- This chapter may also be useful to members of multi-disciplinary teams students who come across online issues within their work, and allied professions such as careers guidance and spiritual direction.

This chapter takes your understanding of the above professional areas as read. The aim of this chapter is very specific: to provide you with a framework that you will be able to use to launch, or improve, your own practice and to think about the issues involved in working online. Not everyone wants to work online; some are already only working online—and there is a growing blend of the two. In reality, the grey area in the diagram will expand dramatically over the years to come, but there may always be a place for F2F work. I use the word "framework" rather than "tools", as I believe in the importance of specialist training for working online and would not wish to spur you to action until you have successfully completed a specific online training.

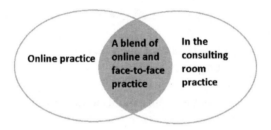

I want to underline the importance of thinking through all the aspects of working online, and of ensuring that you have trained for this and prepared yourself fully. Almost everyone I speak to at the moment who has not trained for working online has not thought through the issues of jurisdiction, insurance, online security, the online therapeutic relationship, or boundaries, but often think that I am exaggerating when I talk about the need for training. A typical therapist exchange might be:

> Gemma was sitting in a counselling conference coffee break recently with a group of three experienced therapists. The conversation turned to online work. All three told her they did some online work. None had checked their insurance or thought about the issues of jurisdiction. In particular, one, David, began by telling her he was newly trained and only worked online using Skype. Gemma replied that this was interesting and asked him to say a little more. David replied that he "only did it with friends"!
>
> Gemma asked David how that worked with insurance (she could have asked many other questions but was rather shocked

regarding the working with a friend) ... At which point David added that he only worked with friends abroad!

The "just working online a little" is a familiar refrain, and in this chapter we'll be showing you why this isn't good enough, and that you are opening yourself up to a myriad of risks.

This book covers in depth, in other chapters, issues which surface in this chapter because, of course, everything is interconnected. Chapter Five, on the subject of challenges and dilemmas in the online consulting room, will give you plenty of food for thought about the day-to-day challenges we face as practitioners. Our intention here is to focus on four key themes that link the online world and our professional practice, in particular in relation to private practice:

- the therapeutic relationship
- professional presence
- context, setting, and format
- business principles.

I have developed a chart below. You should see each of the quadrants as inter-dependent and in no way linear or hierarchical.

You may well already have thought through some of the points, and I have included tick boxes so you can use this as a checklist of key areas to consider in the setting up of your online practice. The only visual distinction I make between the boxes is that the two left-hand boxes relate to the self and the therapeutic relationship, whilst the right-hand boxes relate to external elements.

I suggest that you use this chart to ensure that you have thought out each of the issues. You will find that your knowledge and experience of one of the quadrants will be stronger or weaker than that of the others. Using this chart will help you to know where you need to focus on future development, be it through professional training or business development advice. Of course the positioning of the items in one quadrant rather than another is arbitrary and some could fit comfortably in other quadrants. The key is to think about them and how they relate to you, rather than worrying too much which quadrant they are in, and there may be additional items that you might wish to add to one quadrant or another that are not currently listed. You can download this chart at http://pwtraining.com/resources/.

Checklist: key considerations for an online practice

Professional presence

- ☐ The image we wish to portray, identity
- ☐ Choosing your online social media
- ☐ Managing your online presence
- ☐ Information we wish to share online
- ☐ Adhering to a suitable code of ethics or ethical guideline
- ☐ Contracting that is fit for purpose, including communication between sessions
- ☐ Promotion of cybersafety
- ☐ Pre- and post-qualification specific training for working online and CPD
- ☐ Policy when the technology breaks down
- ☐ Supervision

Business principles

- ☐ Banking and finance
- ☐ Billing and payments
- ☐ Accept international currency
- ☐ Ensuring your tax status
- ☐ Legal structure
- ☐ Legal knowledge of the country you will be "practising" in
- ☐ Business and Professional Indemnity Insurance
- ☐ Security on and offline
- ☐ Administration on and offline
- ☐ Data storage and protection
- ☐ Publicity, PR, advertising, and marketing

Key considerations for an online practice

Therapeutic relationship

- ☐ Establishing the online therapeutic alliance
- ☐ The role of telepresence
- ☐ The use of language, text and emoticons
- ☐ Boundaries—relationship, session, jurisdiction
- ☐ Establishment and maintenance of trust
- ☐ The online consulting room The online therapeutic relationship and its negotiation
- ☐ Disinhibition
- ☐ Transference and counter-transference
- ☐ How different the relationship might be online
- ☐ Advantages and disadvantages
- ☐ The role of fantasy, second life and avatar
- ☐ Working without being physically present
- ☐ Identity—who are we really?
- ☐ The link between personality traits and Internet usage
- ☐ Facilitating a difficult moment for the client

Context, setting and format

- ☐ Your choice of online therapeutic communication

Synchronous   **asynchronous**
Video   Email
conferencing (e.g., VSee)
Text
Secure website
Second Life

- ☐ Your choice of technology and your client's preference
- ☐ Your choice of software
- ☐ Ground rules for how the sessions will take place
- ☐ Issues relating to the specific technologies
- ☐ Security and encryption
- ☐ Differences between online & F2F therapeutic relationship
- ☐ The assessment process
- ☐ Setting out and agreeing the contract, informed consent
- ☐ Confidentiality
- ☐ Record keeping
- ☐ Netiquette

Of course, we are not talking about anything that is very new in terms of information technology in therapeutic practice: telephone counselling has been in existence for many years and the newer web-based methods are largely an extension of the rules that apply to telephone counselling, which is already an important sector in the profession, used widely by EAPs, charities, and the NHS, for example.

All that is new is that we, as practitioners, are, rather late in the day, realising the potential of working online, using a new medium. Psychotherapy in the consulting room has served generations well, as the abundance of training institutes and therapy centres proves. As discussed in Chapter One, it is this very success that has held the profession back from keeping pace with the changes taking place in society at large, especially regarding the rapid progress towards "digitalising" our society and the demand to engage more and more in online services.

Why do clients want to work online when "face-to-face" is apparently working so well?

Anyone growing up in the digital age will probably take for granted that such services exist online. There are a number of specific factors that make working online attractive. These include (this list is not exhaustive):

- ease of access compared with a long weekly journey, with no travelling involved
- flexibility of appointment times
- issues relating to being trapped at home either as a carer or because of conditions such as agoraphobia preventing people from easily leaving the house. Stigma, or disability in some form or another
- people with autism and other conditions finding communication via the Internet less difficult.

Plus, of course, some people (I'm one of them) just love cyberspace and the goodies it brings. Others may be more narcissistic, or indeed into some form of authority issues and want to experience the freedom of disinhibition.

Working therapeutically online opens us to new clients, previously difficult to access or not accessible at all, from a diverse set of backgrounds including country, disability, mobility, poor social skills, stigma, embarrassment and shame, time constraints, ethnic—just to name a few. More importantly these very groups who Walker (2007) called the "silently suffering", have for the first time an opportunity to seek the help and understanding they need.

It also provides the client with a control and power over their choice of help that has previously been the domain of the therapist and some of the grist in the therapeutic process. Different schools of thought may also see online practice as being detrimental to the process of therapy. Whatever the arguments for or against, the demand for online services and help is growing, as Jenny Hyatt of Big White Wall highlights in her commentary at the end of Chapter One.

The rest of the chapter will concentrate on how you might work online.

The four key considerations when establishing up and running your online practice (with the reminder that these should not be viewed as a linear process and that individual items may well cross over into different segments) are: the therapeutic relationship; professional presence; context, setting, and format; and business principles.

THE THERAPEUTIC RELATIONSHIP

The therapeutic alliance

It is widely viewed that the therapeutic alliance is one of the key ingredients for a successful development of the psychotherapeutic relationship (Horvath & Luborsky, 1993), along with the client's capacity and readiness to engage with the process. In Chapter Four and in her research on how meeting online impacts the therapeutic relationship (Dunn, 2011), Kate Dunn discusses the therapeutic relationship within technologically mediated delivery of psychological therapies. Hanley and Reynolds's (2009) review of studies available on research into online outcomes and alliances within text-based therapy appears promising, with the online alliance proving to score higher than the comparison group.

Within the online therapeutic relationship, telepresence, "the feeling (or illusion) of being in someone's presence without sharing any immediate physical space" (Fink, 1999), is emerging as a key consideration to reflect on when making your choice of format for your online practice and how you wish to work with the online therapeutic relationship. Online practitioners such as Dunn, Anthony, and Goss[1] all confirm that the therapeutic relationship is every bit as powerful as the F2F session, developing its own powerful relationship dynamic as a core feature of the online therapeutic relationship.

Taking this further, Starks (2012) identifies that it is "the absence of physical presence, however, and not the specific type of technology used to make the interaction possible, that is a defining characteristic of all distance counselling situations."

Returning to Jackie and Clara's case study:

Q: Do you feel that Jackie and Clara have developed a good working therapeutic relationship?
Q: In Jackie's case, what would it be important for Clara to do or know in order to develop a therapeutic alliance?
Q: How might Clara use the therapeutic alliance in the work that Jackie is doing?

The role of language and non-verbal cues

While the reviews and research seem to indicate that the online therapeutic relationship can work well, there are some major hurdles to overcome in developing the therapeutic relationship online. A practitioner will need to think carefully about these before embarking into the unknown. They include how language varies in different parts of the world, and even between different regions of the United Kingdom, a topic covered in Chapter Six, by Divine Charura, and "non-language", for example the use of "smileys" and emoticons (a sequence of typed characters creating a rough picture of something, such as a facial expression or emotion), text shorthand, text-size, choice of font, colour of text, use of capitals, etc.

Kate Dunn, in a lecture to the UKCP's new media in psychotherapy special interest group (March 2013), beautifully demonstrated the use and role of language and its importance for our online work. The box below gives some examples about how these might be used in therapeutic work.

Consider the following examples—what responses do they evoke in you? How do the different texts/formats/styles affect you?

• I really hate mum for what she did to me … . Abandoning me for all those days, leaving me at home with that nasty neighbour next door … .

- I really hate mum for what she did to me ... . Abandoning me for all those days, leaving me at home with that nasty neighbour next door ... .
- I really hate mum for what she did to me ... . Abandoning me for all those days, leaving me at home with that nasty neighbour next door ... . !!!!!!!
- ih8 HER. ☹

There is a mélange of available fonts, colours, emoticons, and short cuts, each one altering the tone and feel of the sentence. Getting to know your client's ways of using text, acronyms, and text short-hands will be a very important consideration, as we do not all write the same way, just as we don't all speak the same way.

Training will help you learn what works well for you and how to evaluate your use of text. Text has a role for both synchronous video conferencing and for asynchronous emailing and other texts formats where the written word is the only format. I am not a natural writer so my personal preference would always be for video conferencing, but others will prefer the reflexivity of email and other text-based methods, where there is time to think about what you write and how you write it.

It's all too easy to write and send something and regret it afterwards. Fans of email counselling speak of the power of the email, but point out that being in tune, congruent, with your client is very important: I would urge caution and reserve and observe how your client writes in their session and respond accordingly, being reactive to their use of language, text, and style rather than, for example, foisting emoticons on someone who doesn't appreciate short hand paralanguage.

Boundaries

Cyberspace is not border or boundary limited. In *Therapy Today* (September 2013), Colin Feltham interviews Courtland Lee about his involvement in promoting global literacy. Lee states,

> Global literacy extends over the major domains of human diversity. It consists of the basic information that a person needs to know in order to successfully navigate life in the technologically sophisticated, globally interconnected world of the 21st century—a world

in which people from diverse cultural backgrounds interact in ways that were inconceivable in previous centuries. (Lee, 2013)

This borderless geographical, linguistic, and cultural arena presents us, as practitioners, with an exciting challenge and is a great opportunity for the profession but, as the ground rules shift, some practitioners feel uncomfortable. As therapists we are used to having control of our consulting room, and to some extent the process. In this new borderless geography the power has shifted and the delivery of service is adapting to meet this changed shift.

There are three contexts in which boundaries need to be considered: your geographical location and that of your client, which relates to jurisdiction; the type of communication technology used; and the therapeutic relationship. All three need attention and discussion as part of the contractual arrangements discussed at the beginning of therapy process.

Jurisdiction—which country are you working in?

Just because you are in the UK does not mean that UK law is applicable to your sessions where your client is abroad, and vice versa. This is currently untested in the courts, but I am sure you do not wish to be the first case! The general guidance currently is that your contractual arrangements should reflect the country where you reside/practice and that any subsequent complaint/legal case would usually need to be made in that country, and to buttress this you should talk to your insurer and ensure you have the right insurance cover in place. The code of ethics or ethical guidelines for your chosen professional association should be of some assistance here. In addition there are at least two specific

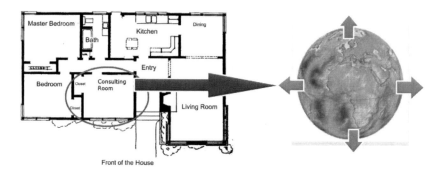

codes/guidelines[2,3,4] available that you can adopt should you feel this is appropriate. Kate Anthony, Stephen Goss and DeeAnna Nagel will give full consideration of these issues in Chapter Nine.

Clara, this has particular poignancy, as California has specific laws relating to practitioners only having the right to practice within the State of California if they are *licenced* to do so within the state. In fact, the general guidance given at the moment is not to work online in North America, as there are specific state licencing laws limited practitioners to only working within State.

We need also to be aware of the laws of the country where the client is based and ensure that we are not breaking that law in working online with them. For example, the general advice is *not* to work with anyone within North America.

You may wish to join an international association such as The European Association for Psychotherapy[5] or The International Society for Mental Health Online (ISMHO).[6]

Q: In the case of Jackie and Clara, which legal jurisdiction are they subject to?
Q: How could Clara best protect her herself in her professional practice?
Q: Do you think Clara should work with Jackie whilst she is in California?

The type(s) of communication technology used within therapeutic session

The therapeutic relationship is built within a context of boundaries; the exploration of these boundaries might need to form part of the therapeutic process. Online work is no different in this respect, but may need some organisation and trust built into it. Let's unpack this a little further with some opening (but not exhaustive) questions:

• What arrangements do you make to ensure you are working with your client and not someone else?
• What arrangements do you make about the confidentiality of the sessions, not only by you but also by your client, as well illustrated by Kevin's story in Chapter Five?

The practical arrangements that you would make are similar; it is the implementation that may be different.

- *Communication technologies including telephone, VoIP, videoconferencing*: in the same way as you would programme time to make appointments and practical arrangements, you will need to allow time to do this online.

  o How do you deal with emergencies?
  o What plans do you have in place for emergency contact either by you in the case of illness or other, or by the client?
  o When working across borders you will need to think about the time zones one person's morning may be another's evening.

- *Text-based sessions*: Starks identified that around fifty per cent of online practitioners used asynchronous email/web for sessions. Kate Dunn in Chapter Four details one such service and her method of working. In essence the important element here is for both parties to agree how an asynchronous service will work. For example, the client might agree to write for about fifty minutes. The practitioner will agree to do the same. What happens if the client writes so much that the therapist cannot possibly deal with it in fifty minutes? As in F2F sessions, the practitioner would need to end the "session" by acknowledging that he/she has not been able to work through all the material, and leave the channels open that this is a subject that they will need to continue on in the next session (although of course by then this material may be redundant as sessions have a way of progressing forward, but that is life too). The important point here is for the therapist to feed back to the client what he/she can manage to work through within the agreed session time and what will happen if this cannot happen, as in the case above.

Q: Thinking through Jackie's story from her point of view (not the therapist's), what sort of online service do you think might suit Jackie best? And why?

For the users of asynchronous therapy through, for example, email, writing in itself is a marvellous tool in the therapy room. I would recommend to you Parts Two and Three of *Writing Cures: Introductory Handbook of Writing in Counselling and Psychotherapy* (Bolton, Howlett, Lago, & Wright, 2004), devoted to writing in therapy and writing online.

The online therapeutic relationship and how this is negotiated

- **Confidentiality**: while this might appear to be no different to a F2F therapeutic relationship, in fact there are other considerations which I have referred to elsewhere in this chapter, such as interruptions (the client's mobile ringing or family members walking in on a session), privacy of content of sessions, but, equally, the safe storage of data. These matters should be addressed in the contract, which should be a paper document/PDF. It is likely that your professional association or training organisation will provide these templates, but please ensure that they include the online aspects of your practice, and if they do not, then think about adding on one of the existing ethical frameworks or codes for working online.
- **Boundary erosion**: I find email invaluable in the planning of my diary—if someone phones to ask me something or for an appointment when I am away from my office, I usually ask them to confirm by email. Email etiquette is one consideration for the practitioner, apart from whether you choose to practice via email (see the separate section for this). However, whilst this sounds straight forward, it may be less so, and open to boundary erosion. Take this example of an email from a client which may go like this:

> Hi—just confirming our conversation and appointment for tomorrow at 10.00 via Skype. By the way, you were right to tell me to leave my partner and I've done this now!

The first sentence is fine, it confirms the arrangement as discussed in the phone call. It's part of the business relationship. The second sentence is wild! First of all, I would never tell a client to do anything— I might list options to help him think about different alternatives, but isn't it interesting how the client hears what I didn't say? In addition, the second sentence is part of the therapy and the boundary has been transgressed and the client is moving discretely and directly into therapeutic territory. How you would react in such circumstances should be set out in the contract between you and the client right at the beginning and reinforced in the discussion you have at the outset about how you work.

The online consulting room—ground rules for therapeutic work

There are a multitude of things to think about, particularly with video conferencing synchronous systems. I will discuss the available video-conferencing software that you can safely use in the section on security, as in particular the most frequently used Skype is not considered sufficiently secure (Quashie, 2013). I will use VSee here for the example:

1. If the technology breaks down, have a back-up plan.
2. You might wish to provide some simple instructions for your client for using VSee (and I am very grateful to Tamara Alferoff for these):

* * *

A few days before your first session, send instructions to your client:

a. Check if your VSee software has an update, and if so, download and install it, and
b. Open your video VSee, click on the Search slot, and find me either by name or by email address (put your own VSee user name here), and send me a Request for Contact. Once I get that, I will Accept. I will then be able to invite you into a call.
[One reason I do it this way is because some people give themselves impenetrable aliases, and there may be, for example, 123 Pippa Weitzes on VSee! As far as I know there is only one of me ...]
c. At the time of the call, 8pm on 8 May, please have your VSee window open, the little lozenge (next to your photo and name top left) green, and your volume so you can hear! Then wait for me to Call you, and click the Accept button.

Additionally, to improve the quality of the call it helps if you:

• have a headset
• close all open browsers
• shut the door on noise and try to keep your room and time private, move cordless or mobile phones *away* from your computer.
• Re: use of camera: If using VSee you can choose whether either or both of you has their camera on. In theory this sounds fine. In practice it can be:
  ○ distracting—if you want to reach for something, find another pen, make notes, you'll be watched
  ○ confusing—the camera will look at you, and you'll be looking at the screen where your client's face is. Thus you will not be looking *at* the client on their screen, and thus be experienced as absented

- o in addition you may feel obliged to stare at the camera, thus not being relaxed or authentically focussed on the process, or present. Surprisingly, you may find that attentive and close listening furnishes a deal more information about what is going on for your client than watching them on camera. In addition, they are likely to feel less self-conscious
- o extraneous—you don't need it, except perhaps to first meet and greet.

* * *

3. You may need to underline the need for the person to be on their own in a room for the whole time without interruption without the flat-mate popping in to do the washing up, prepare the dinner, etc. Believe me, it happens.
4. Equally, you'll need to ensure you can follow the same rules. Partners somehow tend to think that if there isn't a client actually in the room then it's OK to come in, even if they tiptoe. Make some simple rules that your family or housemates know so that you are left in peace for the entire session.
5. Just as you decide what to put in your consulting room, you'll want to decide what you have behind you and what your lighting is like. Both can make a massive impact on the session.
6. Ensure that you keep your picture up small in the corner of your screen so that you can ensure discretely that the client can actually see you—I can't tell you how many VSee meetings I've been involved in where I can see just one eye and a bit of forehead. It's just about getting it right at the beginning, through good training. Once you are used to working with the camera always on you'll take it for granted. Think about how much of you and your body you would like your client to see. It can be quite alarming to see a close-up of someone's face—every crevice isn't always a pretty picture! Think about sitting back a bit and getting your client to do the same, both relaxing into your respective chairs. We tend to lean over our computers—this position may not be conducive to the therapeutic process unless you need to text at the same time. Remember the golden rule to keep an eye on your camera picture to ensure that your client can see you properly: what you see is what your client sees.
7. Just as we would prepare the consulting room—hoover, tidy, puff up cushions, get tissues, etc.—online you need prepare the environment.

Ensure that you clear your desk of all distractions, close all other software and websites, and remove anything distracting, such as mobile phones. Your client will know if your eyes slide off somewhere else!

8. You will need to work out your policy on boundaries, such as if a client rings ten minutes too early, or at any other time for that matter, or is distressed and not ending. What would you do if a client is inappropriately dressed or behaving inappropriately?

Evans (2009) neatly summarises the preparation of the online presence: "Where the nature of the online relationship necessitates a more in-depth understanding of the client and material presented within the interactions, the online practitioner should endeavour to encourage a greater level of personal presence to assist in developing a physical perspective of the client."

The online relationship

Is an identity-fit important?

Earlier on in the chapter I talked about how the therapeutic alliance was a cornerstone in the positive therapeutic relationship, alongside a client's capacity and readiness to engage with the process. A third cornerstone is that of identity and how this is played out online. How we understand our identity indicates how we place ourselves, or feel placed, in the world and the society we live in. When choosing a therapist, it is likely that clients going for therapy, consciously or unconsciously, seek out practitioners' who they think may understand the way they see the world, or who fits with her inner world. The client may looks for clues in the practitioner's profile about his or her background (e.g., sexual orientation, ethnicity) or the client may be looking for evidence of a therapist's proven track record in a certain area of training, such as working with anxiety (such as in Jackie's story). The client may begin his or her sessions thinking he knows quite a lot about you. You too, may wish to check your client out online: what do you think about Googling a client?

How you wish to present yourself and your professional image to the world online, how you manage and protect your identity with regard to social media, marketing, and information about you that may already exist in the virtual world, are other criteria for consideration in the development of the online relationship where trust and the belief that the therapeutic can help the client in difficulty are all essential ingredients. Is the information that is available about you online congruent with what you would like the client to know about you? Can you do anything about this if it is not?

How do I know who you really are?

The question I often hear is: How do we know who the client really is online? That's a bit of a red herring. Do we know who the person is that we meet in the consulting room? We think we do, but people bring to therapy what they need to bring: we don't do an identity check for those coming to F2F therapy, we take them at face value and they provide us with the image of themselves that they wish us to see. And actually, does it matter? A client comes to therapy to work on a particular issue or issues, and if we are able to work satisfactorily on those areas, the rest is probably irrelevant. There has been a lot of discussion about the role of avatar, the development of an alternative identity, usually online, or through Second Life. These issues are explored by Kate Anthony in Chapter Seven and provide some interesting thoughts about identity.

Generally speaking clients engage a therapist initially because they have a problem they wish to address. If they feel judged they will hide behind a constructed identity, and may choose a format for therapy that prevents exposure of the vulnerable part of themselves.

Transference

In his 2004 work Suler indicated that transference dynamics were an important determinant to the potential outcome of a therapeutic relationship and the importance for the practitioner of considering the positive and negatives in the development and maintenance of the online therapeutic relationship. Depending on your modality of therapeutic practice this is an area you will need to think about closely, working out how to work with transference, counter-transference, and projection online. Current research already referred to indicates that working online with issues of transference and countertransference is very positive and there are opportunities to further research into this area to flesh these areas out further.

Overcoming shame and other negative emotions

Another area that would be interesting to research further is what a client chooses to bring to the session online that they might not have explored in the consulting room. One such example of research is the work by Suler (1997) on shame and similar emotions. Online work that allows the client to explore these feelings can be very enabling when clients are not physically present. Equally, Samaritans found this out in the 1980s in their telephone, and later online, work with suicidal young men. We refer below to Dunn's comments on the liberation from embarrassment.

Disinhibition

It's amazing what a difference it makes being liberated from the in-person relationship! I'm not proud of it but I know I've said things on the phone that I would never have the nerve to say in person. Do you recognise this in you?

"In removing the physical aspect of the counselling, the pure expression of mind and soul may be communicated effectively, bypassing the defences of counsellor and client" (Anthony, 2000). Kate Dunn (2013), in a paper delivered to the UKCP new media special interest group, asks whether online disinhibition reveals the true self, and concluded that "a client may write very differently from how they converse, but may feel this represents them *better* as they are not hampered by embarrassment, etc."

Anthony and Nagel (2010) summarise Suler's (2004) work on disinhibition, concluding that anonymity may lead some people to behave with less restraint online. Anthony and Nagel summarise these as follows, and all have some implication for therapeutic relationship:

- "You don't know me" (*dissociative anonymity*), where the client chooses a hidden identity Skype username such as A1B2C3. When separated from their real identity clients feels freer to speak, they feel less vulnerable about sharing information and talking. Of course we all only share what we want to share. Going further they see their behaviour in role as not really being them and they dissociate from their true self.
- "You can't see me" (*invisibility*), where people land up doing things they otherwise wouldn't do, sometimes with undesired results.
- "See you later!" (*asynchronicity*), where communication of the email/ chat is delayed. And the reply is delayed too, allowing time for thought.

- "It's all in my head" (*solipsistic introjection or ego self-absorption*).
- "It's just a game" (*dissociative imagination*), splitting off into the imaginary online world from real life.
- "We're equals" (*minimising authority*).

Anthony and Nagel conclude that together with the various personality factors, issues relating to power, control, authority, dissociation, manipulation, and delusion have a role in disinhibition. Many of the issues to reflect on concerning the online therapeutic relationship parallel the traditional issues in the consulting room but with a twist, mainly involving how to work when the client and practitioner are not in the same physical space, and the consequent issues relating to how we set this up satisfactorily so that the boundaries are solid and the online relationship can develop in a healthy way to achieve success in the therapeutic relationship and a positive outcome for the client. The case study involving Jackie raised important issues regarding jurisdiction, boundaries, and transference, and Clara went wrong at the first hurdle by accepting to work with someone located in California.

Q: How might Clara have set up the therapeutic boundaries and contracting differently?

Q: What would you have done if you had been presented with Jackie?

PROFESSIONAL PRESENCE

Professional Identity

We have already discussed identity within the therapeutic relationship from the point of view of who the client is; now we turn to the practitioner and how you can develop our professional identity. Just as in business, where corporate image is important, so too is developing our professional identity as practitioners. If you have your own consulting room you are likely to have taken a lot of care in the choice of furniture, decoration, positioning, lighting: these all reflect your identity, and are issues that need consideration for online work.

Just as in therapeutic work the client only shows part of their identity, the bit they want us to see, so too will we only wish to show part of our identity. Your job here is to create this and to be sure of what you want to portray and work to portray it! Make sure it is congruent with who you are and what you are.

Preparing the space you will use

- Developing a slick website, but having a fuzzy webcam for online work, or having a teddy bear within sight of the webcam is simply unprofessional. Just as we make a decision about the clothes we wear each day, and the headed note paper that we choose, these are decisions that need to sit comfortably with our personalities. Just because you have an appointment with someone in Australia and it is 3am your time, it is not alright to sit in your pyjamas or onesie with the webcam!

- When setting up the area of the room you are going to work in, if you are working via a webcam, don't just check what you can see in front and around you, check what is visible in the webcam—think about books, pictures, photographs that are behind you. Whatever the client will see in the webcam will tell them a lot about you—every picture tells a story.

- Think too about lighting, not just for you, but how does the lighting in your room affect the webcam. These very simple items of lighting and what's behind you go a long way to setting the scene of the online consulting room.

- Ensure that your computer screen is not visible to anyone it should not be visible to and that it is password protected to protect client information.

- What is on your desk to distract you or to make noise? Maybe papers rustling into the microphone. When running a session, close all other windows on your computer and put away all other distractions including mobile phones. Your client will know instantly if you are even slightly distracted—your eyes will wander!

- Do you fidget? If so, find a way of fidgeting without moving too much and without impact for the webcam or microphone, otherwise it becomes very irritating for the other person.

- Finally, you! How much do you want to reveal? This has already been mentioned but is too important to miss in this section. The problem with desks and laptops is we tend to peer into them, hunched over, leaning forward. Is this the natural position for the therapeutic relationship? Think also about the amount of you that can be seen by the webcam as this will tell the client a lot about your body language. Might it be better to sit in a coffee-table armchair with the laptop around a metre away? Even leaning back on your office chair would be better than leaning forward—have a go and ask some friends to give you their reaction to what looks best.

When you are thinking of setting up your online practice, what do you think might be the major challenges for you?

Would you prefer to work synchronously (e.g., video-conferencing) or asynchronously (e.g., email)? What does this decision say about your preferred style of working, your style of therapy, and your confidence to work in this way? What's stopping you thinking of working in the "other" way?

Thinking back to our case study with Jackie, what do you think might be the important points in terms of your professional practice set-up to be clear on that would enhance the sense of professional presence?

Choosing your social media to reflect your online identity

No one can tell you what to do or which social media to be involved in. But each decision will have a life-long consequence as nothing is easy to erase from the Internet once it is up there.

For example I use Facebook for only personal family usage. It is hidden from view to the public and access is only by invitation.

I have personally chosen to use LinkedIn for professional usage. There are many platforms and social media sites and forums for you to choose from, but choose astutely. I recently searched for the profile of someone key in online psychotherapy and was astounded that he hadn't put up a professional profile, but perhaps this was a deliberate decision on his part. Try and work out what others might expect of your profile, and also what they might expect of your own website. Is it better to be very formal, or less formal? These are all questions of choice and preference, but whatever wording and images you use make sure what you write is inviting and easy to read. Think about who you will be writing for: is it the general public, or a professional service such as NHS contractors? The wording would be quite different.

I also use Naymz to keep me informed about all the activity involving my name on the Internet. It notifies users weekly of any change and enables us to update information on sites we have completely forgotten about. It will also help you measure and manage your social reputation online, particularly with LinkedIn, Facebook, and Twitter.

Also Google yourself—you'll probably be very surprised by how much information there is about you on the Internet, and there's nothing much you can do about it, though you can now search and modify your Facebook through Graph.[7]

How do you get involved in online forums? I read some of the psychotherapy and counselling forums on LinkedIn and am astounded at the unprofessional questions being raised that should be covered in pre-qualification training. But choose your forum carefully—for example, UKCP has its own LinkedIn forum for members—and think about what you put up in web space anywhere—it's highly likely that a client will search for you and find whatever you said.

Be circumspect about what you put online—it's online forever. Even David Cameron and Tony Blair have some historic photos and information they would rather the general public didn't see. Just as an example, on a LinkedIn professional discussion group there was the question "Would you counsel a friend?"

> Friday 11 October's *Evening Standard* had an article entitled "Beware—you're fair game once your data's digital". The central tenet of the article was that future generations of politicians will need to be far more shrewd as to the ubiquity of information readily available about them and their antics, and that this is good news for the "transparency of government". For you and me, on a personal and professional level the implication is,
>
>> The frictionless ease with which a video, photo or comment can be uploaded gives the illusion of ephemerality. There is so much data moving so quickly, we assume it will get lost in the rushing digital stream. But it's all there, all redeemable, those Facebook albums and dating profiles lingering like ghost-clown versions of our past selves, those deleted tweets stored by watchers in the shadows for a rainy day.

Michèle Bartlett reminds us in her commentary at the end of Chapter Ten, on the subject of protecting children and young people from online abuse, that the current prevalence amongst young people of naively sexting is going to create a lifetime of identity problems for these young people as they move through into work and family life.

If you are setting up your website: is this an information-giving website, is it a website where people can blog, interact, or is it a website where you manage your online sessions? Will you provide emergency contact information such as Samaritans and Childline? Will it provide a resource for your clients? Anthony and Nagel (2010) report that "many practitioners translate their online work into academic arenas". Before you go down this route, think about who the readers will be.

Currently there are no UK-based sufficiently robust one-stop-shop websites/online consulting room that you can buy into, but I'm sure that before the ink is dry this will be developing. Even Skype (Quashie, 2013) has come under criticism for not being sufficiently robust as you will read about in more detail in the section on security.

Q: What do you need to consider about your public and professional identities online?
Q: Do you need to make any changes to your privacy settings in social media you are already involved in?
Q: Do you need to work out how to separate your professional and personal online presences?
Q: Have you checked recently what information there is about you online?
Q: How could you market yourself online?

Your professional bodies and codes of practice and ethical guidelines

In this pluralistic world that we live in no two practitioners agree about everything when it comes to codes and ethical guidelines! The Online Therapy Institute has developed an ethical framework for the use of social media by mental health professionals.[8] Those of you belonging to one or more professional associations such as UKCP, BPS, ACTO, or BACP may find that many of the points in the framework are already embedded in existing frameworks and codes. However, there are some extremely useful pointers in this framework that are not yet embedded in the professional associations' ethical guidelines and codes and I would encourage you to use this, until the professional bodies have had a chance to fully engage with their members and appropriately adapt their codes and guidelines. An alternative is the RAMP[9] programme: the Risk Awareness Management Programme written expressly for organisations with online mental health services for provision in a safe and secure manner.

Pre and post qualification training for working online and CPD

Training to work online

As discussed in more detail in Chapter One, online therapy is currently considering as a post-qualification specialism, although there must surely be a place for pre-qualification training courses to include the digital world and online work within their syllabi. If there has been one message throughout this book, it is this: that we all need to do some post-qualification training to prepare us for working online. Clara, in the case study at the beginning of this chapter, would not have made elementary mistakes had she undergone some training, or at the very least some mentoring. In Chapter Three Chris Blackmore and Digby Tantam, and Anne Stokes talk of the importance of proper training for working online. I liken our attitude to working online to being a car driver of twenty-five years' experience. I think I am a good driver, but I was eighteen when I last read the Highway Code. Much has changed in the intervening years, such as no longer stopping by slowing down to second gear! We are too sloppy, also, with our attitude to our online equipment, as we take it for granted. Just as we would never consider that completing a weekend course on art therapy makes us an art therapist, so too with online therapy.

The post-qualification training I have already received (and I plan to do more) has made me think deeply about what I do as a practitioner. It was no rubber-stamping moment. The challenges of thinking through the online relationship are but just one of the most important themes for training to work online. I have spoken to staff and students of the various courses that are around and they have all been most enthusiastic about the courses and the development of their understanding and skills base.

The online training courses I know about are all delivered online. This seems to be sensible, as it gives you the trainee therapist an opportunity to experience the difficulties and challenges that arise for the client, and also to experience the benefits and the richness of this online relationship. Those who work online all talk about the quality of the therapist relationship, but in order to enhance this and use it for the best it is something you need to experience and work on yourself. The very issues that I have detailed elsewhere in this chapter about the online relationship, the creating and fixing of boundaries, working without a physical presence, are therefore the bread and butter of online training. Indeed hardware and software failures happen, and experiencing these and working out your policy in these instances is important.

Continuing professional development

CPD will play its part in two ways. First, through providing us with new skills for working online as the digital world evolves. Second, there is a fabulous opportunity to develop online training which for the moment is largely untapped, with a few notable exceptions. I recently checked a May 2013 issue of one of the main professional journals and counted all the training/CPD adverts at the back. It wasn't very scientific so I may have missed one or two but of approximately fifty adverts only three had any focus on working online! This speaks volumes and training organisations need to act quickly and adapt pre- and post-qualification training. Online working is no longer the country cousin.

Supervision

The rules for supervision are very similar to other areas of online work, so in this section I will merely highlight considerations that are independent of the issues already raised that play an important role of online supervision.

First of all, what do we mean by online supervision? Is it supervision of online therapy taking place online? Is it supervision online of F2F work? Is it F2F supervision of a practitioner who normally works online? As you can see, there are a number of nuances and each of these has its own implications. Is the supervision one-to-one, group, asynchronous, synchronous?

When working in group supervision there are some challenges relating to where each supervisee is geographically located, together with the use of language and traditions. All these are considered within this book, so I merely highlight this as an additional challenge for the online supervisor, who will in particular need to verify her supervisees' identity and ensure that the geographical location does not contravene any national or international law.

All online supervisors and their supervisees will need to think through and consider issues such as client consent, confidentiality and data protection, password security for confidential information, use of emails, just as they would in F2F work, but with the additional dimension of using encryption packages and privacy tools.

Training to be an online supervisor is in its infancy and there's an opening here for some good training courses to be developed.

I refer you to Anne's Stokes section on supervision in Chapter Three for a fuller consideration of supervision, and Anthony and Nagel are currently working on a book on online supervision which will be very useful.

What do you need to think about in your training needs to work online? For example, a specialist course, CPD modules and conferences, additional supervision?

Context, setting, and format

A major point for practitioners will be choice of method used online: the choice is between voice-based technology and text-based technology, with an additional consideration also for the use of an avatar or role in Second Life, a subject discussed in its own right in Chapter Seven by Kate Anthony.

Steve Johnson, in an open letter (2013) to UKCP's new media in psychotherapy special interest group, stated

> I suspect that most psychotherapists when thinking about working "online" or through new media will be thinking about delivering real therapy to real clients in the real world as a real therapist.

The choices you will make about how to practice online will have much to do with you, the practitioner—your personality, your method of working, your mannerisms—but it's important that the choice of technology reflects the wishes of the client. Some will prefer one format over another; to force a format on them because it is what we prefer may alienate the client.

Will you mix F2F work with online work?

Will you choose synchronous (immediacy) or asynchronous (such as email, where a reply has to be waited for)?

One of the early questions was whether therapeutic work online is carried out in the same way as F2F work. Researchers such as Fenichel (Fenichel et al., 2002) confirm that online practice develops in its own way, although online practitioners will of course draw on the therapy and practice that they have been grounded in in their pre-qualification training; online practice itself is developing new methods of working where practitioners will seek out what works best for them, using all the available visual and sound methods in the online world possible, including the most common—videoconferencing, texting, email—whilst respecting the preferred method of their clients.

The first session

The point when your clients first make contact with you is the moment to ascertain how comfortable they are with working via the Internet, with the technology, and what they use the Internet for.

Setting the scene in the first session and enabling clients to feel comfortable about the online format is very helpful, though actually you may find they are more familiar with working and communicating online than you are! In any case, it is important to feel your way in this first session, just as you would in any first session, looking for cues in the clients' use of language—are they very informal or very formal; start the session by acknowledging that they may find online work new and perhaps a little daunting, and this way you'll know their position straight away. Above all, do not force clients to use a form of technology with which they feel uncomfortable.

There is always so much to get into a first session, so, just as in a F2F session, it's important to frame the timing with your client, ensure you get the assessment done, and allow them an opportunity to start off the process—there's going to be a reason why they asked to see you! Ensure that you have laid down the contractual arrangements in your first session so that your clients know exactly what to expect, and that you have adapted your assessment procedures appropriately.

Just as the client needs to check you out, so, you need to check your client out. You may wish to do this prior to the first session, or this may form part of the first session with an understanding, for both of you, that it is a first session and that you will review together the way forward. Actually, there is no difference here, at least in the way I work, as I would always view a first session as an introductory session before engaging fully into the process of therapy.

Working out what to do with technical glitches

Technology problems are a frequent occurrence; whether it is because of a human error or other is really irrelevant. What is important is that you know what to do when one occurs and that you and your client are clear on this, for example, if the Wi-Fi signal is not very good in the hotel where you are conducting your online counselling session with your client. Ensure you have made a plan to cover eventualities such as this and that your client is clear about this: include it in your contracting arrangements so that it is written down. Having each other's mobile phone numbers is one good way to communicate at a time like this.

Assessment, contracting, boundaries, and informed consent

Just as in F2F work, carrying out an assessment when working online is crucial. Not everyone is going to be suitable for therapy, neither is everyone suitable for online therapy (e.g., computer illiteracy, language limitations).

Evans (2009) identifies two additional considerations when doing an online assessment, namely the "potential difficulties in substantiating background information" and, second, "systems required for determining authenticity and suitability of an applicant for online support". You will no doubt already have in place a system for F2F assessments. The question will be, what modifications should you make to this assessment process? Do you already do an intake questionnaire, or do you have a mental tick-list of the key points to cover? Do you see assessment as something you do prior to the client starting their therapeutic work, or do you see it as an ongoing process? How do you view recording the session (either overtly or covertly)?

The other side of the coin is the contracting. This has come up throughout the chapter and sets the foundations in place for the therapeutic relationship. It creates an agreement between you, the practitioner, and your client. It will provide information as to what the client can expect, establishes the boundaries, and sets in place an agreed way of working. It is designed to ensure that the client has enough knowledge and understanding about the way you, the practitioner, are going to work. In addition, it is an important part of informed consent.

It would also be the place, for example, for a discussion about appropriate contact via social media and the privacy levels that you may wish to set. Just as you would discuss with a F2F client how you would act should you meet them at a party, or in the supermarket, so too there needs to be a protocol for similar safeguards online. If your client asked to "Friend" you on Facebook, as Alice does to Lucy in Chapter Seven, how would you respond?

How you develop your boundaries with the client will depend on the type of online work you are offering. In the context of working via email you will perhaps want to clarify how this is going to happen, for example, you might say that once you receive the client's email you will spend fifty or sixty minutes (say) reading it through and replying. The advantage of this approach is that there is no constraint on the client as to how much he writes, but that you, the counsellor will spend fifty or sixty minutes responding and if it requires three times fifty minutes to reply properly, that would constitute three sessions! This is so much more flexible than a synchronous arrangement which is constrained to a certain time and length.

For your emails with clients do you have a secure and separate mailbox for clients? Does each client get his own mailbox or do all the emails go into the same client box? We'll cover more about this in the section on security.

In addition to the points you would usually have in your contract, there are some specific ones to include specifically relating to online work:

- About you and how you work online, synchronously or asynchronously, for example.
- The code of ethics/ethical framework that you adhere to if there is a specific one for your online work.
- What should happen if the technology breaks down, the contingency plan.
- Fees and how you accept payment.
- What to do in an emergency.
- What happens if you are (or your client) for some reason unable to continue (e.g., through illness or death).
- The amount of time for each session (and how that might be handled differently between synchronous and asynchronous).
- Security for confidentiality through encryption and secure sites
- Communication between session, the difference between arrangement-making and "material".
- The privacy of communications between the two of you, for example, not copying others in, or forwarding emails written by you to others.

These should be considered in conjunction with the section on assessment and contracting in Weitz (2006). The issues arising in the area of assessment, contracting, boundaries, and informed consent could fill a book in their own right, and I have only skated over the surface here.

Tamara Alferoff has suggested an agreement that you can use as the basis of the contractual arrangements you might wish to put together. You will need to edit this accordingly to you professional training and style of practice.

Dear [Please put in name]

Thank you for contacting me, you sound very down and lonely, but I want you to know that you are not alone and I really hope I can help you at this difficult time for you. I know just how hard it is to take that first step to ask for help. As this may be your first step towards asking for help, and receiving help online is a bit different I will explain a little about how I work.

Ways we might work online

I work with clients online in the way that you, the client, prefer:
either   via **VSee** (it's like Skype but more secure) where we can talk and use webcams. Each session is 50 minutes.
or   we can **text** via VSee. Each session is 50 minutes.
or   we can **email**. I usually suggest that you write for around 50 minutes and I will engage to reply to you within 2 working days. I too will work on your email and write for around 50 minutes.

I'm really happy to work in the way that you find easiest and most helpful. Please let me know which way of working would work for you … and then we can take it from there. If we are going to work via VSee I will send you the full instructions about how to install it before we start. For email, I use safe-mail.net which is very secure, ensuring the security of our communications.

Number of sessions and availability

I would like to suggest that we start with 6 sessions. We can extend this later on, if we need to. I have some 50 minute sessions available this Thursday or Friday if that would help. Please let me know if you want to book a session, I am free at 4.00pm and 6.00pm on both days.

Questionnaire

The first thing we need to do is to make an agreement about how we are going to work together. Please can I ask you to fill out the short questionnaire below and review the Informed Consent (this sets out everything you need to know) at www.putindomainname.com/informedconsent/ before we start out on the counselling.

Keeping your information safe

As a Registered Member of the BACP, I observe their Guidelines for online counselling and psychotherapy*, and will respect your privacy and your mores at all times. Your communications will remain confidential between us. An exception to this is where I need to take some of the issues to supervision, to ensure that I am counselling in a way that is safe and beneficial to you, as required by my professional code.

If it becomes apparent that a different counsellor or method would suit you better, I will try to assist you in finding the most appropriate way forward.

I will not reveal your identity, and will take all necessary precautions to protect your privacy, and I expect the same from you. The only circumstance where I am obliged to break confidentiality is if you have indicated that there is a risk of harm to yourself or someone else, and I am required by ethics to seek advice and guidance from supervisors or other professionals.

I would need to inform the police in the event that someone might be hurt or a crime be committed from what you tell me I would of course discuss this beforehand with you to obtain your assent.

Emergency support

It may be that you need some support before we can start working together, and if you feel you need urgent help and are in crisis now please contact either www.befrienders.org or www.samaritans.org.

What happens if something goes wrong

In the event of either of us being unable to attend or continue the counselling, we each undertake to let the other know in advance wherever possible. You can call me on [put in your telephone number] in an emergency. If I don't hear from you within a reasonable time, around a week, I will first drop you an email to check out if you are alright. Sometimes things go wrong with technology, so it's important for us to check and please feel to check with me if you feel either that I have not responded as I should have or I have misunderstood something, or if you are unable to continue the counselling for some reason.

Payments

Payment should be made in advance either by personal cheque in sterling, or through Paypal. I will let you have details of how to set this up.

My fees are as follows: [Put in your fees including any concessionary rates]

More about me and how I work

If you would like to read up more about me, and read the full details of how I work, please look at my website www.putindomainname.com .

Do ask me if there is anything you want to check out before we start working together. I'm here to help.

Thank you for asking me to work with you. I look forward to working with you.

Warm regards

Philippa Weitz BEd, MSc, Registered Member BACP
"One step at a time ... ."

*Copies may be obtained from this organisation, also complaints procedures.

Questionnaire:

Please could you copy and paste the questionnaire below into an email, complete it and send it to me at client999@safe-mail.net

:

+   +   +   +   +   +   +   +   +   +   +   +

Name   _____

Contact Number: _____

Address: _____   _____

GP: _____

Prescribed medication you take and how often. _____

I would like to work in our counselling sessions via email / video-conferencing (VSee) / text (VSee)—*please delete as appropriate.*

I agree to _____ (*please put in the number of sessions*) sessions.

I will pay for my counselling in advance using _____ (method).

Date: _____

By copying and pasting this questionnaire into an email and sending it back to my counsellor I confirm that I am over 18 years of age, and am not receiving any treatment for mental illness.

Q: Have you developed a written contract for use with your online clients?

Q: Have you adapted your assessment system for online use?

Q: Do you have any specific items you need to add to your contract that are not covered in the section above?

Q: Thinking of the case study, did Clara suitably contract with Jackie? What might you have done differently?

Security and encryption

At the end of Chapter One I outlined four items on my wish list for online therapy. One of them is a UK-based Internet one-stop-shop for practitioners—the online consulting room, a website, your office—that can be purchased for a monthly fee and provides you with everything you need for working online securely and professionally. This would include a diary, secure storage of your notes, the means of communication via email, text, and web-conferencing, a resources library, and a business section to include accounting, invoicing, and receipts, and credit card/PayPal facility for receiving payments. To illustrate the point, just as the iphone is extremely easy to use, it does of course have extremely complex programming to make this happen. Its design and ease of use is what has made it a household item. My true wish is that we could do the same for an online practitioners' package that would provide a seamless and easy to use front end—and leave the programmers to worry about the back end. (Those working within organisations where their work is evolving online will need their organisations to create a secure and professional online platform; this will include charitable organisations and EAPS.)

This is particularly important in the current climate where doubts have surfaced about the security of using Skype for this purpose. In the recent issue of TILT, Quashie (2013) writes on Skype and the American Health Insurance Portability and Accountability Act (HIPAA) with regard to the rules and regulations concerning privacy and security. Whilst Skype is encrypted it fails at other hurdles that may impact on your practice, namely it is proprietary software (licenced under exclusive legal right of the copyright holder with the intent that the licencee is given the right to use the software only under certain conditions, and restricted from other uses, such as modification, sharing, studying, redistribution, or reverse engineering).[10] In practice, this means that as there is no way of knowing if and what information is stored by Skype, you will be unable to establish an audit trail, or know if there is a breach of security. In short, Skype is currently a tool that you should think carefully about using until these issues are sorted. These issues have been put to Skype by a number of organisations, including Open Technology Institute Reporters Without Borders, but have not yet been addressed satisfactorily. In practice, Skype is the most widely used software, and is likely to be the one you know best. In a Distance Counselling Survey reported in TILT magazine Starks (2012) identifies that 66.3 per cent of practitioners use Skype. If and when you do use Skype please remember the associated concerns, and ensure that you best protect yourself in the way you set up your practice and the security that goes with this and discuss this at the outset with your clients. Kate Anthony recommends VSee which is encrypted (as is Skype) and more secure.

It is indeed very curious that some key trainers training in online work are advocating the use of Skype when the research suggests that this is not sufficiently robust for psychotherapy online. It is for this reason that I have not anywhere in this chapter endorsed or suggested the use of Skype.

If you are working via email then there are two free versions of software that are considered sufficiently robust and secure: Hushmail and safe-mail. Within these encrypted email packages emails can be stored, sent, and received within the encryption site. Jones and Stokes (2009) advocate using a digital signature for the "signing" of the initial counselling contract.

Q: Have you worked out how you will best work securely?
Q: What would be your preferred method to ensure your client's confidentiality?
Q: Did Clara, in as far as we have limited information, think out the issues of security, assessment, and contracting as fully as she might have?

All through the three quadrants so far discussed—the therapeutic relationship, professional presence, and the context—there is an underpinning theme of cybersafety, something we as professionals need to demonstrate in how we set up our online practice, and promote and pursue within our online and face-to-face practice both professionally ourselves and when working with clients.

Business principles

One of the key factors you will need to think about in working online is the administration of your business. Many of these aspects are covered in the books on setting up a practice that I identified at the beginning of the chapter, so I will not repeat them here, except where they need highlighting or are, or may be, different.

Organising your administration online will require thought about encryption and security, especially for payments. The issues around this have been discussed above. The key point to consider here is, where possible, to select a UK-based platform, as it would appear that any legal challenge to your work would need to take place in the UK, if that is where you are practising. If in doubt, discuss with your insurer at the outset.

Is your insurance fit for purpose?

The professional journals are weighed down with ads for professional indemnity insurance. You should ensure that your insurance, both business and professional indemnity, cover what you do, for example, working cross-border, and via different technological conduits whether this be video-conferencing, email, via a forum, text or other. Steve Johnson (2013) of Oxygen commented:

> Psychotherapists are traditionally trained to work either on a one to one or group basis with clients who are present in the same room as the therapist. The main advantage of "New Media" work is also its main drawback—the client is somewhere else! The fact that the client is somewhere else could be a problem and therapists should check with their insurers that their policy covers work where the client might be overseas. The Oxygen policy is worldwide and so this is not a problem for those insured with us. We are also relaxed about the method of delivery of your therapeutic intervention, be it face to face, telephone, Skype, email, or direct messaging but again, our advice is to check with your insurer.

Publicity and promotion

Publicity, PR, advertising, and marketing are all subjects that exist in the real world business plan. However, the Internet leads to new horizons.

The aim of publicity is to attract new customers, but along with the online world of land and plenty there are the dangers of spending a fortune for little return. A good website is invaluable. You will need to decide what you want your website to do: usually a website will educate and inform, gather details, provide sales and have a payments section (ecommerce), and act as a marketing and PR tool. Truffo (2007) states that eighty per cent of the website content should be directed to the client, and only twenty per cent should be about the practitioner. You may want to take some advice before marketing yourself online so that you do not waste money on unnecessary advertising, or make errors in what you put online.

What about joining a directory?

You have done the training, you have set up the system, and now all you need is clients. Whilst established therapists might attract clients without too much difficulty, the rest of us have to follow the usual route and make some pragmatic decisions about how to get going as a business. If you are in that group then you might wish to sign up to a directory or join an e-clinic, rather similar to the one-stop-shop that I've already spoken about, except that they provide the platform, including all those items, and you pay for the benefit of buying into this service. Although there are costs in joining an e-clinic there are also many savings, so for example, you won't need to worry about payments. It's also a good way to start, as you bolt into an existing structure whilst at the same time developing your own website which can be allied to the e-clinic. Anthony and Nagel (2010) highlight eight pointers that you should consider and research when selecting an e-clinic: professional image, practitioner screening, client screening, reputation, solvency, marketing, reliability, record storage including confidentiality and encryption. Examples of online directories and e-clinics in existence are http://www.itsgoodtotalk.org.uk/therapists/, http://psychcentral.com/, http://mytherapynet.com/, http://www.onlineclinics.com/, http://www.acto-uk.org/seekingatherapist.htm. (Please note the inclusion of these web addresses does not constitute endorsement or recommendation by either the author or UKCP.)

The main issue that I have with the e-clinics that I have seen is that none of them are British-based. Legally and contractually I believe that all practitioners need to have their basis for online work through a

UK-based web platform, remembering all the earlier discussion about language, culture, and jurisdiction.

Conclusion

To conclude, I have attempted to give you some insight into all the dimensions and considerations concerning online practice. Any one of these areas is worthy of a chapter or book of its own and should therefore only be viewed as a taster. I hope you will feel sufficiently inspired to explore further, either by reading some of my colleagues' books on the subject or by doing some additional training. One way UKCP members can immediately get some additional support is to join UKCP's new media special interest group. The information is on the UKCP website, http://www.psychotherapy.org.uk/new_media_in_psychotherapy_sig.html

Commentator one: Tamara Alferoff

Before agreeing to work with a client online, I ask her to email me an outline of her main issues. If I decide to take her on, there would have to be a signed contract with a commitment to keep our work private and confidential, to bring to the therapy feelings and difficulties as they arise, and to regularly attend insofar as possible, with an agreed fall-back position for the inevitable hitches in either technology or personal situation of both client and therapist.

It's clear from the information we have about Jackie that she suffers from separation anxiety and consequent panics and rages. The web is not an ideal setting for working with such issues, which indicate a firm container with good boundaries, and a regular contracted series of sessions. It's too easy for Jackie to simply press Delete, or to act out in the public arena her rage and grievances, with potentially destructive consequences for the therapy, the therapist, and Jackie herself (successful matricide). I'd have second thoughts about taking on such a client for online work.

Of course, in-person clients can also simply stop coming, cancel sessions, and tell others how terrible you are, but there is a different quality in the online setting, in that it can be simply a click of a button, an impulsive action, whereas a decision to not show up for your in-person session tends to appear a weightier matter with greater consequences.

Some questions raised by Tamara that may be useful for your consideration

- Your client may ask to Friend you on Facebook. How do you respond?
- You love to post pictures of your family, travel photos, your home, food, evenings out, parties, anecdotes on Facebook. How do you select what is OK, how do you share with those people you want to see them, and not with the whole world (including your clients)?
- You've recently started working online, and realise that some of the history you've shared on Facebook might jeopardise the safety of the therapeutic relationship. What can you do about that?
- Do you know you can open a Facebook Group page that is so secret, no-one can even search for it. You could use this as a secure forum for you and the client to post comments, or to share pictures/quotes. This is also a good forum for an online group to communicate.
- Your client is a dab hand at texting (SMS). She tends to send long messages about her anxiety, or how her relationship is doing, or how she wants to stop seeing you starting with the next session. How can you take pre-emptive measure to ensure that texting doesn't take the place of one-to-one live conversation (whether F2F or online)?
- How will *you* use texting with your clients? Will you?
- Do you have a secure and separate mailbox for clients? Does each client get his or her own mailbox or do all the mails go into the client box?
- If a F2F or Skype client writes a lengthy email, how do you respond? Have you sent up parameters for this eventuality? (I have moved away from email therapy where I started with online work—in favour of the more immediate live real-time methods).
- Silence your phones—but keep them in the room as part of your back-up system if the Internet fails.
- How do you send a recording of the online session to your client? Or do you? Do they record overtly or covertly?

Commentator two: Anne Stokes

It seems that Clare has made the classic mistake of equating good IT skills with an ability to counsel online. While some of the counselling skills are the same as in F2F work, there are also subtle and not so subtle differences when working with clients while using technology. Sound training enables these to be explored, and through role-plays, experience for yourself what it is like to be a client as well as a counsellor. As stated earlier in the chapter, these courses need to take place online, to replicate the issues arising in online work.

Online clients are just as likely to express anger or act out as F2F ones, but they may be tempted to do this in a more public way, as Jackie did. This can be both damaging and painful for the counsellor. In training, such issues are explored; while this cannot entirely prevent clients using social media to discuss counselling, it may go some way to avoiding it. Differences between online and F2F contracts are a key feature in training—so often difficulties arise through poor contracting. If Clare and Jackie had discussed this at the contracting stage, it might not have happened.

Disinhibition is often experienced in training groups, and causes all sorts of interesting group dynamics! While these are hard to work through at the time, they do help counsellors to be more grounded when facing their equivalent with clients. If Clare had trained online, she would be in a better position to move forward with Jackie.

After online training, she could become a member of ACTO (Association for Counsellors and Therapists Online) alongside other professional memberships. It is necessary to have had a specific online training to join. You then have back-up from a professional organisation offering support, a platform (online of course!) to discuss online issues, a network of counsellors working in the same field, and perhaps most importantly, a safety network for clients, with a register of trained online counsellors and a complaints procedure. ACTO also offers a register of online supervisors.

Commentator three: Biljana van Rijn

Philippa raises pertinent questions in this chapter, important for any therapist who works online, whether solely or by mixing online with face-to-face sessions. This area of work is increasingly relevant to any practitioner. As a long-standing psychotherapist and tutor, I have found myself needing to learn about the appropriate use of the new methods of communication in my practice. Reflection on issues of confidentially, boundaries, and risk in each new medium was of utmost importance and usually brought up new learning for me.

The use of online communication is clearly relevant to psychotherapy training. Reflective practice in this realm is as indispensable as it is in any other area of the therapeutic dialogue. Digital communication also has its own characteristics, some of which have been introduced by the author. Therapists and training programmes would benefit from having information about them and an opportunity to reflect on how this impacts the therapeutic frame and the content of the sessions.

Another potential for online work relates to developing psychotherapy training, normally delivered face-to-face. Online media could have a potential to increase access to training, develop curriculum, and share expertise. This raises questions about the appropriateness, the scope, and the teaching methods that could be used. What could be taught online? What would be the ratio of face-to-face training to online material? Would this type of training be more appropriate at a post-qualification level, or could it be useful in earlier training? A combination of online training with face-to-face sessions, already practiced by universities in different fields, could have a potential to increase access to training to people with disabilities, disadvantaged groups, and international students, just as online practice has a potential to increase access to therapy. In my view, we need to step into this field mindfully and explore its potential, whilst maintaining ethical values and principles of psychotherapy and counselling.

Notes

1. Stephen Goss, public comments made at the OCTIA Conference, March 2013, Bristol.
2. Guidelines for online counselling and psychotherapy 3rd edition including Guidelines for online supervision, British Association for Counselling & Psychotherapy, Kate Anthony and Stephen Goss, 2009.
3. http://onlinetherapyinstitute.com/ethical-framework-for-the-use-of-social-media-by-mental-health-professionals/ retrieved 12 May 2013.
4. Dr Rachel O'Connell, Jane Chapman, and Dr Richard Graham https://www.facebook.com/rampguide/
5. http://www.europsyche.org/
6. The International Society for Mental Health Online (ISMHO) https://www.ismho.org/

7. http://uk.news.yahoo.com/facebook-graph-search--how-to-stop-facebook-s-new-search-revealing-your-old-photos-110354038.html
8. http://onlinetherapyinstitute.com/ethical-framework-for-the-use-of-social-media-by-mental-health-professionals/ retrieved 12 May 2013.
9. Dr Rachel O'Connell, Jane Chapman, and Dr Richard Graham https://www.facebook.com/rampguide/
10. http://en.wikipedia.org/wiki/Proprietary_software; retrieved 13 May 2013.

References

Anthony, K. (2000). Counselling in cyberspace. *Counselling, 11*: 625–627.

Anthony, K., & Nagel, D. M. (2010). *Therapy Online: A Practical Guide.* London: Sage.

Bolton, G., Howlett, S., Lago, C., & Wright, J. K. (2004). *Writing Cures: Introductory Handbook of Writing in Counselling and Psychotherapy.* Hove: Brunner-Routledge.

Bor, R., & Stokes, A. (2011). *Setting Up in Independent Practice: A Handbook for Therapy and Psychology Practitioners.* Basingstoke: Palgrave Macmillan.

Buckingham, D. (2013). Making sense of the "digital generation": Growing up with digital media. *Self & Society, 40*: 7–15.

Curtis, N. (2013). Beware—you're fair game once your data's digital. In: *Evening Standard.* Friday 11 October 2013, p. 15.

Dunn, K. (2011). How does meeting online impact the therapeutic relationship? *Counselling & Psychotherapy Research, 22*: 8.

Dunn, K. (2013). The therapeutic alliance online. Paper delivered to the UKCP New Media Special Interest Group 23 March 2013.

Evans, J. (2009). *Online Counselling and Guidance Skills: A Practitioner Resource for Trainees and Practitioners.* London. Sage.

Feltham, C. (2013). We are citizens of the world. An interview with Courtland Lee. *Therapy Today, 24*: 36–37.

Fenichel, M., Suler, J., Barak, A., Zelvin, E., Jones, G., Munro, K., & Walker-Schmucker, W. (2002). Myths and realities of online clinical work. Observations on the phemomena of online behavior, experience and therapeutic relationships. A 3rd year report from ISMHO's Clinical Case Study Group. Retrieved 4 October 2006 from http://www.fenichel.com/myths/

Fink J. (1999). *How to Use Computers and Cyberspace in the Clinical Practice of Psychotherapy.* Northvale, NJ: Aronson.

Hanley T., & Reynolds, D. (2009). Technology and counselling psychology: Therapy, research and practice. *Counselling Psychology Review, 24*: 4–14.

Horvath, A. O., & Luborsky, L. (1993). The role of the therapeutic alliance in psychotherapy. *Journal of Consulting and Clinical Psychology, 61*: 561–573.

Johnson, S. (2013). *Psychotherapy in the New Media—An insurance perspective from Oxygen Insurance.* Unpublished.

Jones, G., & Stokes, A. (2009). *Online Counselling—A Handbook for Practitioners.* London: Palgrave Macmillan.

McMahon, G., Wilding, C., & Palmer, S. (Eds.) (2005). *The Essential Skills for Setting Up a Counselling and Psychotherapy Practice.* London: Routledge.

O'Connell, R., Chapman, J., & Graham, R. https://www.facebook.com/rampguide/ Retrieved 12 May 2013.

http://onlinetherapyinstitute.com/ethical-framework-for-the-use-of-social-media-by-mental-health-professionals/ Retrieved 12 May 2013.

Quashie, R. (2013). Skype & HIPAA: The vexing question. *TILT, 2*: 43–47.

Starks, S. (2012). Distance counselling survey. *TILT, 2*: 59–66.

Suler, J. (1997). Psychological Dynamics of Online Synchronous Conversations in Text-Driven Chat Environments. www.rider.edu/users/suler/psycyber/texttalk.html Retrieved 12 May 2013.

Suler, J. (1997). The Psychology of Cyberspace. www.rider.edu/users/suler/psycyber/presence.html Retrieved 12 May 2013.

Suler, J. (2004). The online disinhibition effect. *CyberPsychology and Behavior, 7*: 321–326.

Truffo, C. (2007). Be a wealthy therapist: Finally you can make a living whilst making a difference. *Psychotherapy Networker, 33*: 42–29.

Walker, M. (2007). *Mental Health Treatment Online.* London: Digital Inclusion Team.

Weitz, P. (2006). *Setting Up and Maintaining an Effective Private Practice: A Practical Workbook for Mental Health Practitioners.* London: Karnac.

http://en.wikipedia.org/wiki/Proprietary_software retrieved 13 May 2013.

PART III

WORKING SAFELY AND LEGALLY IN THE CONTEXT OF INTERNATIONAL LAW

CHAPTER NINE

Developing ethical delivery of cross-border services

Kate Anthony, Stephen Goss, and DeeAnna Nagel

Case study

Jan is an experienced F2F therapist who also has training in life coaching. At a recent conference, she had been talking to a colleague who mentioned that he, Paul, was currently seeing a client who had moved to California, and they discussed how wonderful the Internet is to enable contracts to continue despite geographic difference. Paul was happy to use different ways of communicating with his client—the Googlemail system he uses is adequate, he thinks, and everybody seems to be using Skype these days. He's not sure what chat is, but feels he could probably work it out if clients wanted to use it. He had a website put together by a friend, and charges clients via PayPal. He can fit the work around his full-time job as a clinical service manager if the sessions are email based, and has even heard of people working through avatars in Second Life. When Jan asks him what he did to set up as an online practitioner, he states that he just did it. He only has the one client at the moment, but is looking into using Twitter, Facebook, and LinkedIn to market to clients. He is particularly pleased that he can market to therapy and coach clients at the same time from just the one website.

Jan is very interested in what Paul has to say. She does, however, have a feeling that the simplicity of what he has done may be misleading, and she is not quite sure how client session material going back and forth on the Internet can be kept confidential. She is good at writing, she is aware, and thinks that a therapeutic or coaching relationship done via text would be a good move for her to supplement her face-to-face practice. She is not sure she would want to use video with clients, but is prepared to learn how to do it in the future in case her practice could develop into offering that, once she was used to other methods of using new technologies to communicate. She is comfortable with computers and the Internet, although not as expert as her son and daughter, and starts Googling "online therapy" to find more information.

During her search, she comes across several training programmes that she thinks will inform her practice in going online. She is nervous of just going and doing it, and sees a lot of coach and therapist websites that seem to be rather amateur and lacking information. She considers what she doesn't know, and decides that post-graduate training would be sensible for her. She chooses her trainers and starts her online training course.

The following year, she meets up with Paul again at the same conference. He asks her how work is, and she responds happily, explaining that the chat they had the previous year had completely changed the way she works. She has two websites with a secure encrypted application form for clients to complete, and offers both email work and chat to therapy clients and also coaching clients. She is aware that having one website to cater to both processes was resulting in her own boundaries as to what she was doing—counselling or coaching—being very blurred. She found that having separate websites addressed that.

Her training explained to her the importance of encryption to protect client data, and she understands that crossing global borders is more complicated than it seems because there are different laws in different parts of the world. She knows that while Skype is encrypted, it is not fit for this purpose because Microsoft can access client material as they choose (and might even be in the right if they were to publish it online). She has a Twitter account that she uses to send positive imagery to her followers, but prefers to keep her Facebook account for friends and her LinkedIn profile for colleagues as she has learnt about how quickly dual relationships can form online without a social media policy for clients to read. She uses a Hushmail account for online work sometimes, but also licences a US communication platform as she knows the importance of leaning on experts who develop such platforms ethically. She has a strong support network online and utilises online peer supervision regularly.

While she knows there is no guarantee that there will not be a client complaint regarding her online practice, she is aware that even after completing her training she needs to keep up to speed with research and development. She is relaxed to know that her route to practicing online demonstrates best current practice should there be a complaint.

The authors of this chapter have been engaged in the discussion, creation, and development of ethical guidelines for the use of technology in mental health for over twelve years, dating back to the late 1990s when the International Society for Mental Health Online (ISMHO) created the first distinguishable set of guidelines for mental health professionals.

Traditionally a controversial topic within the profession, there has been much debate as to whether separate guidance is required in using technology to deliver mental health services and, if so, what that guidance should look like. Moreover, with technology creating a fast-paced turnaround of ethical issues to consider, guidance runs the risk of becoming moribund almost as soon as paper publication happens.

The caution with which online counselling has been approached by the profession was well placed. Schools of thought tended to fall into two camps—either, on the one hand, outright rejection of the concept of an electronic element being present in a human-to-human relationship or, on the other, grasping the concept with little thought as to how it should be done ethically.

These are, however, now historical positions to take. What has emerged over the last ten years is a realisation that however we feel about it, technological development in the world is unstoppable. The Internet and mobile technology has changed society radically—it is no longer good enough to ignore it or treat it as something to be enjoyed by geeks. The future generations of clients and counsellors will grow up not knowing an unconnected world. These future digital citizens will find the concept of *not* offering services, or at least researching them, through the Internet extraordinary. When Web 2.0 came into being, this process became complete—humans are much more likely to be in communication electronically than they are F2F. According to research by the networking group Cisco, there will be more Internet connected mobile devices than people in the world by the end of 2013 (Arthur, 2013), and sixty-five per cent of the population in the developed world currently own at least two such devices.

However, we are not here to present an argument against face-to-face physical therapy as it is traditionally understood to take place in the consulting room. Our position is that human therapeutic interaction now has many different ways in which it can be manifested, and one of those technologies is the chair that we and our clients sit upon. As Douglas Adams put it in 1999, we no longer think of chairs as technology, we just think of them as chairs. In this way, and by treating the traditional face-to-face relationship as another technology, the choices we have in being change-agents for our clients in an electronically connected world gives us the potential to cross borders, time zones, disability issues, and to allow this to enable an overhaul of the profession via healthy debate. One aspect of that debate is the provision of ethical guidelines, suggested principals, competency frameworks, and similar.

Historically, professional organisations have been quite dogmatic about giving guidelines to work ethically while delivering services electronically. Increasingly, training is being looked at less as a specialist area and more of a mainstream need. Much of the early guidance such as that from the British Association for Counselling and Psychotherapy (BACP) and the American Psychological Association (APA) carried cautionary notes that the field of online therapy was only just emerging, and that professional organisations carried a desire to reserve judgment until definitive information was available. Early mentions of the concept of electronically delivered services were welcomed, but also provided little insight into how practitioners should handle the particular concerns that doing so raise.

In a global community that is sometimes regulated, as in the USA, with tight legalities such as the Health Insurance Portability and Accountability Act (HIPAA), but is also unregulated in many countries, such as the UK, this way of working brings an awareness of particular ethical concerns. To address ethical considerations of working online from an international perspective, the authors created a framework that could be applied internationally without being dogmatic. The concept of the framework came from taking the best information from five organisations (BACP, NBCC, APA, ISMHO, and EthicsCode.com) and loosening the material enough for practitioners to be able to apply it to their services as they best fit. It is our intention to provide a framework that raises questions and lively debate, such as: What information does a UK practitioner need when the initial enquiry for counselling comes from Africa? At what point can a US therapist cross state lines and take advantage of electronic communication such as email? In a country where therapy is not regulated at all, what is to stop anyone building a website and starting to charge clients to talk to them?

Training in online therapy is not yet a stipulation of practice anywhere in the world. What we do have, however, is a moral compass that guides our work. While not compulsory, seeking training from experts is generally a moral decision, as is choosing all our continuing professional development work in any field. Complaints against practitioners involving the use of electronic devices are growing, and demonstration of best practice dictates seeking knowledge through training. Training programmes have been available internationally for over ten years, both as a stand-alone training and/or part of an organisation's internal human resource provision. Knowledge of ethical thinking over the years is an integral part of offering an ethical online service. In light of that, we offer the ethical framework for the use of technology in mental health (Nagel & Anthony, 2009) to readers to inform and help practice, both for individuals and organisations, hopefully inciting discussion and analysis of best practice procedure.

Ethical framework for the use of technology in mental health

A competent practitioner working online will always adhere to at least the following minimum standards and practices in order to be considered to be working in an ethical manner.

Practitioners require a basic understanding of technology

Technology basics are required for practitioners who choose to deliver therapeutic services via technology. Practitioners will possess a basic understanding of technology as the technology relates to delivery of services:

- **Encryption**: Practitioners understand how to access encrypted services to store records and deliver communication. Records storage can be hosted on a secure server with a third-party, stored on the practitioner's hard drive utilising encrypted folders, or stored on an external drive that is safely stored.
- **Backup systems**: Records and data that are stored on the practitioner's hard drive are backed up either to an external drive or remotely via the Internet.
- **Password protection**: Practitioners take further steps to ensure confidentiality of therapeutic communication and other materials by password-protecting the computer, drives, and stored files or communication websites.
- **Firewalls**: Practitioners utilise firewall protection externally or through web-based programs.
- **Virus protection**: Practitioners protect work computers from viruses that can be received from or transmitted to others, including clients.
- **Hardware**: Practitioners understand the basic running platform of the work computer and know whether or not a client's hardware/platform is compatible with any communication programs the practitioner uses.
- **Software**: Practitioners know how to download and operate software and assist clients with the same when necessary to the delivery of services.
- **Third-party services**: Practitioners utilise third-party services that offer an address and phone number so that contact is possible via means other than email. This offers a modicum of trust in the third party utilised for such services as backup, storage, virus protection, and communication.

Practitioners work within their scope of practice

Scope of practice indicates the specific area to which a practitioner may practice. Scope of practice in many geographic areas also defines where a practitioner may practice; whether the practitioner may practice across various geographical boundaries and within what parameters a practitioner may practice. Practitioners also follow local and regional laws and codes of ethics as applicable:

- **Understanding of boundaries and limitations of one's specific discipline**: Practitioners understand which assessments and interventions are allowed within their specific discipline. For instance, career counsellors who have no training in mental health issues generally do not provide psychotherapy services.
- **Understanding of specific laws or ethics within one's own discipline or geographic location**: Practitioners understand the limits set forth by laws or ethics within the applicable geographic location. For instance, in the United States, licenced professional counsellors cannot call themselves Psychologists, and in the UK the term "Chartered Psychologist" is reserved by law for use only by those with proper recognition from the appropriate authorities. Certain states dictate what a practitioner can be called due to the implementation of title laws. Practice laws may prevent a licenced practitioner from interpreting certain personality tests in one state, yet the same practice may be accepted under practice law in another state.
- **Respect for the specific laws of a potential client's geographic location**: Practitioners understand that different geographic regions may offer additional limits to practice, particularly with regard to jurisdiction. For instance, a counsellor in the UK should be cognisant of the laws of a client who resides in a US state such as California in which the law prohibits consumers residing in California from engaging in counselling from a practitioner who is not licenced in California.

Practitioners seek out training, knowledge, and supervision

Training, knowledge, and supervision regarding mental health and technology is paramount to delivering a standard of care that is considered "best practice" within one's geographic region and within a global context. Practitioners are encouraged to demonstrate proficiency and competency through formal specialist training for online work, books, peer-reviewed literature, and popular media. Clinical and/or peer supervision and support are mandated for practitioners who cannot practice independently within a geographic region and is highly recommended for all practitioners.

- **Formal training**: Practitioners seek out sufficient formal training whenever possible through college, university, or private settings. Formal training is displayed on the practitioner's website.

- **Informal training**: Practitioners seek out continuing education and professional development and conferences, conventions, and workshops.
- **Books**: Practitioners read books written by the general public and professionals.
- **Peer-reviewed literature**: Practitioners read peer-reviewed literature that includes the latest theories and research.
- **Popular media**: Practitioners are informed through popular media such as magazines, newspapers, social networking sites, websites, television, and movies and understand the impact of mental health and technology on popular culture.
- **Clinical/peer supervision**: Practitioners seek clinical supervision whenever the practitioner cannot practice independently within his or her geographic location. Clinical and/or peer supervision is sought by all practitioners who deliver services via technology. Clinical and peer supervision is delivered either face-to-face or via encrypted methods.

Example topics of study related to training, knowledge, and supervision (not an exhaustive list):

- Online therapy
- Online clinical supervision
- Online peer supervision
- Avatar therapy
- Cyberpsychology
- Text-based therapy
- Telehealth
- Behavioural telehealth
- Telepsychiatry
- Internet addictions
- Social media
- Mixed reality
- Online relationships
- Second Life
- Online peer support
- SMS text messaging
- Virtual worlds
- Virtual reality
- Mental health and technology.

*Practitioners display pertinent and necessary
information on websites*

Websites provide access to information for the general public, potential clients, clients, and other professionals:

- **Crisis intervention information**: People may surf the Internet seeking immediate help. Practitioners display crisis intervention information on the home page. Practitioners understand that people in crisis may visit the website from anywhere in the world. Offering global resources such as Befriender's International or Samaritans is the best course of action.

- **Practitioner contact information**: Practitioners offer contact information that includes email, post address, and a telephone or VOIP number. While it is not recommended that post addresses reflect the practitioner's home location, clients should have a post address for formal correspondence related to redress, subpoenas, or other mailings requiring a signature of receipt. Practitioners state the amount of time an individual may wait for a reply to email or voice mail. Best practice indicates a maximum of two business days for therapeutic inquiries.

- **Practitioner education, licence, and/or certification information**: Practitioners list degrees, licences, and/or certifications as well as corresponding numbers. If the licence, certification board, or professional body offers a website that allows the general public to verify information on a particular practitioner the licence and certification listings should link directly to those verifying body websites. Practitioners consider listing other formal education such as college or university courses, online continuing education, and professional development courses, and conference/convention attendance directly related to mental health and technology.

- **Terms of use and privacy policy**: Terms of use, often all or in part, synonymous with a practitioner's informed consent, are available on the website either as a page on the website or a downloadable document. The practitioner's privacy policy is also available in the same way and offers information about if or how email addresses, credit card information, and client records are used, shared, or stored. Practitioners must ensure that they comply with the requirements of the Data Protection Act and other aspects of applicable law, and, in the United States, practitioners display the Notice of Privacy Practices to indicate compliance with HIPAA. Applicable information regarding privacy and confidentiality that are required for patient consent in the geographic location of the practitioner should be posted on the website as well.

- **Encrypted transmission of therapeutic and payment information**: Practitioners offer secure and encrypted means of therapeutic communication and payment transactions. Email and Chat programs, whether embedded within the practitioner site (private practice or e-clinic) or utilising third party platforms such as Hushmail or Cryptoheaven, are explained on the website. Payment methods are explained as well through merchant information or information provided by the practitioner.

Practitioners conduct an initial intake and screening process

The initial screening and intake process begins with the potential client's first contact. The practitioner implements formal and informal measures for screening a client's suitability for delivery of mental health services via technology:

- **Client's technology skills**: Practitioners screen potential client's use of technology through questions at the outset. Questions include but are not limited to an inquiry about the client's experience with online culture e.g., email, chat rooms, forums, social networks, instant messaging, and online purchasing, mobile texting, VOIP, or telephones. Practitioners ensure that the client's platform is compatible with the varying programs and platforms the practitioner may utilise during the course of therapy.
- **Client's language skills**. Practitioners screen for language skills from the initial contact through the first few exchanges. Assessing for language barriers, reading and comprehension skills as well as cultural differences, is part of the screening process. Text-based therapy may also involve screening for keyboarding proficiency.
- **Presenting issue, client identity, and clinical concerns**: Practitioners screen to ensure the presenting issue is within the scope of practice and knowledge base of the practitioner. Screening around issues of suicidality, homicidality, and immediate crisis are formally addressed through an intake questionnaire or first exchange. Practitioners incorporate a mechanism for verifying identity of clients by asking for a formal identification number such as Driver's Licence or other

satisfactory method. The client must not be anonymous, offering at a minimum: first and last name, home address, and phone number for emergency contact. Minors must be identified through parental consent. If client identity is not required, such as is the case with crisis hotlines and triage settings, limitations of the service are stated clearly. Other concerns regarding mental stability are addressed, for example, client currently hallucinating or delusional; actively using drugs and alcohol so that insight-oriented interventions would not be suitable; and any other medical or physical issues that might impede the intervention or require a different method of delivery, for example, disability that impairs typing, rendering a chat exchange cost-prohibitive. Any assessment instruments that are utilised should be approved for online or computer-assisted use according to the test author/publisher.

Practitioners offer an informed consent process

The informed consent process begins when the client contemplates accessing services. Therefore, clear and precise information is accessible via the practitioner's website. The informed consent process includes a formal acknowledgement from the client to the practitioner. This acknowledgement is received via encrypted channels. Informed consent content is revisited during the course of therapy as necessary and beneficial.

The following topics are addressed within informed consent:

- **Possible advantages and disadvantages of online therapy**: Information is disseminated about the pros and cons of online therapy including such disadvantages as lack of visual and auditory cues and the limitations of confidentiality via technology, and advantages that include easy scheduling, time management, and a no need to incur transportation costs.

Confidentiality and technology

- **Encryption**: An explanation about the use of encryption for therapeutic exchanges and lack of encryption if/when unencrypted methods (standard email, forum posts, mobile telephone, SMS texting, social networking) are used for issues such as appointment changes and cancellations.

- **Therapist as owner of the record**: Unless otherwise specified through law in the practitioner's geographic location, the therapist remains the owner of the therapeutic record including all transcripts, notes, and emails. The client is informed that posting direct information about the therapist or verbatim information from sessions is prohibited.
- **File storage procedures**: The client is informed about how records are stored (web-based, third party, or hard-drive/external drive) and for how long the records are maintained. All procedures conform to the standards laid down in applicable law and as required by any relevant authority (such as a professional body) and, at least, include encryption and password protection and a commitment to destroy all records after a given period as required by law/regulation/best practice.
- **Privacy policy**: The practitioner's privacy policy is also included in the informed consent process including information about how email addresses, credit card information, and client records are used, shared, or stored. In the United States, practitioners must include the Notice of Privacy Practices to indicate compliance with HIPAA. Applicable information regarding privacy and confidentiality that are required for patient consent in the geographic location of the practitioner are included in the informed consent process.

Other informed consent issues

- **Practitioner's geographical jurisdiction**: The physical location of the practitioner is offered in the informed consent and if the practitioner is licenced within a specific jurisdiction, the informed consent states that the client understands that services are rendered under the laws or jurisdiction of the relevant country, state, or region.
- **How to proceed during a technology breakdown**: The client is informed about how to proceed if a technology breakdown occurs during a session, for example, "If we disconnect, try to reconnect within ten minutes. If reconnection is not possible, email or call to reschedule an appointment."
- **Emergency contact**: Practitioners offer specific information about who to contact in case of an emergency and set specific rules about emergency emails that the practitioner may not be privy to, for

example, suicidal emails in the middle of the night, threatening posts on a support forum. Practitioners research local resources within the client's geographic area as emergency backup resources.

- **Cultural specifics that may impact treatment**: Practitioners discuss varying time zones, cultural differences, and language barriers that may impact the delivery of services. Practitioners should also ensure at or prior to the start of therapy, that the client's expectations of the service being offered (such as the meaning of the term "counselling", etc.) is sufficiently close to their own understanding and should take into account that different cultures around the world can have very different understandings of these matters.
- **Dual relationships**: Practitioners discuss with clients the expected boundaries and expectations about forming relationships online. Practitioners inform clients that any requests for "friendship", business contacts, direct or @replies, blog responses, or requests for a blog response within social media sites will be ignored to preserve the integrity of the therapeutic relationship and protect confidentiality. If the client has not been formally informed of these boundaries prior to the practitioner receiving the request, the practitioner will ignore the request via the social media site and explain why in subsequent interaction with the client.
- **Insurance, subsidy, or reimbursement information**: If the client resides in a geographic area that generally accepts insurance or other forms of reimbursement for therapy services, the practitioner informs the client of this information. Conversely, if services are delivered via technologies that are not covered at all or at the same rate, the practitioner informs the client of this information also.

Conclusion

Having read the introductory case study and the ethical framework that follows, one can see that not only does the framework offer guidance for the clinician offering services online but also becomes a reference point for other professional organisations that may be grappling with the inclusion of technology delivery into their updated codes and guidelines. Now that a standard of care has been established in the field through peer-reviewed literature including qualitative and quantitative studies,[1] more and more professional organisations that represent the helping professions are willing to embrace the use of technology and encourage the delivery of services through electronic means.

Commentator one: Professor Tim Bond

I recognise the professional landscape and choices set out in this chapter. Online therapy offers both opportunity and threat for therapists. I pitched myself straight into the opposing views on this issue when I was speaking recently at a large meeting of counsellors. In a talk about new technologies and therapy, I suggested that we ought to be mindful of what happens to businesses in other sectors who do not take up the opportunities offered by digital communications and new methods of service delivery. Provocatively, I added, "Do we want to be the next Woolworths?" (This was a large national chain of department stores that disappeared rather unexpectedly but very rapidly because it couldn't update its business practices or take on new technology effectively.) Some therapists were outraged and asserted their commitment to face-to-face ways of working. Others were enthusiastic about escaping some of the physical constraints of the old ways of working but probably not recognising the challenges. These responses fall into the two opposing camps set out in the opening sections of this chapter.

However, there was a new position evident in the room: practitioners who were already engaged with delivering therapy online as part of their work and thoughtfully engaging with the new ethical and technological challenges that they faced. The ethical framework offered in this chapter answers many of the questions that I know preoccupy these early adopters. I am instinctively cautious in reaching ethical conclusions about new fields of activity. Real experience so often contradicts imagined possibilities. However, I think it is becoming clear that that there are no new paradigmatic changes in the ethics of digital and cross-border therapy. Providing a safe and effective therapeutic environment, protecting client privacy, contracting, and managing/avoiding dual relationships, working across cultural and legal differences, are familiar ethical challenges. What this chapter shows is that new means of delivering therapy frequently contain the technological solutions when therapists are resourceful and wise enough to use them. The ethical challenges are familiar; the solutions may be new.

Commentator two: Steve Johnson

If we come at this from the standpoint that anything involving cross-border trading is going to be complex, then the reality might, actually, be a pleasant surprise!

One important thing to think about when working with clients in overseas territories is not necessarily where you are located at the time but where you are based. That will usually mean where you are domiciled or resident, or if you are a limited company, where you are registered. Portable devices and easy Internet access will allow us to work away from our home country and a good professional liability insurer should be ok with that.

Our "home" country is important because that is where any legal action being contemplated against us is likely to be brought. This is because those bringing the legal action will be seeking compensation and the easiest way to achieve that is to bring the legal action in the jurisdiction that is able to enforce any judgements against your assets. Of course, you will have professional liability insurance in place to protect those assets, but the point remains valid.

It is also important that your contract with the client states that the contract is subject to the jurisdiction of the laws of the UK (England and Wales, Scotland, etc., or your home country). While this will not prevent a legal action being taken against you in an unfavourable territory (USA, for example) it will give you grounds to challenge or resist such an action. If in any doubt about this you should consult a lawyer when drafting your contract.

Of course, if you have assets abroad (that holiday home in Florida, perhaps?) and, particularly, if you are doing work with clients who are also based in that territory, bear in mind that they could chose to bring any legal action there and potentially use those assets to secure their compensation. Any combination of assets and work done in overseas territories is definitely something to discuss with your professional liability insurer.

Note

1. Internet Assisted Therapy and Counselling Research Resources at—http://construct.haifa.ac.il/ azy/refthrp.htm and http://www.career.fsu.edu/documents/Distance%20Counseling_7_22.pdf

References

Adams, D. (1999). How to stop worrying and learn to love the internet. At http://www.douglasadams.com/dna/19990901-00-a.html

Arthur, C. (2013). Internet devices soon to outnumber people. *The Guardian*, 9 January 2013.

Internet Assisted Therapy and Counselling Research Resources at http://construct.haifa.ac.il/~azy/refthrp.htm and http://www.career.fsu.edu/documents/Distance%20Counseling_7_22.pdf.

Nagel, D. M., & Anthony, K. (2009). Ethical framework for the use of technology in mental health. In: Anthony, K. & Nagel, D. M. (2009). *Therapy online: A Practical Guide*. London: Sage.

CHAPTER TEN

Protecting children and young people—the "online" generation

Aqualma Murray

Internet abuse is unfortunately extremely common, none more so than for young people who regularly choose to communicate via websites and mobile phones, such as blackberry pin, viber, and whatsapp. Children and young people are extremely vulnerable to Internet abuse, and this directly impinges on child protections issues. For this reason the first section of this chapter is more general, as both the online and the face-to-face practitioner need to be grounded in the issues of child protection and have their internal radars constantly on, with all clients, whether this might be concerning a direct issue as related in a session by a client or an issue further down the line with a family member or friend of the client.

In this chapter we will include: the risks of sexual abuse that children and young people are exposed to; some of the issues that make some children more vulnerable than others to Internet abuse; the difference in how sex offenders target their victims online; what action can be taken to assist children in keeping themselves safe; and the impact of experiencing online abuse and how this may affect the emotional and mental health of children and young people as well as those that are most vulnerable. These sections are included by way of background information necessary for all practitioners, as clues and indicators of child protection and the risks to look out for in clinical practice.

Centrally, the chapter covers methods of keeping children safe and what counsellors and therapists need to be aware of when working with young people and children via online systems.

Technical social media has propelled professionals, therapists, and counsellors to adopt forms of online communication with a range of service users, including children and teenagers. As a result we are faced with the task of considering how these methods of communication can enhance our client contact and some of the pitfalls it may produce.

It is true to say that a number of young people may find it easier to make contact with a therapist via online contact as they are used to communicating this way, and counselling or therapy via this means may feel more acceptable to them rather than the traditional consulting room.

In order for counsellors and therapists to offer a full and comprehensive therapeutic input it is important that online child protection awareness is available and considered by all professionals and those with primary care of children and young people.

Case study

Callum is fifteen years old; he has access to Facebook and other social networking sites. Callum was contacted by a person he believed to be a young woman of fourteen years old who requested that he accept her as a "friend", claiming that she was in contact with some of his other friends on Facebook

Callum accepted her as a "friend" and pretty soon they were chatting away about the local clubs in the area and naming other friends on the site. Sometime soon after they had chatted on a few occasions the girl told Callum that she liked him and wanted him to show her parts of his body on a webcam, and that after agreeing that if he would do so she would also reveal parts of herself.

Callum wanted her to go first, so she sent him some still pictures of herself in a bra. Callum responded by revealing himself in boxers and then he went further and showed himself without clothes on the webcam. Before long Callum was participating in sexual acts such as masturbation on the webcam, believing that he was seducing a young woman of fourteen years old, whom he had seen pictures of and chatted to online for a number of weeks.

One day the police arrived at Callum's home and asked his mother if they could talk to him alone. The mother refused the police the opportunity to speak with her son alone, but agreed that he could be interviewed in her presence.

The police informed Callum that a girl called Lorraine had been encouraging a number of boys to reveal their sexual parts on webcam and also taking part in sexual acts such as touching themselves and masturbating on webcam. At this stage in the investigation the police did not want to reveal that they knew Lorraine was really a man, until they were sure that Callum was indeed a victim of the offender.

Callum revealed that he had been talking to Lorraine on webcam and Facebook and that he met her on Facebook via other friends on the site; however, he denied revealing any parts of his body or masturbating on webcam. The police enquired if he had any pictures of Lorraine and he said yes. The police then enquired if he had shared any of these pictures of Lorraine without clothes on with others, to which Callum said no.

Factual information

The child abuse investigation team had discovered that a man was posing as a teenage girl called Lorraine; this man had contacted some 200 boys online, posing as a girl in order to fulfil his paedophile fantasies. The abuser also had information about some of the young people he had made contact with via his community links with a number of the boys.

Due to the ongoing investigation and information-gathering, the police did not, at this stage, want to reveal to the boys and their families that the offender was in fact a grown man rather than a young girl.

The computer was confiscated by the police for further investigation.

Child abuse

When an adult with intentions to hurt and manipulate children takes steps to make contact with children and young people online, it is just as dangerous and abusive as when a potential abuser attempts to meet a child in public or in a family home, and some would argue that it could be even more dangerous, as the abuser has much quicker access and is able to make contact with a much larger number or children in a shorter space of time. If that child or young person is exposed to sexual images or acts of a sexual nature, then the abuse is just as damaging as all other types of abuse.

We will look at the impact of Internet abuse by considering the four main categories of abuse, namely physical, sexual, and neglect and emotional abuse, and we will examine how the abuse experienced by Callum in the case study might impact on him.

Physical abuse

When we consider physical abuse we do not usually equate it with online abuse; however, if young people are encouraged into touching themselves on webcam, this amounts to physical abuse. Children may also be lured into meeting the abuser in person, which may result in further sexual and physical abuse.

The impact of physical abuse could affect young people by causing them actual bodily harm, and will also have an emotional impact on them which could impact negatively on their mental well-being, causing depression, anxiety, distress, phobias, and uncontrollable fears.

Sexual abuse

The greatest risk to children via online abuse is that of sexual abuse, both virtually and face-to-face, as well as the fact that images of children in sexually compromised positions may be kept and distributed by the offender, which results in a permanent image of the child being available and accessible to other sex offenders online. Hence when children and young people are sexually abused online they may be aware that the images of them will never go away and can be accessed by any person which could leave them with a feeling that the abuse is on-going, even after the event and that at any time the images of the abuse can reappear causing them on-going distress, humiliation and shame. Some children and young people may even feel guilty for having taking an active part in the abuse at the instructions of the abuser. Children and young people should always be made to know that they are not to blame for the abusive actions, threats or encouragement that have been wielded by the virtual abuser.

Neglect and emotional abuse

If children are left to access web pages on the Internet without appropriate guidance from the caregivers and adults in their lives then their well-being is at risk of being neglected. Where a child is exposed to online abuse this may have a negative effect on their self-esteem and may ultimately result in emotional turmoil, causing the child to be exposed to a level of emotional abuse. When children are the victims of online abuse they experience layers of abuse consisting of a number of the four main categories mentioned above.

Children need to be protected from abuse, as the consequences of childhood abuse may be longterm and can negatively impact on their adult lives, causing mental health issues, social difficulties, and affecting the ability to function as useful adults in society. As noted in the Home Office publication, "Child Protection Messages":

> Links between childhood experiences and adult adjustments are debatable, but it is generally agreed that abuse is a serious risk factor. Abused children appear more likely to suffer intellectually and as social beings and to display affective and behaviour disorders by comparison with non-abused children from similar backgrounds. (1995, p. 42)

The most vulnerable children

In general children that are left unsupervised for long periods and late at night are at greater risk of being contacted by potential abusers. Some children are unable to make friends easily and find they are lonely, which makes them prime targets for abusers who will take advantage of their availability and lack of social support from friends. The most vulnerable children are those who are looked after by the local authority, as they may already have experienced abuse and may have low self-esteem, feel isolated from friends and family, and may be less confident about the support they can gain from the adults in their lives, amongst other issues of distress that they are attempting to deal with on a day-to-day basis. Some of these children may also have learning disabilities which would place them at grave risk of becoming victims of online abuse. As stated in a publication that offers safeguarding guidance to professionals,

> Many disabled children are at an increased likelihood of being socially isolated with fewer outside contacts than non-disabled children. ... Safeguarding disabled children's welfare is everybody's responsibility, given that we know that disabled children are more vulnerable to abuse than non-disabled children, awareness amongst professionals, about safeguarding disabled children and what constitutes best practice is essential. (Murray & Osbourne, 2009, p. 35)

The guidance also states: "Ensure disabled children are taken into account when developing local e-safety strategies" (p. 34).

Online grooming

Grooming is the process by which a potential sex offender prepares a child to be sexually abused. It is acknowledged that in order to groom a child the abuser has to gain the trust of those around the child; this usually consists of making himself useful and helpful to those around the child. For example, in a family the child may be groomed by the abuser making sure that he is available to the family and can assist either by offering money, skills, or time. Hence, the adults will gain some trust in the potential abuser and this will offer him some degree of power and access to the child whom he plans to abuse. Once that power has been gained the abuser will then attempt to isolate the potential victim or ensure that he has access to the victim, and then progress to perpetrate the abuse.

In relation to online grooming this takes a slightly different form, as abusers are not in a position to groom the adults around the child. Hence, they target children who are not sufficiently protected by adults or children who are vulnerable to contact with online friends; otherwise they merely trick the children into thinking they are someone the child may wish to relate to, which amounts to a large number of children and young people being at risk from online abusers. Research co-funded by the European Union has noted that

Online groomers talked about spending seconds, minutes, days, months and even years talking to young people. For those offending quickly, the Internet has speeded up the process of child sexual abuse. That is, the anonymous, disinhibiting properties of the Internet are allowing offenders to behave in a sexually explicit way, at a speed that would be almost impossible to replicate F2F with a stranger offline. (Davidson et al., 2011, p. 9)

We will consider the children who are at most risk later. So how does the online abuser groom the child for abuse?

In order to prepare children for online abuse the potential abuser will groom them by attempting to befriend them online, often stating that he is a friend of their friends online or giving compliments about the pictures he has seen online. The abuser may make contact in a chat room situation and then invite the young person or child into a private discussion or phone call. The abuser will then maintain regular and frequent contact with the potential victim as a means of building up a somewhat trusted relationship. For children who may feel lonely or vulnerable for whatever reason, the consistent contact from one Internet friend can be very attractive and encouraging, especially if the online abuser treats them as special and continues to give them a lot of attention which is lacking in their day-to day life. Once the abuser has gained knowledge, information, or even indecent images of the child or young person, he may become quite controlling, threatening or bullying in order to get the young person either to introduce him to other young people or to meet in reality with a view to escalating the abusive relationship. Vulnerable young people may be placed in a position of fear or admiration of the abuser, which may lead them to continue being at risk of the abuser and or of other abusers, as sex offenders are known to work together in order to access and abuse children and young people.

As stated above, when children or young people experience abuse they are at risk of suffering, emotionally, physically, and sexually. In the case of Callum, who was taken in by a stranger pretending to be a young girl of a similar age, if and when he discovers that he was deceived for the purposes of another person's sexual gratification, he may feel that it is very difficult to trust others in future and will experience a sense of personal violation. As well as the direct feeling of being exploited and abused by the man pretending to be a girl online, Callum may also feel a deep sense of shame and guilt for allowing this person to have his online way with him. This could result in Callum withdrawing from the outside world for fear of ridicule and embarrassment. He may also experience a level of depression, coupled with humiliation, as a result of not being wise enough to have avoided the online grooming performed by the man pretending to be Lorraine. Another consequence for Callum is that his parents and family will also be alerted to the details of the abuse, which could amount to public humiliation for him, as the family, police, and social workers will want to discuss the matter with Callum.

Some children may be so upset by such an ordeal that they can become suicidal or experience mental health issues. Another common reaction to having experienced sexual abuse of any type is to self-harm. Children and young people who self-harm report that they experience the most horrible feelings inside of being dirty, confused, fearful, and empty. These feelings of internal disgust and fear can be so overwhelming that those who self-harm will take action to hurt themselves as a way of feeling something that relieve the horrible internal pain, if only for a few short seconds. Self-harming is a dangerous action that can put the lives and well-being of children and young people at risk; it should be taken very seriously and professional help must be acquired as soon as possible. The greatest risk is that some young people and children will self-harm in secret, even though they desperately need help.

It is important for professionals and parents to be sensitive to the possible consequences for a child and to limit the number of people that are made aware of what the child has experienced, while taking appropriate steps to ensure the child's safety in future.

Access to information about potential child victims of online abuse

On some occasions, online abusers will have had some contact with the child in reality, so may know the child's vulnerabilities, for example, a child who is being bullied in school, or struggling with a physical or learning difficulty, as well as experiencing aloneness and isolation from his or her peer group. On other occasions the abuser will pick up clues about children's vulnerabilities by what they have posted online, such as comments about being dumped by a boyfriend or seeking friends to go to shows with, or information about being in foster care or in a residential setting.

Some abusers will search the web for additional information about the children they wish to target, such as what area they live in, the type of music they like, and other interest they may have. Therefore it is important that children and young people are told to limit the amount of information about themselves that they put online. People like to say what is going on in their lives by online blogging and by using social networking sites to post pictures of events and recent experiences, both good and bad. This can give potential abusers a great deal of information about a potential victim that they might use in getting to know a young person or in encouraging that young person to befriend and ultimately trust them.

Callum, however, was quite fortunate that the abuse was detected and stopped before he was lured into meeting the abuser. Some children are not so fortunate, and the abuser will continue to befriend them online until the child feels confident enough to meet the abuser, placing the child at risk of actual abuse and/or murder.

The impact of sexual abuse may leave children feeling that they cannot cope with overwhelming feelings such as fear, anxiety, dirtiness, shame, and guilt and some children may resort to self-harming behaviour in order to relieve themselves of such horrible feelings. Other children may become quite withdrawn and others may act out. If a child suddenly changes character or behaviour then we are to be concerned that the child may be responding to abuse or to another type of trauma or distress.

In order to counteract the negative experience of sexual abuse, some children may find that they act out sexually, as a way of trying to make sense of their experience and gain a greater understanding of the motives of the abuser. Sexually active children may place themselves at greater risk by making themselves more available to those who might hurt and abuse them.

How professional counsellors and therapists can help keep children safe and maintain professional boundaries while offering online support

In order for therapists and counsellors to offer a safe and transparent online counselling service to children and young people, who may be at risk of online abuse, it is important for them to have relevant training that will offer them insight and equip them with a thorough understanding of the extent of the risk of possible online abuse to children and young people. The police organisation known as the Child Exploitation and Online Protection Centre (CEOP), offers face-to-face and group training as well as on line guidance and advises in relation to information and methods of how to keep children safe online. CEOP has provided material suitable for professionals, teachers, parents, and younger and older children, that keeps children safe online; their campaign has assisted many in learning more about the current situation, including online bullying, sexual abuse, and sexual exploitation, and is a valuable resource. CEOP aims to alert parents and professionals to the dangers of internet abuse and offers methods of protection for children and young people from online abuse. Therapists and counsellors would also benefit from learning about the emotional impact that children experience when communicating or viewing material online. It is therefore important for counsellors and therapists to access up to date research that considers the emotional impact of online interaction as experienced by children. A research paper produced in February 2013, by EU Kids Online, consulted almost 10,000 children who noted that their main concerns were pornography and violence online. The report also noted the difference between boys' and girls' emotional responses and has some reference to how children reacted in different countries. This paper gives a realistic insight into the views, concerns, and worries of children when communicating online.

The traditional counselling process, of sitting together in a cosy room opposite the client in a chair, may not be the method of choice for a large number of young people at this time. Young people are becoming more and more skilled at expressing themselves via chat rooms, texting, and other means of short word dialogue. I recall a time when a young woman who had experienced rape would text me once a week to let me know how she was feeling. On one occasion she texted me and said that she felt like killing herself. The question is, how do you respond to such a text? When children and young people speak of suicide, the first thing we need to establish is that they are safe, and then we need to gain insight into the present level of risk to life. In order to gain the information I needed to in order to know that this young woman was not about to take her life on this particular day, I chose to respond to her using the method by which she had contacted me. My thinking was that either she could not speak to me at that moment or chose not to, so, rather than run the risk of alienating her, I responded by text and asked her, on a scale of one to ten, with ten being the highest, how much did she feel like killing herself. The young woman responded very quickly with a firm "Seven". I then asked her if there was any one else she felt like killing and she responded by saying "Yes him, the rapist". I asked how much and she responded by saying "Ten and more". From this, I deduced that she was feeling more anger than despair and was, therefore, less likely to take her life that day. My next response was to say "I am pleased that you are angry, what he did was wrong, but if you hurt yourself, that would be giving him more power, and he does not deserve to have so much power. Let's focus on what you can do to take back control of your life." 'I then said, "When can I call you to discuss this further?" She gave me a time and we spoke later that day.

The added value of responding by text is that the young person can keep the text and re-read it as and when she wants to. What we know about trauma is that it makes it difficult for people to absorb and truly hear what is being said to them while they are feeling distressed, anxious, and confused. The text or email allows the young person to revisit the support that has been offered by the counsellor/therapist at a time when they may be feeling more able to focus on the words and can allow a vulnerable, scared young person to have a form of ongoing support when the therapist is not there. Hence, we need to be very careful about how we respond via texting, emails, or other means of Internet interaction.

Therapists and counsellors also need to be aware that a conversation that takes place via text and or other types of writing can be kept by young people and shared with others. So we need to be specific and make sure that the words we use are clear and non-ambiguous so that the meaning is transparent to all. We also need to guard against writing anything that might be offensive to close family members—who might be offering support to the young distressed person—if the email or text is read out of context of the relationship that one has with the young person. A good rule of thumb is not to use jargon of any type when sending text and also not to use any text abbreviations which may be ambiguous, such as "lol", which in text speak could mean either "laugh out loud" or "lots of love".

Therapists and counsellors also need to maintain an appropriate boundary when communicating via Internet or phone, be it Skype meetings, emails, or texting. It is important that young people only contact you by a medium that is for professional use only and is not used for your social or personal life. Be wary of Internet accounts such as Facebook which allow others to know about and share information. Be mindful of how you will maintain confidentiality when communicating via the web or mobile phone messaging. Counsellors must ensure that a manager, senior, or supervisor is alerted to the fact that communication is taking place with a client via Internet or phone access and that appropriate safety issues have been thought about and are in place, both for the young person and for the therapist/counsellor.

It is important that you discuss timeframes with young people so that they are aware of when you will and won't respond and that they are alerted to other resources and systems of support that they may access at times when you are not available, such as Childline and Samaritans.

There are innate difficulties about communicating through a medium whereby you cannot see the client/service user. One such difficulty is that you cannot be one hundred per cent sure that you are in fact talking only to your client/service user. A few young people (I think not the majority) may invite a friend to view their online dialogue with their therapist, but a number of children and young people may have such worrying issues that they would not choose to share this with others. However, some may try to normalise their dilemmas by sharing with someone they think understands their situation or is a good friend, and as a way of trying to normalise the experience of having a counsellor. It is therefore important that explicit ground rules, with explanations as to the reason for them, are drawn up between the counsellor/therapist and the client/service user.

Another concern that therapists and counsellors should be alerted to in relation to Internet dialogue with young service users is that of potential allegations of abuse or bullying by therapist and counsellors. What we know about children and young people who make false allegations against professionals is that, once they have developed a trusting relationship with a professional and find that they are ready to reveal information about a situation of abuse that they have experienced in the past, some young people find it easier to talk about their experience of abuse by keeping the identity of the abuser, who may well be somebody they love and are dependent on, such a mother, father or a powerful individual in their lives, concealed. So in order to talk about their experience of abuse they may say that the now trusted therapist or counsellor is in fact the perpetrator of the historical abuse. Some of the unconscious thinking behind young people making such allegations against a therapist/counsellor they have grown to trust and value, may well be that the young person is aware that the therapist/counsellor will not be punitive when they are named as the alleged abuser; or it may be that the experience of growing close and developing a level of trust with the therapist/counsellor is too uncomfortable for the young person to manage, and that the disclosure of abuse may be something of an ultimate test to see if the therapist is really someone who can be trusted and who will not hurt or leave the young person.

It is my view that children and young people do not accuse their counsellors consciously but are confused and torn by a number of internal feelings and desires that drive them to disclose in a way that leaves them feeling overwhelmed and confused; hence, memories and feelings become jumbled inside the young person and, in a quest to relieve himself of all of these awkward feelings, he may say things that contain an element of truth, but not in the order that he has revealed it. It is therefore very important that professionals who work with children who have experienced abuse, especially online abuse, are clear about following procedures, sticking to boundaries, and ensuring that a senior worker is aware of what they are doing.

The progression of technology and the need to protect

As we are unaware of just where technology might lead and how young people and children may prefer to communicate next, professionals need to be flexible in their approach and ready to try new methods of interaction while holding on to the core values of respecting the client and listening effectively via all the means of communication available to us, keeping our code of ethics in mind.

For those of us who are working with adults who may also be vulnerable to online abusers and, on occasion, perpetrating the abuse, it is important that we have some insight into this issue and are aware of the ethics and policies that offer guidance as to how we should respond if we become aware that a child or vulnerable adult is at risk of online abuse.

Conclusion

Within this chapter we have considered a method of online abuse and child protection issues via the exploration of a case study. In order to appreciate the gravity of online abuse we discussed the four main categories of abuse, namely physical, sexual, and neglect and emotional abuse as a method of understanding how this impacts on children who are abused via the Internet and other technical means.

The gravity of online abuse was discussed by taking a look at the most vulnerable children, with an acknowledgement that all children need to be protected from such abuse.

Offenders of such abuse, and the methods they may use, were discussed by looking at the process of online grooming in order to gain insight into the extent of the risk to children, so that we are armed with knowledge that we can share with children and young people in order to afford them some protection.

Professionals also need to consider protecting themselves from allegations of abuse and to be aware of how their online interaction may be negatively used by some clients and service users. It is important to note that most children and young people who may seek help will not abuse this method of support.

Finally, online counselling is a wonderful new method of support for a wide number of people and hence it is important for us as professionals to continue to debate the issue of how to ensure that this method of communication keeps children and young people safe in this time of amazing inventions and swift change.

Commentator one: Michèle Bartlett

Aqualma Murray has raised a number of different issues relating to the potential vulnerability of children and young people to online abuse and exploitation.

Whilst it is true that the Internet provides a potential platform for sex offenders to access children, one aspect that I feel warrants more attention is the potential risk not from the adult stranger (as depicted in Callum's story) but from peer-to-peer abuse.

Callum puts himself at risk because he shares intimate pictures of himself with someone he believes to be his own age. This trend is becoming more prevalent amongst adolescents. Excellent research by the NSPCC (Ringrose, Gill, Livingstone, & Harvey, 2012) on "sexting" (the practice of sharing sexually suggestive nude or nearly nude images) found that the primary threat was peer-to-peer, rather than from strangers. The researchers also found that sexting was often coercive in nature and adversely affected more girls than boys. Once images are shared, they are readily disseminated around a school year group or further, and they exist in cyberspace forever.

Young people need education in how to manage their online profile and how to be cautious about what they share and with whom.

It would be possible to write a whole chapter (at least) dedicated to protecting children from each other online, not just in terms of sexting but also in terms of the perils of cyberbullying via social media such as Facebook and whatsapp.

Commentator two: Eduardo Pitchon

The first thing psychotherapists learn in their training is the importance of early life and childhood experiences. They are the foundation of the mental and emotional edifice that we build in later life.

In our practice we have always been aware of the harm that abuse of any kind causes in the sensitive psyche and the life of our patients. Pain, trauma, and emotional wounds are issues that psychotherapists confront daily in their consulting rooms.

Because of our work we know how easy it is to cause harm to a person, and we have learned to our cost how hard it is to help repair the damage.

As human beings we are fragile creatures, and the more open, less defended, and less experienced we are, the more we will be exposed to abuses and vulnerable to attacks of all sorts.

Child psychotherapists undergo a long and arduous training which enables them to work with young children and adolescents in various settings. We come across abused, neglected, and wounded children all the time. That is why they come to us. These issues can come from different sources, whether it is parental neglect, family conflicts, educational problems at school, or problems of socialisation, to name a few. We know from experience that there are a multitude of ways in which a child's trust and faith in himself and in human kindness can be damaged.

In this chapter Aqualma Murray indicates the dangers that modern technology poses. As with everything else, the Internet and online connections and communications can be a mixed blessing. We all use the Internet every day. I use modern communications in my practice, for example, using my mobile phone to text patients, and supervising students via Skype who live in faraway countries, such as Mexico or the United States.

Aqualma Murray draws our attention to "the dark side of the moon". This is the perverse use of the Internet and the harm it can cause. It is a timely article and a clear exposition of how times have changed and the risks that this new technology can bring in its wake.

Children and young people are familiar nowadays with computers and feel confident and comfortable navigating the Internet, and this is the real danger, because they are not aware of the inherent risks.

Aqualma Murray's article makes for chilling reading. In it she discusses a case in which a young boy of fifteen was being groomed by an older man who passed himself off as a young girl. Fortunately for the boy, in this case, the situation was discovered by the police at a relatively early stage, and it was resolved before the child had a chance to meet the perpetrator. The child's trust and his sense of security, having been so badly shaken, must have caused deep psychological scars which will need attending to.

The author then discusses different types of online abuse, which according to her can be physical, sexual, and emotional. She says, quite rightly, "Children need to be protected from abuse as the consequences of child abuse may have long-term effects which could negatively impact on their adult lives, causing mental health issues, social difficulties, and the ability to function as useful members of society." She then discusses different ways of online grooming and the need to protect and supervise children. She ends her article by discussing how technology can help counsellors and therapists in communicating with young patients.

To conclude, I would like to add that as an older therapist of a different generation I have found this article enlightening, disturbing, and most useful.

References

Bryce, J. (2009). Online sexual exploitation of children and young people. In: Y. Jewkes & M. Yar, *Handbook of Internet Crime*. Cullompton: Willan Publishing.

Child Exploitation and Online Protection (CEOP) Centre (2007). *Strategic Overview 2006–2007*. London: Child Exploitation and Online Protection Centre.

Davidson, J., Grove-Hills, J., et al. (2011). Online abuse: Literature review and policy context. European Online Grooming Project. Co-funded by the European Union.

EU Kids Online (2013). www.eukidsonline.net

Murray, M., & Osbourne, C. (2009). Safeguarding disabled children. Practice Guidance. The department for Children, Schools, and Families. HMSO.

Ringrose, J., Gill, R., Livingstone, S., & Harvey, L. (2012). A qualitative study of children, young people and "sexting": a report prepared for the NSPCC. London: NSPCC.

CHAPTER ELEVEN

The way forward

Aaron Balick and Philippa Weitz

Philippa Weitz

Writing this book has been a journey in itself. It started out, in my mind, as a simple guide to setting up an online practice. The result is a great deal more powerful and wide-reaching.

The chapters and their authors have made journeys through the many lands of the digital age, and the many challenges and dilemmas that these present to psychotherapy. I believe that the digital age is the single most exciting "happening" for psychotherapy since Freud. I hear many of you groaning in the aisles now! But just as you cannot put toothpaste back in the tube, psychotherapy has changed forever.

Psychotherapy 2.0 is the space where psychotherapy and technology meet. The cover of this book attempts to convey this but trying to capture the essence of Psychotherapy 2.0 and bottle it is almost impossible as the subject is far reaching and diverse as cyberspace itself. These are exciting times for those who wish to walk this digital path and enter the Psychotherapy 2.0 space. For those practitioners who choose not to I hope this book will equip them with some knowledge to work with their clients who are most likely to be digital natives.

Virtually everyone I speak to about this book and about psychotherapy online gives me one of those funny looks that show doubt and raise questions such as "How can you trust someone you have never met?", "How could a relationship online be as powerful, or even more powerful, than a F2F meeting?" I'm not going to attempt to answer these questions, as that's been the role of this book. But this book will have given the doubters a run for their money. It is enlightening and refreshing to read Kate Dunn's account on the depth and intensity of the psychotherapeutic encounter through asynchronous methods: using email. Her research (Dunn, 2012) is illuminating and challenging to those who believe the old ways are the best. Psychotherapy 2.0 is not an "also-ran", a second-best; it is already providing inspiration to many clients who may never have received help before. Aqualma Murray in her chapter reminds us that many young people might actually find the consulting room far more daunting than online help. The online world is also expanding our ways of working with many new platforms such as Big White Wall and MindFull. This is really exciting for clients, as they are now able to access the help they so desperately need which is currently so limited in availability within the NHS.

Some of the contributors to this book will tell you that this is the only way they work now, that they find the online psychotherapeutic encounter so strong, the asynchronous method using email escaping the noise of the consulting room and enabling the client to think and feel at his/her own speed.

It is clear that there is an exciting future for those therapists who wish to work digitally. It will not be every practitioner's choice of means of working. However, those who stick their heads in the sand and refuse to engage in and research all things digital is doing their client a great disservice. Kate Anthony's chapter on avatars demonstrated beautifully the practitioner's gap in knowledge of Second Life, but equally the humility with which she was prepared to admit she did not know enough to be able to help her client, and then go off and research this fully so that she could help. And then what a journey they took together.

Whether we choose to work online is one decision, but the world has gone digital, which means that somehow, and in many ways unanticipated, this will implode on our clinical practice: the client arriving having been bullied online, or having been fraped, or even had their identity stolen. These are all daily occurrences in the newspapers and our clients will be experiencing them too. We need to know about these things so we are better able to help our clients.

Finally, the "R" word. Yes, research. There is already a mass of excellent research out there. This book was only possible because of the research of others. Some of it is ground-breaking. All of it is extremely important to the robustness of the future of the profession. I urge you to think about getting involved in research into all matters digital as they relate to psychotherapy. If Kate Dunn had written her chapter only based on opinion and clinical experience it would not hold the power that it does hold, because it is grounded in solid research.

At UKCP we have a new media special interest group and we would be delighted to guide and be guided in the development of research and clinical practice online. It's such an exciting time to be involved in psychotherapy and I hope you'll join us in taking the profession forward in Psychotherapy 2.0.

Aaron Balick

My role as a consulting editor for this book has been an interesting one, and one that I would like to use this conclusion to reflect upon. While Philippa can take credit for the vast proportion of the elbow grease in making this book happen, my role was rather more at a distance. It was my job to brainstorm with Philippa on the possible structure the book would take; to consider the broader sections, authors, and structure; and to offer a general kind of oversight with regard to psychotherapy as a whole in relation to the continued emergence, change, and growth of the digital world. My interest, as declared in my own chapter, is primarily with regard to using our skills as psychotherapists to theorise the meaning that developing new media has not just on our profession, but on society as a whole. The sections of this book that referred to online practice were as new and educational to me as they will be to most of our readers.

If I am honest with the reader, many of the chapters left me with a sense of anxiety. I am certainly no Luddite when it comes to new technologies. In fact, you might call me an early adoptor. Over the past two years I have devoted myself to understanding this brave new world through the psychotherapeutic lens in my own book *The Psychodynamics of Social Networking: Connected-up Instantaneous Culture and the Self* (Balick, 2014) and through my role in this and other related projects.

What I continue to learn is that keeping up with the pace of change is nearly impossible, hence my sense of anxiety.

Though online practice is not my modus operandi, I, like many of the readers of this book, have necessarily utilised networked technologies as part of my work. Email, text, and Skype all sit rather comfortably in the domain of my regular F2F practice, despite my not having conceptualised this as "online practice." However, I have learned by way of this process that this "dabbling" has more consequences than I had anticipated. While for many years I have kept notes on an encrypted hard-drive, I had not considered too deeply how I deal with my day-to-day emails, nor the Skype that I regularly use to communicate with clients and supervisees. Though I feel relatively "with the programme" on this sort of stuff, reading this book has really opened up my eyes—and, furthermore, has alerted me to the fact that as a profession many of us are sleepwalking into the use of technologies without the requisite information from which to make ethical and appropriate decisions. Welcome another dose of anxiety!

In my own book I did my best to take the familiar position of "non-judgement" with regard to the goods or evils of our sometimes-incomprehensible brave new connected-up world. There is so much to be excited about, but at the same time, this notion of sleepwalking into something unknown became a spectre that began to cast a shadow over my neutral positioning. Social technologies both enable and disable. It is easy to take a position in which the enabling or disabling casts the bigger shadow, but we must always hold both in mind. The one thing that we cannot deny is that the scene is set, we cannot go back, and as responsible clinicians we must come to the forefront of this technological nexus of psychology and technology and develop the very best way forward that we can.

While I carry the excitement of a great many of our writers about this project, I also feel that we cannot move forward without acknowledging some degree of loss. While technology is enabling, it is also impinging; while it opens up our individual space to a wider world, it also brings this wider world into our personal space; while it widens routes of access to psychotherapy, it also changes the nature of what psychotherapy is. I love technology. I have every shiny gadget and app that I can get my hands on, and yet I also have an attachment to "old world" psychotherapy, and I don't want to give that up.

From the sci-fi world of *Star Trek* I quote from the most socially networked race encountered, the Borg: "Resistance is futile." Web 2.0 is here and is quickly moving to Web 2.1; Web 3.0 will shortly follow, a development that is likely to include "wearable tech" in which even more details of our lives will be compiled and uploaded into the cloud. It is incumbent upon us as psychotherapists, primarily, to understand this and, second, to engage with it productively, and at some times, yes, to resist: but to resist in the context of what is real, not of what we do not understand. The chapter authors are at the vanguard in relation to this pairing of technological networked psychotherapy. Readers will be making their own choices about how much and in what ways they engage in this paradigm.

The lesson I take away from this is that as a profession we must also make our choices with respect to the reality principle: the contemporary nexus of technology and psychotherapy. One may choose to completely embrace this digital world and operate in almost complete synchrony with it, at times challenging the very notions of what psychotherapy is. Others may resist that draw and operate in the traditional fashion, utilising the technological world only where absolutely necessary. My sense is that so long as these choices are made in relation to a deep and thoughtful consideration of their consequences rather than as a knee-jerk response out of fear of the new, or indeed as glassy-eyed seduction by the excitement of it, then these choices are for clinicians to make. These authors have taken a bold step in formulating not just thinking but also action in this brave new world, and we should carry on doing so in the face of such overwhelming change.

References

Balick, A. (2014). *The Psychodynamics of Social Networking: Connected-up Instantaneous Culture and the Self*. London: Karnac.

Dunn, K. (2012). A qualitative investigation into the online counselling relationship: To meet or not to meet, that is the question. *Counselling and Psychotherapy Research, 12*: 316–326.

GLOSSARY

Words, context, meanings, and acronyms

Asynchronous   Not synchronised, using online resources for therapeutic purposes such as email where the therapy is not in real time

Avatar   A computerised representation of the self

Chat   Internet Relay Chat (IRC) e.g., Skype, VSee (or similar) written messages

Cloud   A network of remote servers hosting web-based tools and applications hosted on the Internet to store, manage, and process data (your information and files), rather than a local server or a personal computer. Working via the Cloud enables you to access your own data as long as your electronic device has access to the web, so that you can work remotely

Download   A document drawn down from the Internet such as a PDF, a film, music, photos, or software programs that can be received and saved

e-learning   Technology-enhanced learning (TEL)

Emails   Emails

Encryption   The process of encoding messages (or information) so that hackers cannot read them, but so that authorised parties can

F2F   Face to face, in person

Fraping   The act of changing the details on someone's Facebook page when they leave it open

Hardware   Computer equipment, including drives, storage devices, gismos, gadgets, mobile phones, computers, hand-held devices, etc.

Internet   Global system of inter-connected computer network which provides a basis for all data and communication including email

ISP   Internet service provider

Netiquette   Paralleling the rules of etiquette is society, netiquette involves the rules of social conventions online via networks

Offline   When you are disconnected to the Internet

Online   When you are connected to the Internet, particularly important for working in a synchronous way

Platform   A framework on which software or hardware applications may be run

Practitioner   The therapist, counsellor, or psychotherapist, irrespective of tradition

Search engine   Online software that enables you to search on the Internet, e.g., Google, Bing, MSN

Sexting   Sending sexually explicit messages and/or photographs, primarily between mobile phones

Software   A set of machine-readable instructions (e.g., a computer program) directing a computer's processor to perform specific tasks. Software may be written for many different hardware units, including those of Apple iPhones/iPads, etc., Android intelligent phones, and the like, as well as for suites of program to support office workers, accountants, and many others. Software is also written to control and run social media sites

Streaming   Data and material received from the Internet to be used immediately but cannot be saved

Synchronous   Synchronized, in real time such as video-conferencing

Text (or SMS)   Mobile phone message

Video conferencing   Communication via the Internet e.g., VSee, Skype, in real time with video and sound

Virtual world   Computer-simulated environment

Webcam   A camera that you use in conjunction with your PC or laptop to transmit images in real time over the Internet. Used for real time conversations through software, such as Skype.

INDEX